Tinkering with the System

Tinkering with the System

Technological Innovations in
State and Local Services

Robert K. Yin
Karen A. Heald
Mary E. Vogel

Lexington Books
D.C. Heath and Company
Lexington, Massachusetts
Toronto

Library of Congress Cataloging in Publication Data

Yin, Robert K.
  Tinkering with the system.

  Bibliography: p.
  Includes index.
  1. Local   government—United   States.   2. State   governments.
3. Technological innovations—United States—Case studiés. I. Heald, Karen
A., joint author. II. Vogel, Mary E., joint author. III. Title.
JS341.Y563   361.6'0973   76-57903
ISBN 0-669-01360-9

Contents

List of Figures and Tables

Preface

The national view of state and local service delivery has always been a frustrating one. Federal resources—in the form of support for research, implementation, or evaluation—have too often led to disappointing results, as state and local services frequently appear to operate independently of any federal influence. Yet, for exploring the potential of new technology, an active federal role is essential, because most state or local jurisdictions do not have the technical expertise or financial resources to adequately develop and test a wide range of potential innovations. Thus federal policymakers are continually searching for new clues about the innovative process in state and local services. The eternal hope is that a productive partnership between federal agencies on the one hand and state and local services on the other can eventually be forged.

The purpose of this study is to improve federal policymaking by increasing our understanding of how state and local services implement and incorporate innovations. This objective was accomplished through a review and analysis of 140 case studies of a state or local organization's first experience with a new technological device. The review is the first occasion, as far as we are aware, that the often disparate literature of site-specific experiences has been brought together for synthesis and analysis. A similar approach was used in a previous study of nontechnical innovations in local services (see Robert K. Yin and Douglas Yates, 1975), and we view the present effort as a complement to the previous one. Both attempt to elucidate the innovative process in state and local agencies.

This study was previously reported in a different version, entitled "A Review of Case Studies of Technological Innovations in State and Local Services," The Rand Corporation, R-1870-NSF, Santa Monica (February 1976). The change in title reflects significant substantive changes in the text. Chapter 1 has been revised to develop more fully the notion of "tinkering" in a positive sense that views incrementalism as the normative pace of innovation. Numerous changes have been made in the description of the study design and reporting of the data so that the salient points are clearer. The discussion in Chapter 5 has been rewritten to focus attention directly on the most theoretically significant contribution of our study, which is the suggested distinction between bureaucratic self-interest and production efficiency as two innovative processes. Finally, Chapter 6 has been entirely revised to make the potential options for new federal policies clearer to the nonspecialist.

In sum, the problem of state and local innovation is a most difficult one and deserves continued attention. This does not mean that we are simply advocating change for change's sake; rather, we hope that our notion of "tinkering" adequately conveys a constructive and appreciative view of how services must operate. The natural environment within which services operate has changed rapidly, first with residential dissatisfaction and civil disorders, and now with energy problems and increasingly stringent financial constraints. To innovate under these circumstances, making services more attuned to external reality, thus may not be just a matter of bureaucratic amenity. Innovation may be necessary for the very survival of certain basic services.

Acknowledgments

This study has benefited from the advice and assistance of many people, although the authors alone are responsible for the final version.

J. David Roessner played a key role throughout the study, helping to conceptualize the initial issues, commenting on the research design and analysis, and reviewing preliminary drafts. We wish to thank Dave and the others at NSF's Office of R&D Assessment (Leonard Lederman, Alden Bean, and Mary Mogee) for providing a stimulating milieu within which this study could be carried out. However, neither these project officers nor the National Science Foundation, which provided support under grant No. RDA 75-04134, bear any responsibility for the views expressed in the final text. The Rand Corporation also provided financial support for the writing of the book.

Among our colleagues at Rand, Peter Szanton and Roger Levien stimulated our initial interest in urban innovations. Although neither was at Rand at the project's end, Peter Szanton shared with us his own rendition of the unique role of The New York City-Rand Institute. The Institute will remain a special urban innovation for many of us who worked there. Similarly, Roger Levien shared his insights and perspectives on federal R&D management and the relationship between federal policies and urban innovations. Others at Rand who made helpful suggestions or comments were John Wirt, William Lucas, Peter de Leon, William Hederman, Barbara Williams, Milbrey McLaughlin, Edward Merrow, and Richard Rettig. The last mentioned made especially useful comments on an earlier draft.

We have also been fortunate to have had the sage advice of several experts in the field. Everett Rogers (Stanford University) gave a close reading to an earlier draft and both improved the study and tried to make it more consistent with his own interpretation of the innovation field. (We did not always follow his advice but hope that the study will nevertheless find its way into his "core" bibliography.) Irwin Feller (Pennsylvania State University), Richard Bingham (Marquette University), Donald Menzel (University of West Virginia), W. Henry Lambright (Syracuse University), Wayne Kimmel (The Urban Institute), and Alfonso Linhares (U.S. Department of Transportation) were all more than generous with their comments on the research design and other portions of the manuscript.

Special thanks are due to Kim Morrissey and Sally Maitland Bosken (of Rand), and Vicky Agee and Carol Pyke (of The Urban Institute), who helped to track down many of the case studies and necessary supporting materials; many officials and researchers (listed in Appendix A) who also helped us to identify relevant information; Eveleen Bingham (of the Department of Urban Studies and Planning, M.I.T.) for writing the initial drafts of the reviews in Appendix F; Anne Stevenson, who did all of the computer programming needed to carry out the analyses; and Ellen Marks and Erma Packman, who made the whole text legible. We must also point out the supportive environment at Rand's Washington office where this study was done (2100 M Street, N.W., Washington, D.C.) and where a small group of people can have a quiet yet stimulating and nonbureaucratic setting in which to do their research. Finally, the hidden partners in this whole effort were the authors of the original case studies who, by making their studies available to the public, also allowed each case study to contribute to a larger story. We hope that the larger story will be more than the sum of its parts, but that it will not violate the integrity of any of those parts.

Tinkering with the System

1

Urban Technology: Promise and Problems

The Role of Innovations in State and Local Services

Rising Demands for Service

In the last twenty years, state and local governments have been subjected to a continued and sharp rise in demand for services. The strains resulting from this rise have been evident in several ways. The governors and mayors of large states and cities have been prominent on the national scene, usually pleading for more assistance in dealing with their problems. The emergence of public unions has fundamentally changed the nature of service relationships, and employee strikes have occurred. In addition, citizen dissatisfaction with services has replaced an earlier mood of complacency. State and local services, in short, have been confronted with an enormous performance gap[a] between the services needed and those provided (Downs, 1967) that has resulted in new responses and new stresses.

The increased demands are easily documented. Whether they concern rising crime rates, increased production of solid wastes, more frequent use of highways for personal travel, or new needs for housing and family support services, the demands have placed a greater burden on all facets of state and local government (e.g., Gordon, 1965; Marris and Rein, 1967; Hadden et al., 1971; and David and Peterson, 1973). Civil disorders brought national attention to these needs and sharpened the pressure for governmental action at all levels (*Report of the National Advisory Commission on Civil Disorders*, 1968). Population growth in the suburbs and in some rapidly expanding central cities has also served to increase demands for public services. However, even cities with declining populations have experienced rises in demands for service.

Much of the demand appears related to four factors: changes in consumer behavior, migratory patterns that have brought many poor families to urbanized areas, the simple aging of urban physical plants, and increased reliance on public agents for services that might have been privately provided in the past. To mention a few examples of this last factor, increases in the need for public health clinics, teachers, and sanitation workers may in part reflect the decreased numbers of druggists, clergy, building superintendents, janitors, and other artisans

---

[a]This concept currently appears frequently in the public organization literature. It is similar to the notion of "optimal stress" as defined by March and Simon (1958, pp. 182-184), but the first actual use of the term seems to be attributable to Anthony Downs (1967, p. 169).

1

traditionally found in the neighborhood (Banfield, 1970). Moreover, the federal government has frequently played a role in increasing the demands (see Sundquist, 1969; and Levitan, 1973). In many cases, as in education and social welfare programs, new federal resources have accompanied new legislation calling for increased services. However, the responsibility for organizing and administering the services has fallen on state and local governments. In other cases, as in the establishment of new regulations and standards in air or water pollution or in the provision of additional monies directly to the citizen as part of Medicaid and Medicare programs, the federal actions have not necessarily been accompanied by sufficient resources to alleviate the additional administrative burdens on state and local governments.[b]

Up to a point, the standard and not unreasonable response to these rising demands has been to increase the amount and coverage of government services. One of the distinctive features on the state and local scene has been the rapid growth of local services—e.g., from 1.8 policemen per 1000 population in 1958 to 2.4 in 1973, and from $511 per pupil spent for public elementary and secondary schools in 1958 to $1026 in equivalent dollars in 1973.[c] Together with the rise in services, an expansion has occurred at all levels in the administrative hierarchy, with central planning and budget functions, for instance, becoming more specialized and imposing more rules and regulations that in turn result in further needs for counterpart staffs at the agency level. This standard response of increasing governmental services remains the common alternative whenever demands for services increase. However, since resources are not unlimited, and since the costs of services have also been rising, continued expansion of governmental services has become difficult to sustain. In a few dramatic situations such as New York City, the service budgets have finally outdistanced the city's revenue and credit resources to such an extent as to threaten the city government with bankruptcy. Most cities have in fact begun to look seriously for ways of reducing their budgets or holding them down to previous levels without affecting services.

Alternative Responses

The inability to close the performance gap by the sheer increase in services has been the main reason that governments have continually searched for new ways

[b]There has been little assessment of the overall organizational effect of federal activities on states and cities. Some works have reviewed the needs for greater federal support (e.g., National Commission on Urban Problems, 1968). Other works have discussed the federal effects, but only in relation to specific programs such as the Community Action programs, Model Cities program, or revenue sharing (e.g., Sundquist, 1969; Farkas, 1971; and Reagan, 1972). Moreover, in most of these works the potential effect on state government problems has generally been ignored.

[c]The police data are from the U.S. Department of Justice, *Uniform Crime Reports, 1958*, and *1973* (1959 and 1974); the education data are from *Digest of Educational Statistics, 1973*, U.S. Department of Health, Education, and Welfare, Office of Education (1974), table 78.

to enhance service effectiveness and efficiency. The search has focused on identifying workable innovations that allow an agency to provide either improved services at the same cost or the same services at reduced cost. Typically, municipal governments at their early stages of development have pursued annexation or redistricting policies to increase their tax base or to reduce the per capita costs of services through economies of scale, and thereby to create improvements for all agencies in one fell swoop. Beyond annexation, governments have continued to experiment with other innovations. In the last decade, examples of these innovations have been new technological devices in transportation and traffic services, program budgeting, decentralization of command to the district level, centralization of command to superagencies, the use of operations research and other quantitative models, new public health techniques, the installation of computer systems to improve administrative efficiency, and a host of new types of equipment in public safety and curriculum changes in education. Despite their apparent diversity, these innovations may be said to fall into three broad categories, depending upon the type of device that is the object of the innovative effort: technological innovations, managerial innovations, and client-oriented innovations.

Technological innovations involve some technological process, defined as a specific machine, material, chemical, computer system, or set of analytic routines. Typically, a local agency attempts to install such a new device—e.g., a computer, a new apparatus for making health diagnoses, or an algorithm for placing mobile units in the field—to make direct improvements in service coverage or to provide a new service (e.g., The Urban Institute, 1971; and Council of State Governments, 1972). With the success of the aerospace program in landing a man on the moon, and with the presumed primitive state of affairs in the use of technology in local services (where, for instance, basic firefighting or solid waste collection techniques have not changed much in fifty years), there have been high hopes, still largely unfulfilled (Nelson, 1974), for demonstrating the beneficial effects of new technology in state and local government. The installation of a technological device, however, is not necessarily a mere mechanical procedure. New jobs, new assignments for existing jobs, and new relationships among employees are also involved. In short, although the innovation concerns a specific technological device, its installation or implementation entails changes in bureaucratic structure and behavioral roles that are often overlooked. The innovative process must therefore be understood in terms of both the innovative device and the concomitant organizational changes.

With *managerial innovations*, the new device is usually a specific administrative mechanism or policy that in turn requires further bureaucratic changes to be implemented. The desire to install program budgeting in local agencies, team teaching in schools, or productivity improvements in sanitation departments are examples of managerial devices (e.g., Hatry, 1971; Hamilton, 1972; Lucey, 1972; and Hawley and Rogers, 1974). Similarly, the use of well-defined techniques of program evaluation in what has become a surge of interest in evaluation research (e.g., Hatry et al., 1973) may also be considered a managerial innovation aimed at improving public services. In some cases, managerial innovations may overlap with technological ones. For instance, a new computer may be installed as part of a management information system. Whenever such an overlap occurs, the innovation for present purposes is regarded as a technological innovation.

Client-oriented innovations, in contrast to the first two types, do not have the improvement of services as their sole objective, but also seek to increase the influence of clients over services or even to place clients in service positions (e.g., Hallman, 1970; Lipsky, 1971; Yin et al., 1973; Hallman, 1974; and Yin and Yates, 1975). Once again, a specific device serves as the focus of the innovative effort. The creation of a client-elected governing board or the hiring of clients into paraprofessional positions are devices that deal directly with both the service and client control objectives. Devices that are less direct include citizen complaint procedures or the movement of service facilities to geographic locations that are close to the clients being served; in these situations, more information about client problems and more intense client contact are presumed to make the services more responsive to client needs. In general, any movement toward citizen participation in local services actually consists of one or more attempts at client-oriented innovations. However, as in the case of the first two types of innovations, the client-oriented ones also require changes in bureaucratic structure and procedure to be implemented.

Tinkering with the System: Incrementalism Revisited

Independent of these three categories is the basic issue of the anticipated impact of local service innovations. An air of expectancy, directly attributable to the successful efforts in space exploration, has led us to believe that revolutionary changes in local services can occur overnight. Our imagination has been teased by visions of such new services as solid waste collection through a system of pneumatic tubes, policemen who are at once effective at dealing with different cultural groups, are well armed, and are quick responders to calls, and schools that will facilitate upward social mobility for even the most impoverished students. In fact, however, as of the mid-1970s, policemen still protect the streets, sanitation men still collect the garbage, and teachers still train students much as they did even two decades ago.

There have nevertheless been many innovations. Individually, however, most innovative efforts appear to have brought only marginal improvements to services. Some innovations, such as the use of quantitative fire deployment models, have increased safety but have left the basic firefighting job unchanged. Where actual firefighting practices have had to be changed to use a new technological device such as the jet-axe, there has been resistance to its use, and only a small percentage of fire departments have adopted the innovation

(Frohman et al., 1972). Other innovations, such as program budgeting, appear to have been accepted but later modified in such a way to restore the practices in effect before the innovation. Finally, many educational innovations, including attempts to change curriculums and improve teaching practices, have been found to cease after a short demonstration period, usually in relation to the cessation of federal funding.

The apparent marginality of these efforts leaves the impression that innovations in state and local governments have had little effect. However, our expectations of revolutionary changes as a result of technological, managerial, or client-oriented innovations may reflect an unrealistic and misleading generalization from the space effort.[d] The more relevant interpretation of innovative efforts in private or public organizations may be based on the cumulative impact of incremental changes. For instance, if one takes the long view and considers changes in law enforcement (as do the authors of an eminent textbook in the following quote), the degree of change is startling:

Police methods have changed greatly during the past hundred years. The police today use almost every conceivable means of transportation and communication. The horse patrol and nightstick on-the-pavement have given way to automobiles containing teleprinters, helicopters with television, and jet flying belts. Modern communication centers tape-record telephone messages and complaints as well as radio dispatches. . . . Police dispatchers now have access to computer-based visual-display terminals giving identification data, records of wanted property, and other information of great tactical value. Telephonic devices can automatically record on dictating machines reports made by officers from any telephone, and these reports can be transcribed onto a master from which any desired number of copies of the report may be reproduced. These systems are gradually replacing the typing of reports by the officers themselves as well as eliminating the frequently illegible copies of reports that resulted from the use of carbon paper. Television-based filing and retrieval systems now permit nearly instantaneous capture, storage, and random-access retrieval of documents with resolution high enough to permit classification of fingerprints transmitted by the system (Wilson and McLaren, 1972, pp. 8-9).

Thus the full impact of innovations may only be realized over a long period of time and may only consist of the aggregate effect of many minor changes. Innovations in state and local services may indeed only work in an incremental manner, adding in an almost marginal capacity to the organization's functions. Due to the complexity, inertia, disagreement over major objectives, and difficulty in gathering comprehensive information, organizational change itself may be considered an incremental process (Lindblom, 1959). To this extent, the degree of change may appear at any single point in time as having the effect of *tinkering with the system*; on the one hand, dramatic changes occur infrequently, but on the other hand the existing service system can sustain many changes without being entirely supplanted, destroyed, or rendered ineffective.

[d]For one who believes to the contrary, that the space experience is eminently generalizable as a paradigm for change, see Schulman (1975).

Given this view, an important goal of research is to provide an understanding of the tinkering process, for this process can still be made more (or less) effective through policy actions. To study the process, we have chosen to focus on recent attempts at technological innovations by state and local services.

Despite some disappointments in the past and some continued cynicism about future technological applications (e.g., see Nieburg, 1969), technological innovations hold the greatest interest for two reasons. First, the technological achievements in private industry and the continued high labor costs of public services suggest that there may be large payoffs if new technology can successfully produce savings in manpower in local services (e.g., Committee on Intergovernmental Science Relations, 1972; and Crawford, 1973). Other innovations could increase services without necessarily increasing manpower requirements. Integrated utilities, cable-based remote audio and visual contacts between service providers and clients, more effective burglar alarm systems, the tailoring of services to individual needs as in dial-a-ride systems, home health care diagnosis through remote communications, or personalized educational opportunities could all result in such improvements. Such claims are not to say that productivity improvements might not also follow from managerial or client-oriented innovations. However, there has been much experience with technological innovations, and these experiences deserve to be reviewed.

Second, a continuing public policy problem is to identify ways of making the federal role more effective in improving state and local services. On the surface, at least, the federal role may be more appropriate for technological innovations than for the other two types. Technological innovations, unlike the other two, may require large-scale efforts frequently beyond the means of a local government. In comparison with individual state and local governments, the federal government may more easily conduct new research and development, support tests of innovations at specific sites, provide technical assistance, or set product control standards. Thus any improved understanding of the innovative process is likely to be more relevant to federal policymaking if technological innovations are the major focus.

In brief, this study assesses previous experiences with technological innovations in state and local services and identifies those factors that have resulted in the successful (and unsuccessful) use of these innovations. Although there have been many reports about such innovations, especially on a case-by-case basis, there have been few assessments of the aggregate experience.[e] This study develops an aggregate perspective by summarizing 140 case studies of individual attempts to use technological innovations. These innovations cover such devices as new computer systems, new analytic routines or quantitative models, new service equipment for fire or police departments, the use of interactive

---

[e]In contrast, there are several good assessments of managerial innovations (e.g., Kimmel et al., 1974) and client-oriented innovations (e.g., Yin and Yates, 1975; Cole, 1974; and Washnis, 1974).

(two-way) television, and the use of new diagnostic equipment or information systems in hospitals. The case studies are all part of the existing literature (published and unpublished), written by many authors.

The Study of the Innovative Process in State and Local Services

Any attempt to assess the use of technological innovations bears directly on the problem of understanding organizational change. Our current understanding of the change process, however, is still very rudimentary. Little is known about how state and local governments innovate, or whether they can be induced to innovate. This knowledge is critical because it underlies certain strategies for change—e.g., those involving an active role by external organizations, such as the federal government. If such strategies are improperly designed or grounded on fallacious assumptions, then their implementation may not only be ineffective, but may even be counterproductive.

Traditional Approaches

Basic to the problem has been the apparent ineffectiveness of three traditional approaches used for describing and studying the innovative process. These approaches have not been adequate for explaining or predicting the use of innovations in such local organizations as schools, police departments, hospitals, or county agencies. On the basis of an exhaustive review of the organizational literature, Havelock (1969) described these three approaches as:[f]

The research, development, and diffusion approach;

The social interaction approach; and

The problem-solver approach.

Of these three, only the last begins to provide a realistic perspective for understanding innovative efforts in local organizations. However, even it has several major shortcomings. A review of the main features and problems with each approach follows.

The Research, Development, and Diffusion Approach. The first approach posits a staged sequence of events in which an innovation (a new artifact or technique) is: (1) discovered or tested in the laboratory, (2) further tested and demonstrated in the field, (3) communicated or diffused to potential users, (4) tested

---

[f]Havelock also suggested a fourth approach (the linkage approach), but this approach is not discussed because it was a hybrid of the first three.

by the users, and (5) adopted or rejected by the users on the basis of their testing. According to this approach, the more successfully the innovation passes through each of the first stages (based on actual evaluation), the more pervasive adoption will be. Havelock (1969) describes how this approach has been used in attempts to explain the innovative process in private industry R&D (Havelock and Benne, 1969), in the U.S. agricultural research and extension system, and in educational organizations (Brickell, 1964; and Clark and Guba, 1965). In addition, other investigators continue to subscribe to this view in examining the effects of such federal policies as the use and design of demonstration programs (e.g., Baer et al., 1976). However, at least in the case of local organizations, the approach has not satisfactorily explained why some innovative efforts succeed and others fail (House, 1974). The main problem is that experience has shown little relationship between the successful progression of an innovation through the first three stages and the ultimate extent of adoption.

One reason for this failure to explain innovative efforts in local organizations is that the approach assumes, first, the transferability of innovative experiences from one site to another and, second, a passive role by the ultimate adopter or user (House, 1974). Because of these two assumptions, the approach grossly overlooks implementation factors, and these very factors may be the reason that otherwise demonstrably worthy innovations are not adopted. The factors include such issues as:

> The adopter may have contrary or competing interests to pursue (e.g., maintaining organizational power) and hence an entirely different set of incentives than is assumed;

> The innovation may require substantial redesign to be suited to the local organization's needs;

> There may be resistance in some parts of the local organization to the use of the innovation; and

> Implementation may have simply not been competently guided or monitored.

The importance of these implementation factors does not merely imply that another stage—implementation—should be inserted into the original research, development, and diffusion approach. The more serious argument can be made that innovative efforts in local organizations do not follow the staged sequence at all but that, for instance, initiatives by the adopter may precede research and development.

Such arguments begin to challenge the utility of applying the whole research, development, and diffusion approach to local organizations. The basic features of an organization and its local setting, as well as the manner in which an innovation is introduced, may even outweigh the importance of research, development, or diffusion. Certainly there may be as many cases in which innovations with dubious merit (by R&D standards) were adopted by local organizations as there are cases of meritorious innovations having been adopted. To investigate how innovative efforts in local organizations may succeed, the study would therefore not be based on innovations as units of analysis (as implied by the research, development, and diffusion approach); it would rest more appropriately on organizations or types of local organizations as the units of analysis.

The Social Interaction Approach. Havelock (1969) uses this term to describe the classic diffusion approach, as represented especially in the work of Everett Rogers (e.g., Rogers and Shoemaker, 1971). The dominant concern in diffusion studies is the nature of communication within social networks of potential adopters. The approach is compatible with the research, development, and diffusion approach but interprets the innovative process from the standpoint of the individual adopter. It includes a staged sequence of events in which innovations: (1) come into the potential adopter's realm of awareness, (2) arouse the adopter's interest, (3) are evaluated by the adopter, (4) are given a trial, and (5) are finally adopted or rejected. The social interaction approach fosters the study of adoption in relation to the characteristics of the individual adopter, the communication channels, and the adopter's use of these channels. The approach has been fruitfully applied to the spread of scientific information (e.g., Crane, 1972), of innovations in agricultural practice (e.g., Rogers, 1962), of cultural innovations (e.g., Barnett, 1953), and of new health care practices among physicians (e.g., Coleman et al., 1966). A typical finding has been that certain cosmopolite traits—e.g., membership in an informal but professional communication network—are likely to be associated with individuals who are early adopters of an innovation (Rogers and Shoemaker, 1971).

This second approach has also been used to study the innovative process in situations where the adopter is not a single individual. In some cases, the adopter is the local populace expressing its desires in a referendum, and the innovations have included such decisions as the one to adopt fluoridation (e.g., Crain, 1966). In other cases, the adopter is a local organization, and the innovation has been a new service program (e.g., Mohr, 1969). The application of the social interaction approach to innovative efforts by organizations, however, has several shortcomings (Warner, 1974).

First, the innovations themselves may be misclassified. For instance, such innovations as the initiation of new programs or the use of some analytic model or technique may be traced across many agencies. This tracking procedure, however, rarely allows for mutations in the innovation from site to site, so that unless the tracking is done with considerable care to avoid misleading verbal labels, some agencies may get undue credit as an adopter of the innovation because they were overgenerous in interpreting the label, whereas other agencies may be ignored because they adopted the innovation but under a different label. Second, the approach is based on the premise that an adopter is an individual person, even though innovative efforts in organizations are not usually a unitary act of adoption by a single adopter. Those using the social interaction approach often have to select the adopter arbitrarily within the organization (usually the head of the local agency), and this results in a misleading oversimplification of the innovative process. Third, the approach also tends to underplay implementation factors. Typically, the approach arbitrarily assumes the agency head to be the adopter and then gives great emphasis to the adopter's external communication links; little attention is given to the distribution of power or resources within the organization. Examination of the implementation process, however, might reveal that the innovation had led to behavioral changes within the organization that were entirely unexpected and that serve as the most important facet of the innovation's effect.

To deal with these shortcomings, there have been attempts to modify the social interaction approach to make it more applicable to the study of the innovative process in organizations. Rogers and Eveland (1975), for instance, suggest that one possibility is to add the implementation stage to the original approach, making the decision to adopt merely an intervening variable, and defining permanent changes in organizational practice as a new set of dependent variables.ᵍ This and other elaborations still do not, however, make the social interaction approach suitable. Even with the elaborations, the approach tends to obscure the problem of the shifting nature of the innovation from site to site, the problem that innovative efforts are not the result of a unitary act of adoption by a single adopter, and the possibility that implementation factors may once again play an important role much earlier in the staged sequence and not merely after the decision to adopt has been made. An alternative conclusion would be to challenge the overall utility of the social interaction approach rather than to modify it, and to look for other ways of studying innovation in local organizations.

The Problem-Solver Approach. The third approach differs considerably from either of the first two, for it accepts a broad definition of an innovative effort that makes such an effort almost indistinguishable from the continued process of organizational change (e.g., Miles, 1965). Where the first two approaches tend to define an innovative effort as involving a device that is new to the whole set of organizations either in the same industry or providing the same type of public service (e.g., Becker and Whisler, 1967), the problem-solver approach regards an

---

ᵍThe brevity of these remarks should not be misleading. The Rogers and Eveland (1975) piece is a thoughtful and instructive reanalysis of the original diffusion paradigm, of its shortcomings in relation to organizational innovations, and of the potential need for a new paradigm.

innovative event as being the first use of a new device by the organization itself, regardless of the previous history of use by other organizations (e.g., Zaltman et al., 1973). Given this definition, the approach interprets the innovative process from the standpoint of a decisionmaker or group of individuals within the organization that: (1) recognizes or feels a need for change; (2) examines the problem and identifies alternative solutions; (3) selects an alternative and implements it by initiating organizational changes; and (4) evaluates the changes while making sure that the organization has achieved a new level of stability. In all of these activities, outside assistance may be used in a catalytic or consulting role, but the basic emphasis is on the organization's own initiative and understanding of the problem and solution and on a reliance on internal rather than external resources. The more these conditions prevail, the more likely the innovative effort will succeed (Havelock, 1969).

The potential usefulness of this third approach appears on the surface to be supported by recent experiences in state and local governments. Time and again there have been reports that the key to a successful innovative effort was the existence of an acknowledged need, the presence of a capable official within the organization who could actually resolve the problem by himself if he had the time, and the presence of a strong decisionmaker having the power to implement the solution (e.g., Radnor et al., 1970; Ernst, 1972; and Szanton, 1972). In addition, a separate review of the literature on the innovative process in the public sector resulted in a scheme that was identical in its main features to the problem-solver approach (Robbins et al., 1973). The problem-solver approach, however, makes the key assumptions that most if not all organizational changes stem from the existence of a problem, and that the service-improving innovation will be fully implemented by the organization once the service improvement has been initially demonstrated. In fact, some innovations may occur independently of any problem, and there may be conditions other than service improvement (as we see especially in Chapter 5) that can lead to the implementation of an innovation. Nevertheless, the problem-solver approach may provide more conceptually useful clues about the innovative process in local organizations than either of the first two approaches.

In relation to the other two approaches, one important deficiency of the problem-solver approach has been its lack of operational criteria and hence its inability to support empirical research. In fact, Havelock's review of the literature (1969) indicated that the problem-solver approach, unlike the other two, was not the outgrowth of extensive empirical efforts—even in organizations at other than the local level.

The operational shortcomings of the problem-solver approach begin with the problem of the unit of analysis. The obvious units of study are organizational events, and hence organizations, rather than the innovative device. The specific organizational events, however, are extremely difficult to define. The effort to create organizational change could be one appropriate definition of the innovative effort, but organizations are continually changing, and without further guidance one does not know the boundaries by which to define any specific change effort. Such boundaries, even artificially defined, would be needed just so a study could begin. Second, the approach creates a need to define specific organizational end states by which to gauge the effect of an innovative effort. In the first two approaches, the decision to adopt is usually arbitrarily defined as the end state and therefore can serve as a dependent variable for any research study. With the problem-solver approach, even if the change effort were adequately defined, rules would have to be developed for the specific behaviors or organizational states that would be regarded as outcome variables—e.g., changed behavior on the part of the practitioners in the organization, improvements in service performance, or the making of some internal set of decisions.

Recent attempts to revise and improve this approach have unfortunately not compensated for the lack of operational criteria. Berman and McLaughlin (1974), for instance, have developed a conceptual framework in which the relevant conceptual stages are support, implementation, and incorporation. Although these stages appear to be an accurate representation of the appropriate sets of organizational issues, and although the stages are basically compatible with the problem-solver approach,[h] their framework explicitly addresses neither the unit of analysis nor end-state problems, but merely lists a wide variety of organizational characteristics that are to be monitored. The exhaustive listing of such characteristics is inadequate, since in the case of local organizations these characteristics can continue endlessly to cover not only the innovating agency but also the larger district or superagency of which it is part, the executive office of the jurisdiction (the mayor's or governor's office), and other legislative and administrative bodies in the political process. With local organizations, in other words, some theory must guide the appropriate definition of an end state and the key organizational factors to be assessed.

In summary, although the problem-solver approach does not have the same conceptual flaws as the first two approaches, its operational inadequacy has reduced its usefulness as a research paradigm. The approach has failed to sustain large numbers of research investigations, but more critical, since each investigation has usually had to develop an idiosyncratic research framework, the evidence and conclusions from the studies have been difficult to compare and aggregate. As judged by Kuhn's (1962) view of the role that scientific paradigms play in creating convergence, scientific progress, and ultimately new knowledge, research using the problem-solver perspective is still in its preparadigmatic stage.

[h]Berman and McLaughlin would probably argue this point. For them, the problem-solver approach is still built around the act of adoption, whereas their own framework is built around the process of implementation. Our interpretation is that the problem-solver approach does in fact include implementation factors, but that in any case the main shortcoming of the approach is its lack of operational criteria and not its conceptual deficiency.

This is in marked contrast to the social interaction approach, for instance, where a single paradigm has become useful for studying any number of diffusion phenomena, and where investigators of diffusion phenomena are able to communicate easily and may actually form an invisible college (Crane, 1972) that cuts across the disciplines of economics, sociology, and political science (Rogers and Eveland, 1975).

Implementation

As a result of the dissatisfaction with these three approaches, attention has focused on developing a better understanding of the *implementation* process, and many investigators have recently stressed the importance of understanding the implementation process in local organizations (e.g., Gross et al., 1971; Pressman and Wildavsky, 1973; Zaltman et al., 1973; and Berman and McLaughlin, 1974). The implementation orientation explicitly begins with the peculiar bureaucratic characteristics of local organizations as the context for change. For instance, most local agencies have minimal opportunities for the lateral entry of new personnel at higher positions, have few incentives for making innovative efforts, and are dominated by a strong chain of command hierarchy (Archibald and Hoffman, 1969). Furthermore, the predisposition of the local organization to pursue the bureaucratic goals of self-preservation and autonomy may mean that the organization will tend to favor certain types of innovations—e.g., those that lead to a larger annual budget, or those that do not affect the basic resource mix or role relationships within the organization (Downs, 1967; and Pincus, 1974). The initiation of change, the generation of internal support for change, and the mounting of resources available for making changes are therefore key factors, and all form part of an *initiation* stage that is critical but has seldom been studied.

The implementation theme also deals explicitly with the problem of creating change on a permanent basis. New projects, especially those with external sources of financial support (as in federal programs implemented at the local level), have often been unexpectedly transient. Even though successful for a period of time, the projects fail to become a permanent part of the local organization once the external support has been removed or reduced. This has been true of numerous local services, varying from such innovations as new information and referral services placed in a branch library (Yin et al., 1974) to innovations in the education system (Berman and McLaughlin, 1974). Other innovations may last the duration of a specific political leader's tenure in office, even for more than one term, and then disappear (Costello, 1971). To understand how permanent change occurs, investigators have increasingly become concerned with the process of *incorporation*, or the ways in which new changes become a permanent part of the organization's bureaucratic fabric.

Falling between the stages of initiation and incorporation are many other events, such as changes in the amount of time pressure or in the number of decisions that are required. Pressman and Wildavsky (1973) point out in one case study that the time pressures were so severe and the required number of decision points so numerous that the innovation was doomed to failure, regardless of its merit. Other important factors include the degree of professional organization and the reward structure among service practitioners (Utech and Utech, 1973), the amount of client contact and influence (Lipsky, 1971; and Fainstein and Fainstein, 1972), and the traditions and other inherent organizational differences among the different types of local services (Yin and Yates, 1975).

The implementation theme appears to have captured more of the complex, behavioral nature of local organizations than have the traditional approaches. However, the theme has yet to become a paradigm for studying the innovative process in organizations. As with the problem-solver approach, too many important concepts have not been specified in operational terms. It is not easy to tell, for instance, where the various stages of initiation and incorporation begin or end, or what units are the appropriate subjects for analysis. Similarly, the breadth of outcomes needed to assess organizational end states also remains unspecified.

To this extent, anyone who studies the innovative process in state and local services is confronted with a dilemma. On the one hand, the two approaches that have proved most suitable for studying innovative efforts by individuals or in the private sector—namely research, development, and diffusion; and social interaction—are conceptually inappropriate for studying innovations in local organizations. On the other hand, the two approaches—problem solver and implementation—which appear more conceptually appropriate have not yet been the subject of intensive empirical investigation, and the problems of developing measures for key concepts may even be insurmountable. This dilemma certainly draws attention to the fact that (from Kuhn's perspective again) research on innovations in local (or even all) organizations may be regarded as having arrived at a critical juncture where a new paradigm may soon emerge. However, and more important for the current study, the dilemma also means that any new study of innovations in local organizations—including a study focusing on the use of technological innovations—must explicitly describe its conceptual framework.

The Study Design

Although Chapter 2 describes the complete methodology of our study, the basic conceptual framework for the study may be described as follows. The study took as its unit of analysis a site-specific innovative experience by a state or local government agency as recorded and described in an existing case study. This definition was intended to include any innovative experience, regardless of the type of technological device involved. To this extent, the goal was to analyze the peculiar organizational experiences for a variety of technological innovations. The choice of the unit of analysis was intended to reflect a greater interest in the innovative process in local organizations, and less interest in relating the diffusion experience of single technologies.

The evidence to be examined in each case study dealt with the identification of: (1) the outcomes of attempts at implementing technological innovations and (2) the relationship between these outcomes and other factors in the case setting. Successful attempts were defined in terms of four conditions. Each condition represented a different combination of the degree to which an innovation was found beneficial—i.e., produced a service improvement of any sort, whether of an input or output nature—and the degree to which it was incorporated into the daily activities of the local agency. The four conditions involved situations in which:

An innovation produces a service improvement, and it is also incorporated;

The innovation does not produce any improvement, and it is also not incorporated;

The innovation produces an improvement, but is not incorporated; and

The innovation does not produce an improvement, but is nevertheless incorporated.

The four conditions were judged, of course, from the perspective of the case study's evidence, which was not necessarily the same as the perspective of the organization in which the innovative effort has occurred.[i] From the case study's perspective, the first two conditions were regarded as successes. A successful technological innovation, in other words, was defined for the purpose of this study as either a meritorious innovation that had been incorporated ($success_1$), or a nonmeritorious innovation that had not been incorporated ($success_2$). The third and fourth conditions were regarded as failures.[j] Technology that was incorporated although there was no evidence of a service improvement, or, where there was such improvement, was not incorporated, was regarded as counterproductive.[k] The four conditions may be depicted as in Figure 1-1.

---

[i]This is mainly a reminder that the organization may or may not have been aware of the case study, and its administrators may, if given the opportunity, have disagreed with the findings of the case study.

[j]This use of the terms "success" and "failure," of course, is made only for the purpose of the present study. For other investigations, the different combinations of outcomes might be designated with an entirely different set of labels, and a combination considered a failure here may be considered a success under some other circumstance.

[k]In assessing these outcomes, it is important to remember that our main evidence is a body of 140 existing case studies. The outcomes therefore reflect the state of an innovative effort at the time that a particular case study was written. Since the case studies were not uniformly written in relation to a specific stage in the innovative process, and since most of the studies were written only a short time (one or two years) after the innovative effort began, our outcomes reflect only the state of the effort at the end of each case study.

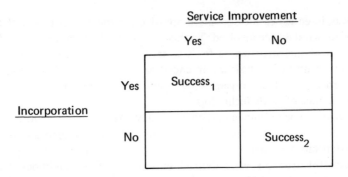

Figure 1-1. Definition of Successful Outcomes of Innovative Efforts.

To understand why any one of these conditions occurred in a particular setting, the factors associated with either the successful or unsuccessful outcomes were explored. The factors considered were all drawn from the existing literature on organizational innovation and thus individually constitute a reexamination of most of the prominent ideas regarding the innovative process. One set of factors dealt with the characteristics of the innovative device (Chapter 3). Then other background factors (i.e., characteristics of the community and the stable state of the organization) and implementation factors (i.e., characteristics of the specific innovative effort) were examined independently and in comparison with the characteristics of the device (Chapter 4). The comparative analysis of these factors attempted to identify the optimal set of conditions associated with successful outcomes. Throughout the comparisons, our major hypothesis was that the *implementation* factors would be the most important. The hypothesis draws directly from the observed failure by either the research, development, and diffusion approach or the social interaction approach to account for innovation in local organizations, as well as from the mounting evidence concerning the importance of implementation factors.

As one result of this framework, the study does not examine the origins of the technological devices, the research or development efforts associated with the devices, or the other factors generally associated with the research, development, and diffusion approach. Instead, the major theoretical contribution is on organizational change. Chapter 5 suggests that two different sets of conditions—and hence possibly two different organizational processes—are related to the two components of the success outcome. In other words, the second major hypothesis of our study was that the two components of success—evidence of a service improvement and evidence of incorporation into the daily activities of the organization—were themselves outcomes of *two different innovative processes*, and that successful use of technological innovations in local services requires an understanding of both of these processes.

Finally, the role of federal policies has been examined separately by analyzing the association between specific types of federal policies and successful and unsuccessful outcomes (Chapter 6). Any direct associations would tell us about the role that federal policies have played in the past and could provide some guidelines for the desired nature of federal intervention in the future. A third hypothesis of our study related to this analysis of federal policies. Once again, because of the increasing evidence on the importance of implementation factors—especially within each local setting—we hypothesized that federal policies would not be notably correlated with the outcomes of innovative efforts. Such policies may have been implicitly based on the research, development, and diffusion approach or the social interaction approach, and these approaches appear not to account for innovative changes in local organizations. The analysis and conclusions in Chapter 6 therefore bear the major policies implications for the entire study.

The basic analytic strategy was to note the relationships among key characteristics of the innovative process in each case study and to aggregate the frequency of these relationships. Thus the main conclusions of our study are based on the aggregate nature of the case studies. Our overall objective has been to generalize from case studies on the use of technological innovations in local organizations, but in a more rigorous fashion than previous investigations that have aggregated evidence from individual cases in the private sector (e.g., Myers and Marquis, 1969; Cahn, 1970; Utterback, 1974; and Gayer, 1974). The next chapter discusses the process of searching for case studies, the nature and quality of the evidence they presented, and the method we used to aggregate the evidence.

2

The Nature of the Evidence

Case Studies as Evidence

The analytic goal of the present study was to examine the innovative process by aggregating evidence from case studies of technological innovations in state and local governments. Viewed one way, such a review of case studies basically represents another type of literature review, in which the main goal is to develop conclusions about what the available research already says. Viewed another way, the aggregate picture, because it is based on an innovative and methodologically rigorous procedure (see Yin and Heald, 1975), represents a replicable and significant contribution. To appreciate the latter view more fully requires a description of the case studies and the process by which they were identified, as well as the *case survey method* by which the aggregate picture was developed.

The case studies may have served originally as a formal evaluation, as an observer's report about a situation, or even as a grantee's report submitted upon the completion of a project. Whatever the purpose, the case study has had wide use because it can focus on an organizational change and can cover the peculiar flavor, setting, and people that are likely to explain what happened and why. A good case study attempts to capture the unique blend of events occurring in an organization, much as the clinical approach in psychology is able to present the unique situation and personal background involved in analyzing an individual's behavior. Although a case study may end at an arbitrary point and therefore preclude followup analysis or the examination of secondary effects, the case study nevertheless usually traces organizational events over time (up to its arbitrary end point) and hence provides insights into the actual process of organizational change.

Since existing case studies of technological innovations were the basic evidence of our study, the cases served in a formal sense as the universe or population of concern. The conclusions and generalizations drawn from our analysis therefore pertain to what the case study literature says. For obvious reasons, the case study literature, as with any research literature, is likely to provide a biased picture of the actual innovative experience. For instance, some experiences may not have been documented, authors of case studies may have been disproportionately attracted to successful experiences, or certain services, such as education, may have more frequently been the subject of a case study because of the availability of federal funds to support the writing of the case study. Since the full extent and nature of these biases are unknown, the conclusions from an analysis of case studies, as in any other review of the literature, cannot be directly related to the actual innovative experience. However, even given this limitation, the case study literature is still invaluable in that it provides a rich range of experiences from which to analyze the innovative process. No other source of evidence describes in detail the innovative experiences for such a wide variety of locales, innovative devices, or service sectors. This contrasts with most other studies of technological innovation, which are often limited to either one or two types of innovation or service sectors.

The aggregation and analysis of the evidence in the case studies involved two procedures: (1) the definition and the identification of case studies describing factors in the innovative process, and (2) the systematic extraction of the information from each case study to allow subsequent aggregation.

Definition and Identification of Case Studies

Any attempt to generalize from a sample to the universe of case studies must deal first with the problem of defining the specific sample to be analyzed. In the ideal situation, the sample must be defined so that its relationship to the universe of all case studies is known—e.g., it is a representative sample. Unfortunately, no rigorous method is available for defining this relationship.

There are two ways of attempting to deal with the problem, both of which are followed in the present study. The first is to conduct a search for case studies that is as *exhaustive* as possible, so that the final sample to be analyzed may constitute a majority of the entire population of case studies. If the sample is a dominant portion of the population, then the precise relationship between the sample and the population becomes less critical. The second is to conduct a search for case studies that is as *unbiased* as possible with regard to the use of sources and citations, so that no single type of case study is more likely to be identified than any other type of case study (e.g., books as well as unpublished reports, or studies conducted by sociologists as well as those by political scientists). To deal with the sampling problem, one must therefore establish an orderly procedure of searching for and identifying case studies—a step that is usually given only superficial attention in traditional assessments of research literatures.

In the present study, the search began with several criteria for defining a case study. To qualify as a case study, a written report had to describe the organizational events in a specific local agency (e.g., school, police department, or county or state office). Further, these events had to cover:

The organization's first experience with a new machine, material, chemical, computer system, or quantitative analysis; and

An experience in which the innovation had actually been tested for use or implemented within the organizational context and not merely studied, as in a feasibility study, or tested in a quasi-laboratory or experimental situation.

In addition, even though written reports that were unpublished or in manuscript (prepublication) form were accepted as case studies, written reports were excluded from consideration if they appeared: (1) in trade journals or magazines (typically published by nonacademic institutions); (2) only as a result of a conference; or (3) before 1965. The first two exclusions were made because of the generally fragmentary nature of such reports. As the third exclusion, it was decided to limit the search to the last ten years because of a restriction on available resources.

Search Process

Given these ground rules, an attempt was made to conduct an exhaustive and unbiased (with the one exclusion noted later) search covering the ten-year period from 1965 to 1975. This search included four main sources of information. First, available libraries and bibliographic services—such as the National Technical Information Service—were examined, using such subject headings as urban technology, technology transfer, innovations, urban models, and public technology. Second, citations contained in individual works were examined for references to potential case studies. Third, a large number of relevant journals was examined, issue by issue, for case studies appearing as articles during the years 1965-1975. Fourth, numerous individuals were contacted and asked about their knowledge of case studies. These individuals generally fell into one of two groups: officials of federal agencies likely to support technological innovations of their study, and professionals in universities, national organizations, or consortia of local governments who were likely to conduct tests or studies of technological innovations. Appendix A lists the bibliographic sources, the journals searched, and the individuals contacted. As the one exception in the search process, local agency officials who might have known about case studies in their locale were systematically excluded because of resource limitations. Any attempt to survey this population would have required an overwhelming number of individual contacts.

Wherever a title or abstract appeared relevant, the full written report was examined to determine if it suited the definition for a case study. This search procedure produced a total of 140 case studies. In addition, the search procedure uncovered many written reports that ultimately did not qualify as case studies. In most instances, disqualification resulted because the written report either did not concern a technological innovation or the report did not describe an innovation that had been intended for implementation. In other instances, an implemented innovation was described, but only as a steady-state characteristic, excluding any discussion of the organization's first experience with the innovation. In yet other instances, the case study mainly described the technical and not the organizational aspects of the innovative effort, a characteristic that in fact is quite common among cases of technological innovation (Douds and Rubenstein, 1975).

The search procedure also produced reports that were actually multisite or multiorganization studies. In these reports, the characteristics of individual sites or organizational settings were usually covered only by the use of aggregate statistics and therefore could not be analyzed in the same manner as the single case studies. These multisite reports remain an important part of the literature on organizational innovation, however, and the methods and findings for each report are summarized in Appendix F. Since this classification of the written reports into case studies, non-case studies, and multisite studies was a critical product of the search procedure, Appendix B lists the final collection of case studies as well as the other two categories of written reports.

Nature of the Case Studies Identified

The 140 case studies that were collected had the following characteristics:[a]

69 percent appeared in an unpublished form, 31 percent as journal articles or books;

46 percent were dated from 1973 to the present, and 43 percent were dated 1971 or 1972;

64 percent of the studies were conducted with partial or total support from the federal government (independent of whether federal funds were also used to support the innovative effort);

69 percent reported on efforts in agencies in the central city; the remainder on activities in states, countries, and metropolitan jurisdictions, such as councils of governments;

The majority of the case studies reported on innovative efforts in the eastern portion of the country;

Roughly similar proportions of the studies covered small, medium, and large jurisdictions; and

[a]See Appendix C for the instrument used in collecting information from the case study and section A in particular for the frequency distribution of responses to each question about case study characteristics.

Roughly 20 percent of the studies covered each of five different types of state and local services (police and fire, education, health, transportation and public works, and planning and miscellaneous).

Judged by these characteristics, the case studies tended to be official but unpublished reports, dated during the last four years, and supported by federal funds. The typical study reported on an innovative effort in an agency of a central city located in the eastern United States.

Factors in the Innovative Process

The analysis of the case studies attempted to identify key factors in the innovative experience for each case. The key factors were based on the mentioning of a key word or phrase in the case study. The analysis was therefore based on the actual reporting of an event or organizational characteristic by the case study. (Obviously, there may have been instances where an event occurred but was not reported.) The procedure does not therefore represent an analysis of the hypotheses presented by the case studies themselves (many of which had no real hypotheses). The main goal was to define the potential causal factors that produced the successful use of new technology for each case study, and then to aggregate the findings for the body of case studies as a whole. In theory, an understanding of the innovative process could then lead to the design of effective strategies for change, particularly in using federal resources (or showing where they should not be used) as instruments of change. In practice, our analysis could identify only those factors *associated with* success or failure. Although such associational links are not sufficient grounds for establishing causal relations, the failure to find a consistent associational link between a given factor and either a successful or unsuccessful outcome is sufficient grounds for rejecting that factor as causal in the innovative process.

A list of potentially relevant factors to be sought in the case studies was based on a thorough review of recent studies of organizational efforts to innovate, especially those using technological devices. Various studies have emphasized different factors, but four sets of factors appear to be most frequently discussed and most relevant.[b] These factors are described in detail in subsequent chapters and are introduced only briefly here. In addition, to give the reader concrete examples of the case study evidence, Appendix E presents some of the items that were coded from the case studies that reflected these factors.

---

[b]Although many of the empirical studies may focus on only one or two factors at a time, recent reviews of the literature (e.g., Rothman, 1974; Zaltman et al., 1973; Rowe and Boise, 1973; and Roessner, 1974) have generally covered these same four sets.

First, the *innovative device* itself has many characteristics that may or may not be important for successful outcomes. For instance, hardware-oriented innovations such as two-way telecommunications networks in health care systems (Rockoff, 1975) may lead to different results than software-oriented innovations such as operations research analysis (Rosenbloom and Russell, 1971). Furthermore, a device's technological merit and its political visibility may account for differences in outcomes. The long-term merit of an innovation in relation to existing practices may normally lead to its acceptance; however, given the current political conditions in most cities, innovations combining short-term gains with high visibility may be more likely to be implemented (Costello, 1971).

A second set of factors has to do with the *innovating agency*. Typically, with local organizations, the concern has been that the agency's formal structure, budgetary constraints, or bureaucratic incentives serve mainly as barriers to innovation, and these barriers are likely to be found throughout local services—public safety departments, schools, hospitals, social welfare agencies, and public works agencies (Laudon, 1974; Pincus, 1974; U.S. Department of Justice, 1973a and 1973b; The Urban Institute, 1971; and Frohman et al., 1972). The personnel structure of local organizations has also been cited as a barrier to innovation, with line agencies dominated by single practitioner specialties rather than a diverse set of professional occupations that could expose employees to different perspectives (Alesch, 1971; Gordon, 1973; and Savas and Ginsburg, 1973).

The *external conditions* related to the innovative effort are yet a third set of factors. These factors include the general social and political conditions that may reflect needs for more service improvements and hence provide an incentive for a local agency to consider an innovation; the market conditions that affect the participation of private industry in the manufacturing and testing of innovations (Lambright and Teich, 1974); the role of professional and other external organizations in fostering an innovative environment (Feller et al., 1974); and communications among service practitioners in similar agencies but different jurisdictions (Utech and Utech, 1973; and Cohn and Manning, 1974). Viewed another way, a variety of institutions participate directly or indirectly in the decision to innovate. For instance, Arthur Ezra (1975) has described the institutional participants in a technology delivery system for a solar energy innovation in the housing industry as including the homeowner, the homebuilders and developers, equipment manufacturers, lending institutions, local government codes and regulations, and architectural and engineering companies. In addition, federal agencies have become an increasingly important part of the technology delivery system in almost every local service, whether concerned with highway safety, solid waste collection and disposal, public safety, education, or health. The federal role, both in managing federal programs that call for local innovations and in influencing procurement standards and other regulations that will affect the innovative process, needs to be studied explicitly.

A fourth set of factors concerns the *implementation process*, or the process of testing a technological innovation and integrating it into an agency's organization. Implementation factors involve a mix of characteristics of the innovating agency and external conditions. Within the innovating agency, for instance, the management and monitoring of implementation (Gross et al., 1971), the participation of service practitioners in early planning and testing (House, 1974), and the timing of the innovation to suit specific decisionmaking needs (Radnor et al., 1970; and Burt et al., 1972) all appear to be important to successful innovative efforts. Outside of the agency, the commitment and leadership by top executives, whether the elected head of the jurisdiction or a city elected school board, often appear essential (International City Management Association, 1972; and Yin et al., 1974). In addition, attention has focused on the role of specific actors during implementation. The personal attributes of an innovator or of an implementer can contribute substantially to the innovative effort (Hayes and Rasmussen, 1972). Similarly, the role of an externally based change agent who operates within the innovating agency has frequently been considered important for changes in the educational system (Carlson et al., 1965).

These four sets of factors, then, appear to characterize innovative efforts in local organizations and to include the potentially important causal factors that produce success or failure. To extract these factors from each case study, a standardized checklist of closed-ended questions was developed. Appendix C contains the checklist that was used, with questions concerning the outcomes reflected in section F of the checklist and questions concerning the innovative device, the innovating agency, the external conditions, and the implementation process in the checklist's other sections.

The Case Survey Method

The final set of 140 case studies on technological innovation became the main units of analysis in our study, and the information extracted in a uniform manner from each case study constituted the data. The data could then be aggregated to provide conclusions about the sample of case studies as a whole. This method of aggregation and analysis, which is known as the *case survey method*, has been applied previously to a study of urban decentralization and citizen participation, in which the information from 269 case studies was analyzed and aggregated (Yin and Yates, 1975). The rationale and procedures for the case survey method have been fully reported elsewhere (Lucas, 1974; and Yin and Heald, 1975), but its main features are worth reviewing.

The case survey method involves the use of a checklist of closed-ended questions. The questions are designed to cover both the characteristics of the case study (e.g., the date and type of publication) and the information reported in the case study (e.g., the type of innovation being studied and the outcomes of the implementation experience). For each case study, a reader-analyst answers the checklist questions and gives a level-of-confidence rating ("sure" or "not sure") for each answer.[c] The reader-analyst also has the option of answering any question "impossible to answer" if the case study does not provide any suitable information. Since the questions are closed-ended, the information from each case study can then be tabulated and aggregated.

Because the case survey procedures are explicit, the entire review process may be replicated. A comparison of the responses of two different analysts can also indicate the reliability of the method. In the present study, a random sample of 23 of the 140 case studies was selected for reliability analysis. To determine interanalyst agreement, two analysts independently read each study and completed a checklist. Among all checklist items for which both analysts gave a substantive response (i.e., neither responded "impossible to answer"), the agreement between analysts was 71.9 percent (see Table 2-1). (When "impossible to answer" responses were considered in the total, the overall reliability dropped to 62.1 percent.) When the level-of-confidence rating is taken into account, the degree of agreement diverges as expected: for answers with a "sure" level of confidence, interanalyst agreement reached 77.1 percent; for answers with a "not sure" level of confidence, agreement dropped to 59.8 percent.[d] These levels of agreement may be considered quite satisfactory, since almost all of the

Table 2-1
Reliability Analysis of Twenty-three Case Studies Based on Ratings of Two Analysts

Level of Confidence*	Percentage of Responses	Percentage of Agreement	
		Mean	Standard Deviation
Sure	74.4	77.1	7.8
Not sure	25.6	59.8	15.7
Total	100.0	71.9	6.5

*"Sure" includes those responses for which both reader-analysts were sure; "not sure" includes those responses where one or both reader-analysts were not sure. The total does not include responses for which either analyst considered the question impossible to answer.

[c]The reader analyst is both the experimentor and the subject of experimentation. The only prerequisites for filling such a role are that a person be familiar with the general issues and literature being studied, and that he/she follow some simple instructions (e.g., "fill in every box on the checklist"). No training is needed that is specific to the investigation at hand.

[d]Since the "sure" responses were more reliable, one can accept with more confidence the data from questions for which the percentage of "sure" responses was high. To provide such information about the relative reliability of the case survey data, the checklist in Appendix C also presents the percentage of "sure" responses given for each checklist question. In general, one should note, however, that the percentage of "sure" responses was quite high and varied little for most of the questions.

questions on the checklist involved multiple response categories, placing the expected (random) level of agreement well below 50 percent. Moreover, these figures compare quite closely to the reliability estimates obtained (82.4 and 60.2 percent, respectively, for "sure" and "not sure" answers) in a previous application of the case survey method to case studies of urban decentralization (Yin and Yates, 1975; and Yin and Heald, 1975).

Quality of the Case Studies

A methodological advantage of the case survey method is that it allows one to examine and evaluate the information reported in the case study in light of the quality of the study. In contrast, traditional reviews have suffered from a procedural defect that occurs after the initial body of literature has been assembled: *The investigator typically discards the poorer quality studies without describing the discard procedures.* Since the review then covers only a fraction of the literature initially gathered, the effects of the discard procedure are left unknown.

To overcome this defect requires the development of explicit criteria for assessing the research quality of a given case study. The investigator can apply these criteria to every study uncovered by the initial search and can then compare the quality of each study to its substantive characteristics and conclusions. This capability leads to two options: if different quality studies do not vary in their range of innovative experiences covered, then the lower quality studies may be discarded or given less weight, with the discard or weighting procedure now made explicit; if different quality studies vary in such coverage, then all the studies ought to be retained, but a quality check needs to be given with each substantive finding, so that the effects of quality on each finding can be identified.

The assessment of the research quality of policy studies has only recently attracted serious scholarly attention. For the most part, the concern has been with the assessment of evaluation studies, since so many such studies were initiated along with federal social welfare programs of the last decade. The antipoverty programs in particular included significant support for evaluation studies to assist policymakers in deciding what variants of different programs were most worth continuing or expanding (Ferman, 1969). However, even though the number of evaluation studies on antipoverty and other programs grew, only a small percentage of the studies had any effect on decisionmaking, and as one result, questions were raised regarding the quality of the studies (Wholey et al., 1970).

The 140 case studies we have gathered on technological innovations do not in any way represent a body of evaluation studies. Nevertheless, it is useful to organize our analysis by following the same concerns as typically found in *evaluations of evaluations:*[e] (1) the criteria for judging quality, (2) the proportion of case studies that are found to be of adequate quality, (3) a comparison between this proportion and those found in other studies, and (4) the substantive case study characteristics that vary with the quality of the study, leading to a decision about which studies, if any, should be discarded.

Criteria for Judging Quality

Most studies of evaluation research (see the articles in Caro, 1971; Rossi and Williams, 1972; Weiss, 1972; and Caporaso and Roos, 1973) have called attention to two criteria that appear to be important in judging the quality of evaluation studies:

> The measures used, or the degree to which both the intervention process and its outcomes were measured with reliable and valid instruments (Riecken and Boruch, 1974); and

> The research design used, or the degree to which the evaluation study followed the paradigm for experimental research and has internal and external validity (Campbell and Stanley, 1966).

Implicit in these criteria are notions of hypothesis testing and theory building about the intervention process, although the main objective of an evaluation study may simply be to determine whether an intervention works as expected without regard to any understanding of the process.

The concern for adequate measures and research design is reflected in every evaluation of evaluations. Different approaches to assessing their adequacy, however, have been used. In one approach, Gilbert et al. (1974) limited their review of twenty-nine highly rated evaluation studies to those studies that at a minimum involved a randomized, controlled field trial. In another approach, investigators (Mann, 1972; Bernstein and Freeman, 1975; and Yin and Yates, 1975) categorized studies according to the presence or absence of quantitative measures and research design, with those studies using operational measures and some acceptable experimental or quasi-experimental design (Campbell, 1957; Campbell and Stanley, 1966; and Campbell, 1969) being regarded as having the highest quality, and those studies using either little quantitative evidence or some weak research design, such as a one-shot case study, usually being regarded

---

[e]This term will be used to refer to other aggregative studies that have dealt with some large group of individual evaluation studies, even though the term has also referred to single reassessments of single evaluations. Five aggregative studies will be referred to in particular: Wholey et al. (1970); Mann (1972); Gilbert et al. (1974); Bernstein and Freeman (1975); and Gordon and Morse (1975). A sixth study (Yin and Yates, 1975), an evaluation of case studies, will also be referred to.

as having the lowest quality. In yet a third approach, Gordon and Morse (1975) used a combined quality score that was based on a subjective rating. Each evaluation study was judged on a five-point scale for the appropriateness of the study's conclusions in relation to its research findings. Gordon and Morse aptly point out that they ". . . felt it necessary to do this because research quality is dependent upon appropriate use of technique rather than simply the presence or absence of a given technique."

In addition to judgments concerning the quality of the measures and research design used, a third criterion for research quality has been identified, especially for evaluation studies, but has seldom been applied:

> Research utilization, or the degree to which an evaluation study has addressed decisionmaking issues and provided relevant findings in a timely manner.

In contrast to the first two criteria, which tend to reflect academic concerns in assessing research quality, the research utilization criterion calls attention to the fact that evaluation studies are not conducted for purely academic reasons, but are usually intended for use by some decisionmaker. The quality of an evaluation study should therefore be judged according to some criterion of policy relevance, over and above the first two criteria of measurement and research design. Thus, for instance, Roos (1973) has suggested that evaluation studies must: (1) address the decisionmaker's objectives, (2) examine programmatically relevant alternatives, and (3) arrive at results in a timely fashion, presented intelligibly for use by the decisionmaker.

Of the existing evaluations of evaluations, only one investigation (Wholey et al., 1970) made any attempt to assess the studies according to any research utilization criterion. The criterion was a stringent one: the evaluation study had to have a direct effect on changes in program policies or resource allocations. The authors found that, by this criterion, there was a dearth of successful evaluation studies, with the main reasons for failure being the resistance to change by the decisionmaker and the irrelevant research design of the study. The failure to finish research in a timely manner or to communicate the results to the decisionmaker have also been cited as common reasons that evaluation studies do not meet the research utilization criterion (Weiss, 1971).

Besides these first three criteria for assessing research quality, others have been suggested, reflecting concerns about value judgments, the selection of variables to be studied, and the type of organizations and investigators that carry out the research. However, since most case study research still does not follow the basic requirements for establishing internally valid studies, any assessment of research quality must still emphasize the first two criteria—i.e., the appropriate use of research measures and design. The present review of 140 case studies thus attempted to develop several measures for these two criteria. These measures both addressed the simple presence of a methodological characteristic and provided a subjective rating of the methodological adequacy:

1. The presence of operational measures for both the innovative device and the outcomes of the innovative effort (question A-7[f] of the checklist)
2. The presence of a relevant research design (question A-8);
3. A subjective rating, similar to the one used by Gordon and Morse (1975), of the adequacy of the study's overall evidence in relation to its conclusions (question F-13); and
4. A series of subjective ratings of the adequacy of the evidence presented for each of the study's major stated outcomes (question F-4).

Because the case studies were mainly intended as reports of innovative experiences, no attempt was made to apply the third criterion of research utilization. As with a previous review of case studies of urban decentralization and citizen participation experiences (Yin and Yates, 1975), the case studies of technological innovations had a variety of audiences, with only a few instances where a specific study was intended to serve a specific decisionmaking need.

Proportion of Case Studies of Adequate Quality

A case study of adequate quality may be presumed to be one that scores at the top of all four of these measures. Let us first look at the distribution for each measure singly and then determine the fraction of case studies that scored at the top on all measures.

Based on the two measures of quality that concern the presence or absence of methodological features, the 140 case studies fell into the following categories (see Table 2-2): ninety-four (or about 66 percent) provided an operational description of both the innovative device and its performance; fifty-seven (or about 40 percent) contained some relevant research design, usually a before-versus-after set of observations, but without any control or comparison group; and forty-three case studies (or about 30 percent) of the studies had both the operational description and relevant research design. As for the two subjective ratings, the full distribution of the rating categories is shown in Table 2-3, with the main finding that twenty-two (or about 15 percent) of the studies were given an overall rating for having good support for the conclusions drawn, whereas fifty (or about 35 percent) had a high rating for having good support for each stated outcome.

If the degree of overlap among all four measures is examined, an initial

---

[f]This notation refers to the original question in the checklist and is used throughout the report to guide the reader who wants to examine the question and its alternate answers. See Appendix C for the checklist.

Table 2-2

Distribution of Case Studies According to Presence of Two Methodological Characteristics

(N = 140)

	Research Design				
Measures	*Some Relevant Design*	*Line of Argument No Design*	*Coherent Descrip- tion*	*None of These*	*Total*
Operational description of both innovative device and outcomes	43	30	17	4	94
Operational description of performance only	10	4	4	3	21
Operational description of innovative device only	3	2	8	2	15
None of above	1	3	5	1	10
Total	57	39	34	10	140

Table 2-3

Distribution of Case Studies According to Two Subjective Ratings of Research Quality

(N = 140)

	Number of Case Studies	
Rating	*Overall Conclusions*	*Support for Each Stated Outcome*
Good support for conclusions; alternative explanations ruled out	22 ⎫	50
Some support	61 ⎰	
Neutral	44	57
Evidence for minor points is contrary to conclusions	11 ⎫	
Evidence for major points is strongly contrary to conclusions	2 ⎰	33
Total	140	140

finding is that the four measures were significantly related to each other in a positive direction. Table 2-4 shows a matrix of χ^2 values for the simple pairwise relationships among the four measures; the actual contingency tables are given in Appendix D.[g] A second finding is that fifteen (or 10.7 percent) of the studies can

[g] Key contingency tables appear in the text; all supplementary tables appear in Appendix D.

Table 2-4

Positive Relationships Among Four Measures of Research Quality

(x^2 values, N = 140)[a]

Measure	Operational Measures	Relevant Research Design	Overall Adequacy	Adequacy for Each Outcome
Presence of operational measures of innovative device and outcomes				
Presence of some relevant research design	$x^2 = 20.20$[b] df = 9			
Rating for overall adequacy of evidence in relation to conclusions	$x^2 = 22.83$[b] df = 12	$x^2 = 46.00$[c] df = 12		
Rating for adequacy of evidence in relation to each stated outcome	$x^2 = 13.05$[b] df = 6	$x^2 = 29.83$[c] df = 6	$x^2 = 40.73$[c] df = 8	

[a]The x^2 is used throughout the data analysis even though the collection of case studies is not a random sample. The reader is therefore cautioned to examine the raw observations closely (see the contingency tables in Appendix D) and to use the x^2 calculations only as a guideline for interpreting the data.

[b]$p < 0.05$.

[c]$p < 0.001$.

be regarded as having adequate quality in that they scored at the top of all four measures and therefore had: (a) operational measures of both the innovative device and its outcomes, (b) some relevant research design, (c) the highest subjective rating for providing overall support for the conclusions drawn, and (d) the highest subjective rating for providing support for each stated outcome. In other words, if an investigation of the 140 case studies were to restrict its analysis to those case studies of acceptable quality, the original case load would be reduced from 140 to fifteen.

Two major questions remain. First, how does the proportion of case studies of adequate quality compare with the experiences of other evaluations of evaluations; and second, what difference, if any, does variation in research quality make in relation to the other characteristics of the case study?

Comparison with Evaluations of Evaluations

At first glance, the fact that only 10.7 percent of the studies were deemed of adequate research quality suggests that the case studies under review were of poorer quality than other collections of evaluation studies. To a certain extent, this was true simply because most of the case studies were not intended to serve as evaluations. Nevertheless, a comparison between this proportion and those found by evaluations of evaluation studies shows some similarities in the proportion of studies ultimately found to be of acceptable research quality.

In one evaluation of evaluations, Bernstein and Freeman (1975) contacted all FY 1970 awardees of federal projects concerned with evaluating a large-scale action program. Of the original 318 awardees who returned a questionnaire, eighty-two (or 26 percent) claimed that they did not feel that they were doing or planning an evaluation study. Bernstein and Freeman note (p. 28) that these eight-two studies "... might properly be considered of 'low' quality." They suggest also (p. 34) that, of the remaining 236 studies, "... if there is a bias, it is toward the studies appearing more technically sophisticated and complete than they actually are," since many awardees were still reporting about their plans and not about what they had done.

Concerning the 236 studies, eighty-four lacked a measure of the intervention process or its outcomes (or both), and the remaining 152 studies were ranked according to their adequacy for six methodological features, including research design, sampling, measures used, and data analysis and statistical procedures. The rankings showed that seventy-six studies were adequate on over four of these six features, and seventy-six studies were adequate on four or fewer. Table 2-5 summarizes the total number of evaluation studies for different types of quality. The table shows that out of a collection of federally funded evaluation studies (and given a bias toward the studies appearing to be of higher quality than they actually were), only 23.9 percent of all of Bernstein and Freeman's evaluation studies could be characterized as having adequate research quality.

In a second evaluation of evaluations, Gordon and Morse (1975) analyzed a

Table 2-5
Quality of Federal Evaluation Awards, FY 1970

Quality Category	Quality	Number of Awards	Percent of Total
Not a real evaluation study	Low	82	25.8
No measure of intervention process or outcomes	Low	84	26.4
Ranked low on adequacy of methodology	Low	76	23.9
Ranked high on adequacy of methodology	Adequate	76	23.9

Source: Data for table were taken from Ilene N. Bernstein and Howard E. Freeman, *Academic and Entrepreneurial Research: The Consequences of Diversity in Federal Evaluation Studies* (New York: Russell Sage Foundation, 1975), pp. 28-29, 65-66, 84-85, 102-103.

sample of all evaluation studies appearing in sociological journals from 1969 through 1973. The authors noted that since their source was *Sociological Abstracts* and the studies were thus published in the major sociology journals, the final sample of ninety-three studies should have represented the better evaluation studies done in the field of sociology. Nevertheless, Gordon and Morse found that only twenty-one, or 22.6 percent of the studies met the *minimal* methodological criteria of having: (1) operational definitions of the intervention process and its outcomes, (2) control groups or a sampling design, and (3) appropriate tests of significance or measures of association.

Similarly low proportions have been reported by other investigators. Mann (1972) examined evaluation studies in the predominantly psychology-oriented literatures on psychotherapy, counseling, human relations training, and personality testing. In spite of the fact that these evaluations were published and most were carried out under favorable research conditions—i.e., in a laboratory, classroom, or hospital, and with well-developed testing procedures—only 181, or less than 30 percent of the original studies were regarded as being of sufficient methodological quality, although Mann left unclear his criteria for judging quality. Finally, Yin and Yates (1975), dealing with the case study rather than the evaluation study literature of urban decentralization and citizen participation, found thirty-three (or about 12 percent) of their case studies had an acceptable research design and adequate operational measures. Most of the other case studies, of course, followed the typical one-shot case study design.

In summary, although only a small proportion of the 140 case studies on technological innovations was of acceptable research quality, analyses of other literatures that a priori should have been of the highest caliber have not revealed much better results. Only about one-fourth of the evaluation studies published in the sociology and psychology fields have been found to have sound methodological characteristics.

These comparisons are nevertheless not intended to justify the continued writing of case studies of the same quality on technological innovations. The innovation literature is probably far too dominated by a "demonstration" spirit, in which the main goal is to demonstrate the feasibility of a new device, and the development of adequate evaluation techniques has lagged behind. In this respect, the technological innovation literature ironically contains fewer "technical" case studies than do some of the nontechnological topics represented by neighborhood health center programs, compensatory education programs, and the like. Since field experiments to test the use of a new technology in a local service setting are likely to continue in the future, and since the case study form of analysis still has no counterpart in capturing the intricacy of key events during an innovative experience, some attempt should be made to improve the quality of the case studies that will be written in the future.

Our review of the existing 140 case studies suggests that, in the future, the quality of such studies can be immediately enhanced by one easily implemented change [h] The studies should have some comparative reference for the intervention or treatment population. This need not be a control group in the strict sense (although such a group would be desirable), but can merely be a before-versus-after comparison of the treatment population's experiences with the trends in the other sections of the city or among other aspects of agency operations. In too many of the existing case studies, in other words, the effects of the innovation have been reported without any clue as to the other changes that might have occurred independent of the innovative effort itself. As one result, the studies have been unable to address the problem of alternative explanations, if even in a less rigorous mode. (For other suggestions concerning improved case study methods, see the discussion in Chapter 7.)

Case Study Characteristics that Vary with Quality

Our comments up to this point have been directed at the issue of what can be said about the overall research quality of the 140 case studies. The main reason for having assessed the research quality of the body of studies, however, was to determine what characteristics, if any, varied with that quality. In other words, did studies of different quality: (1) systematically differ in their other ascriptive characteristics, (2) cover different universes of innovative experiences, or (3) present different success rates for the outcomes?

For the purposes of investigating these issues, we divided the 140 case studies into three categories (moderate—fifty cases; low—fifty-seven cases, and poor—thirty-three cases),[i] based on one of the quality measures—the subjective rating for the adequacy of the evidence presented for each outcome (see Table 2-3, column 2, which draws on question F-4 of the checklist). This particular index of quality was used because preliminary analysis showed it to be more sensitive to variations in the other case study characteristics than the other three measures (i.e., more of the relationships between the index and the case study characteristics were statistically significant, though the direction of the relationship by no means differed from those of the other quality measures).

Ascriptive Characteristics. Previous investigations have found that certain ascriptive characteristics (e.g., source of funds, type and length of award; principal investigator's discipline, highest degree, and institutional affiliation) can vary

[h]The discussion deliberately focuses on an implementable and low-cost change. The most desirable changes—from the standpoint of research quality—would of course involve features that are much more difficult to implement; i.e., an adequate research design with random sampling (Gilbert et al., 1974; Abert and Kamrass, 1974; and Riecken and Boruch, 1974).

[i]The moderate quality studies contain both the fifteen studies of acceptable quality and thirty-five other studies that rated high on the subjective scale. Separate analyses showed few significant differences between these two groups, and the desire to work with a larger number of cases for statistical purposes dictated the combining of the two groups.

with quality. Bernstein and Freeman (1975) found that the higher quality evaluation studies in their sample were usually carried out as a grant from a particular federal agency (the National Institutes of Health) and had a principal investigator who was trained in psychology, had a Ph.D., and was academically based. In a similar vein, Yin and Yates (1975) found that the higher quality case studies in their sample were usually carried out with federal (as opposed to nonfederal) financial support and by academically affiliated investigators. Their investigation found no relationship between quality and the author's relationship to the intervention program. While none of the other evaluations of evaluations discussed here examined the ascriptive characteristics of the studies in relation to quality, the obvious conclusion from the existing evidence appears to be that, insofar as these characteristics are concerned, higher quality studies are conducted by investigators who are more highly research trained, who work in research institutions, and who are therefore most likely to be supported by federal agencies that are also research oriented.

In the present study, research quality was found to be related only to one ascriptive characteristic: If the author was an evaluator of the innovative effort and was neither merely an observer nor affiliated in any way with the effort (question A-6), the study was likely to be of higher quality (see Table 2-6). No significant relationships were found between research quality and: (1) whether the study was published or unpublished, (2) the date of the study, (3) the source of funds for the study, or (4) the author's institutional affiliation. (See tables in Appendix D.)

Universe of Innovative Experiences. For the purpose of assessing the importance of variations in quality, characteristics dealing with the universe of innovative experiences and with the outcomes presented are more important than these ascriptive characteristics. The universe or scope of study is important if it turns out that the quality (higher or lower) of the study is associated with specific

Table 2-6
Relationship between Author's Relationship to Innovative Effort and Quality of Study
(N = 140)

	Quality of Study (Question F-4)		
Author's Relationship (Question A-6)	*Moderate*	*Low*	*Poor*
Part of evaluation only	19	7	8
Observer or reporter	6	18	15
Involved in effort	25	32	9
Impossible to answer	0	0	1

Note: $\chi^2 = 19.59$, df = 4, $p < 0.001$ (excludes impossible-to-answer case).

types of interventions or geographic settings. To the extent that this is true and lower quality cases are discarded, the generalizations that can be made will apply to different universes of experiences. In the only previous study that examined the universe of experiences in relation to quality, Yin and Yates (1975) found no relationships between quality and the type of local service, the size of the city, the regional location of the city, or the intervention strategy being studied. They concluded that the universe or scope of study did not change—even though their study went on to discard the lower quality cases.

In the present study, research quality was found to be related to several characteristics of the universe. First, if all the innovative devices being studied are divided into three categories—hardware and machinery (excluding computer systems), computer systems, and data analytic innovations—the higher quality studies are associated with the hardware category (see Table 2-7). Similarly, higher quality studies were significantly associated with: public works and transportation studies, federal financial support for the innovative effort (as opposed to support for the writing of the case study), large-scale support for the effort (over $50,000 as opposed to less than $50,000), and case studies in which there was some formal citizen or client participation. Quality was not related either to the size or the regional location of the city being studied.

Of these characteristics of the universe, one in particular is potentially important for policy reasons. This is the presence of federal financial support for the innovative effort. Its relationship to quality suggests the possibility that such federal support may be a causal factor in helping to produce higher quality studies. To explore this possibility, the quality of the study was analyzed according to the functional use of the federal funds—i.e., whether the funds tended to be associated with the R&D for the service, information dissemination, technical assistance, training of local personnel, evaluation, work by a research organization or university, or the general implementation of the effort (see question D-14 of the checklist). Of these functions, none was significantly related to quality except for general implementation support. This result suggests that the initially observed association between federal funding of the

Table 2-7
Relationship Between Type of Innovative Device and Quality of Study
(N = 140)

Type of Device (Question A-5)	Quality of Study (Question F-4)		
	Moderate	Low	Poor
Hardware	25	23	6
Computer system	15	16	15
Data analysis	10	18	12

Note: $\chi^2 = 9.60$, df $= 4$, $p < 0.05$.

innovative effort and higher quality studies, if at all a causal link, is not a direct one—otherwise some relationship between quality and either the evaluative function or the role of a research organization should have been evident. If there is a causal link, the general presence of federal support may be serving to make more resources generally available and hence to make better case studies possible, but nothing more. If there is no causal link, then the relationship simply means that federal support happens to occur at the same sites as higher quality case studies. More speculatively, if the direction of the causal link is reversed, then one explanation would be that the planning of a higher quality case study or evaluation facilitates the awarding of federal funds to support the innovative effort.

Outcomes. The final set of characteristics deals with the outcomes and conclusions reported by the case study. Among the previous investigations that have examined quality in relation to outcomes, Mann (1972) found no relationship between various aspects of research quality and negative or positive outcomes. Two other investigations, however, found significant relationships in opposite directions. In the first, Yin and Yates (1975) reported that higher quality studies tended to be associated with a higher frequency of positive change in client attitudes as a result of the intervention; higher quality studies were also positively related to a judgment of successful intervention by the author of the case study. Higher quality studies, in other words, were associated with more positive outcomes. In the second investigation, Gordon and Morse (1975) found that higher quality studies were *inversely* related to a judgment of successful intervention on the part of the author. One possible explanation for this contrasting result is that the Yin and Yates case studies covered interventions that resulted in much more positive outcomes than those covered by Gordon and Morse, so that higher quality studies were appropriately reaching more positive conclusions in the former work and more negative conclusions in the latter. Unfortunately, Gordon and Morse made no attempt to assess the nature of the outcomes reported by the studies in their review, so that this hypothesis cannot be tested.

The present investigation of technological innovations found that there was a positive trend but no statistically significant relationship between quality and the outcomes involving incorporation and service improvement (again, see Appendix D for tables). Quality became significantly related in a positive direction, however, when these two outcomes were combined to define our success outcome. Higher quality studies, in other words, reported a higher frequency of *successful outcomes.* The present study also found a significantly positive relationship between the quality of the study and the author's judgment that the innovative experience had been successful.

An additional point may be made about the author's judgment regarding the success of a case: its frequency was positively correlated with the author's having close contact with the innovative effort in either an evaluative or participatory role (see Table 2-8). Moreover, our results suggest that university-based authors, if involved in the innovative effort as well, were just as susceptible to this tendency as nonuniversity-based authors. These findings are consistent with previous studies (Yin and Yates, 1975; and Gordon and Morse, 1975) and suggest, at a minimum, that agencies supporting case study research in the future may want to consider a dual award, asking two investigators—one affiliated with the project, and the other not—to conduct two independent case studies. Such a procedure would certainly be more costly. However, it might be one solution to a perennial problem: If an evaluator and an evaluation study are independent of and not funded by the decisionmaker's organization—i.e., the one supposed to make policy changes—the study takes the risk of not being policy relevant; if the decisionmaker's organization sponsors or funds the study, it is more likely to be policy relevant but may not be able to propose any changes that threaten the position of the decisionmaker (Ward and Kassenbaum, 1972; and Bogdan, 1975). By having two case studies, either of these conditions may be more easily avoided.

Summary. Table 2-9 summarizes the significant relationships between the quality of the case study and the other characteristics of the study that have been discussed. Since many of the characteristics that are significantly related to quality have to do with the scope or universe of innovative experiences, the effect of discarding lower quality studies would be to limit the innovative experiences examined to those involving hardware innovations, public works and transportation services, efforts supported by federal funds, larger sized efforts in terms of dollar support, and efforts with client participation. To the extent that one objective of our investigation was to examine the widest possible range of reported innovative experiences, there appears to be strong reason not to discard the lower quality studies. All subsequent analysis will therefore be carried out with the full caseload of 140 studies.

Table 2-8
Relationship Between Author's Relationship to Innovative Effort and Author's Judgment of Success
(N = 140)

	Author's Judgment of Project (Question F-11)		
Author's Relationship (Question A-6)	*Success*	*Failure*	*Impossible to Answer*
Part of evaluation only	25	9	0
Observer or reporter	20	18	1
Involved in effort	59	8	0

Note: $\chi^2 = 16.19$, df = 2, $p < 0.001$ (excludes impossible-to-answer case).

Table 2-9
Summary of Characteristics Related to Studies of Higher Quality

Characteristic	Statistical Significance of Relationship (x^2)
Ascriptive Characteristics of Study	
Study is published (question A-1)	n.s.
Study was dated in past three years (question A-2)	n.s.
Study was supported by federal funds (question A-3)	n.s.
Author was an evaluator, not merely an observer or someone involved with the project (question A-6)	$p < 0.001$
Author was affiliated with an academic institution (question A-4)	n.s.
Universe of Innovative Experiences	
Population of city was over 500,000 (question G-2)	n.s.
City was in North Central United States (question G-7)	n.s.
Innovation involved public works or transportation services (question B-2)	$p < 0.01$
Innovation involved hardware, and not merely a computer system or data analysis (question A-5)	$p < 0.05$
Innovative effort was supported by federal funds (question B-5)	$p < 0.05$
Funds for the innovative effort were over $50,000 (question B-6)	$p < 0.01$
Some formal client participation (question B-7)	$p < 0.01$
Outcomes	
Innovation was incorporated into agency's routine (question F-1)	n.s.
Innovation resulted in service improvements (question F-5)	n.s.
Innovation resulted in incorporation and service improvement (success$_1$) or no incorporation and no service improvement success$_2$) (question H-12)	$p < 0.05$
Author judged innovative effort to be successful (question F-11)	$p < 0.05$

Note: n.s. = not significant.

At the same time, the relationship between quality and the success outcome suggests that any interactions among two or more variables may be related to quality. This means that a correlation, for instance, between the occurrence of client participation and service improvement may be more frequently found among the higher quality than the lower quality case studies. For this reason, it will be important to report the relationship to quality for each interaction examined in the following chapters. This will be done by noting at the bottom of each contingency table whether the conclusions would have differed if the analysis had been limited to only the adequate quality cases.[j]

Conclusions on Quality

The present study is based on a review of 140 case studies. Although these case studies—if judged by rigorous standards of research design—are generally of low quality, the analysis of other collections of previous research that have been published in the form of evaluation studies has shown similarly low proportions of adequate quality studies. The case studies should thus be taken as a body of evidence similar to most research on site-specific experiences. Nevertheless, to mediate between the desire to maintain high research standards and to report the content of the existing research, our analysis will indicate the results from the whole body of case studies, but at the same time indicate whether the conclusions would have been different if only the adequate quality studies had been examined.

[j]There are three types of notes: (1) where analysis of only the adequate quality cases significantly supports the relationship between the two variables shown by all the cases, (2) where such analysis shows no significant relationship between those variables, and (3) where such analysis indicates a significant relationship not indicated by all the cases. Because of the small number of higher quality cases ($n = 50$), a significance level of $p < 0.20$ was arbitrarily chosen just to give as much room for contrary findings as possible. Of all the cross-tabulations in the remainder of the text, 71.8 percent had the first note, 25.6 percent the second note, and 2.6 percent the third note.

3

The Nature of the Innovations

Even though local service agencies as a group have not adopted a large or dramatic array of technological innovations, many of these agencies have nevertheless attempted individually to adopt some innovations. The innovations that have been attempted are diverse, ranging from computer-assisted instruction and multimedia programs in the schools to the use of mathematical manpower deployment models and helicopter patrols by criminal justice agencies. Hospitals and health agencies have experimented with methadone maintenance and computerized blood-bank inventory systems; planning groups have tried land use and urban growth models; and transportation agencies have included dial-a-ride systems in their attempts to upgrade urban mass transportation. Among the technologies propounded by public works departments have been mercury and sodium vapor lights, as well as fully mechanized residential refuse collection vehicles, and several firefighting agencies have experimented with "rapid water."

In this chapter, we first describe some illustrative examples of these devices in greater detail, and then we relate the experiences with these devices to the major outcomes of the innovative effort. Along the way, the chapter also reviews some of the prominent relationships between the characteristics of the innovative device and success$_1$, success$_2$, and failure, as reported in the case studies.

The Innovations

Definition of Technological Innovations

There are several different ways of defining a technological innovation. The term *innovation* alone, whether the innovation be technological or not, can refer to several different concepts. Innovation may be conceived of as an organizational process or a technological product or process. For instance, Myers and Marquis (1969) interpret innovation as an organizational process that ". . . is a complex activity which proceeds from the conceptualization of a new idea to a solution of the problem, and then to actual utilization of a new item of economic or social value." In the present study, however, we consider innovation to refer only to a specific technological product, device, or process; the organizational process of innovation is referred to as the innovative effort. The term *innovation* can also be ambiguous with reference to the degree of newness. For instance, Becker and Whisler (1967) define innovation as "the first or early use of an idea

43

by one of a set of organizations with similar goals." In this view, a device only qualifies as an innovation if it is new to an industry or to a family of public agencies (e.g., all police departments). An alternative view, however, broadens the definition of innovation to include "any idea, practice, or material artifact perceived to be new by the relevant unit of adoption" (Zaltman et al., 1973; see also Barnett, 1953). Because of our interest in how individual agencies have dealt with technological innovations, we use innovation in this broader sense.

In short, within the context of this study, innovation includes any discrete idea, practice, or material artifact that is introduced for the first time into a local agency and is seemingly discontinuous with past practice. The term *technological innovation*, moreover, refers to those innovations that consist of: (1) an artifact or material; (2) a computer system; or (3) an analytic idea or practice that lends itself to quantitative symbolization. Technological innovations consisting of artifacts or materials have been termed *hardware* innovations. Innovations that are ideas or practices are called *data analysis* innovations and include such items as algorithms for ambulance dispatch and the optimum location of fire stations. In distinguishing among types of technologies, the hardware-data analysis distinction is of particular interest. Utterback (1974), among others, suggests that data analysis (software) innovations tend to be adopted more readily and successfully than hardware innovations, although Feller et al. (1974) found no strong differences between the two types in their study of diffusion among state agencies. At the same time, *computer systems* have been categorized as a third general type of innovation, both because they have commonly been regarded as a special family of innovations and because they typically involve both hardware and software components (Kraemer et al., 1974).

Illustrative Examples

Table 3-1 indicates the range of innovations in the 140 case studies that were found to fit this definition of technological innovation. To give us some flavor of the innovative devices and the situations in which they were used, however, we briefly describe five innovations here: a closed circuit television system, a mechanical refuse collection vehicle, a computer-assisted instructional program, a fire station location analysis, and an urban activity allocation model. Although the descriptions refer only to these innovations as they were tried at one site, in fact the case studies may have included similar attempts with the same device at other sites.

Closed Circuit Television. An example of a two-way, closed circuit television system is one that was installed in New Hampshire to extend psychiatric consultation into a rural area. Although the area contained one mental health clinic staffed by two psychologists, it had no resident psychiatrist. The objective of the innovative effort was to supplement the care provided by family physicians and the small mental health clinic with psychiatric consultation and advice from a spatially remote psychiatric staff.

The closed circuit system consisted of two television studios—one located in the Psychiatry Department at Dartmouth Medical School in Hanover, New Hampshire, and a second studio with an adjacent observation room in the small industrial town of Claremont, twenty-six miles away. Transmissions were facilitated by two microwave signal relay stations. During 1969 alone, 199 consultations were held. The system subsequently received substantial financial support from the National Institute of Mental Health. In this instance, the innovative device, while somewhat of a newcomer to the field of psychiatry, had amassed a long history of experimental use prior to its adoption by the New Hampshire group. In addition, several members of the Dartmouth staff were familiar with "limited but intriguing [psychiatric] application(s)." The New Hampshire case thus appears to constitute a situation of early clinical use of closed circuit television in the field of psychiatry.

Mechanized Refuse Collection Vehicle. Another type of hardware, but one that was attempted by a public works rather than a health agency, was first tried in Scottsdale, Arizona. The device was a mechanized residential refuse collection vehicle (Godzilla). The new vehicle differed from the standard refuse collection vehicle in that one man could operate the truck, which mechanically lifted trash from a location near the curb into the body of the truck. As part of the innovation, the city also had to develop a suitably durable polyethylene trash container.

The leader of the innovative effort appears to have been the head of the department of public works. However, the city manager and numerous industrial designers also participated in the development of the new vehicle. Funds for the development of the Godzilla vehicles were obtained by the city from the U.S. Environmental Protection Agency in the form of a $172,000 demonstration grant that was matched by Scottsdale funds. Perhaps the most severe difficulty encountered by the project was locating a manufacturer to construct the vehicle and its related equipment. The root of this supply problem may have been the fact that Godzilla was a prototype—the first fully mechanized residential refuse collection vehicle to be constructed—and represented an unknown commodity. Unlike the closed circuit television application, Godzilla exemplifies an innovation that was both a new innovation and a device tried by a local service.

Computer-Assisted Instructional Program. One such innovation was attempted by the Board of Education in Cincinnati, Ohio. Developed especially for use with blind and deaf children, the computer-assisted instruction (CAI) system offered teachers an opportunity to individualize instruction for their sensory-impaired students; further, it provided a computer software capacity for

Table 3-1
Range of Innovations Represented in the Case Studies

Criminal Justice and Fire	Transportation and Public Works	Health	Education	Planning and Other
Hardware				
Police helicopter patrol	Bay Area Rapid Transit System (BART)	Two-way closed circuit television for psychiatric consultation	Closed circuit television	Two-way cable television for intergovernmental communication
Automated status reporting and emergency signaling system for mobile patrol units	Dynamic traffic safety displays (lighted signs, improved road illumination, buzzers, etc.)	Vital function telemetry	Multimedia educational program	Computer-assisted information system to dispatch multiagency response vehicles
Rapid water	Dial-a-ride system	Technique to extract acid from urine to measure lead in humans	Televote system	
Universal emergency telephone number (911)	Mercury and sodium street lights	New equipment to streamline ordering, procuring, and distribution of medication	Silent alarm system	
	Grider sewage pumps	Methadone maintenance program		
	Godzilla vehicle system for fully mechanized refuse collection			
Computer Systems				
Remote access infrared data file and search system	Information system for dynamic deployment of police traffic patrols in response to traffic flows	Automated medical history system (AMH)	Computer-assisted instruction	Integrated municipal information system
Criminal justice identification system		Patient monitoring system	School information system (SIS) to assist decision-making in school administration	Minicomputer to automate library acquisition system
		Computer-assisted system to analyze electrocardiograms		Computer program to assist in housing-policy decisions

Computer programs to allocate manpower and devise proportional police rotation schedules

Technique to reduce court appearances required of police

Police deployment technique

Analysis of firefighting resources deployment

Mathematical models to test effects on service of fire company locations

Computer algorithm to assign bus drivers to routes

Cost-effectiveness analysis of a water supply system

Manpower scheduling system

Data Analysis

Model for distribution of mental health funds

Automated patient registration, identification, and appointment system

Blood inventory and information system (BIIS) (computerized clearinghouse of information on regional blood inventory)

Hospital information system (medication charts)

Teleprocessing information system to provide data processing to multiple school districts

Computer-assisted testing

Information retrieval system to assist decision-making in five-county area

Computer integrated into science and math curricula

Computer system to process complaints and violation notices and issue activity sheets to housing inspectors

Urban dynamics model

EMPIRIC (land use planning model)

Computer simulation for renewal policymaking

Computer simulation model to test new investment and urban change hypotheses

Computer simulation of emergency service operations

translating English language instructions and materials into Grade II Braille with a twenty-four-hour turnaround. The system, which used a Hewlett-Packard 2000 F computer, was also employed to furnish teachers with in-service training in the use of CAI with sensory-impaired children.

The U.S. Office of Education provided financial support for creation of the system in the form of a $91,000 grant under the Elementary and Secondary Education Act, Title III. Initially, pupils participated for ten to fifteen minutes each day and covered the same programmed lessons in reading or mathematics. As the system developed, individualized tutorial lessons were added. Although general educational experience with CAI has a long history, its use with sensory-impaired children was a new undertaking. The Cincinnati experience thus represents an example of the early use of a specialized application in computer technology.

Fire Station Location Analysis. Several of the data analysis innovations concerned the problem of facility location. One of the analyses to address a location problem was a New York City-Rand Institute analysis of the deployment of firefighting resources in Wilmington, Delaware. In 1966, a Wilmington Community Renewal Program study of the city's firefighting resources concluded that most of the city's firehouses, all of which were over sixty-five years old, needed to be replaced. At that time, a capital improvement plan was developed. Several years later, however, a reassessment revealed that only one of those stations had been built. The city then reexamined the projected costs of constructing the remaining stations and found itself faced with a potential cost overrun of more than 100 percent. Budget constraints, coupled with the desire of a newly elected mayor to reassess the city's firefighting operations, as well as a challenge by the new fire chief about the suitability of some of the proposed construction sites, caused the suspension of further construction plans until the situation could be reevaluated. The New York City-Rand Institute was retained under a contract from the U.S. Department of Housing and Urban Development to perform the assessment.

After six months of study in which various quantitative methods were used, Rand concluded that the locations of existing fire companies were approximately correct, but recommended some adjustments in the location pattern for new construction sites. The analysis further contended that the budget problems could be reduced by eliminating one or two fire companies, and that the elimination would create no significant reduction in the level of service. The two models that formed the basis for the analysis were a parametric allocation model and a firehouse-site evaluation model. The allocation model was used to determine the optimum distribution of companies across the city's four fire-service demand regions. The site evaluation model, by contrast, was used to assess and evaluate the effects on service of specific site alternatives. The analytic techniques, although new to Wilmington, had been extensively tested and applied by the New York City Fire Department and other fire departments. The Wilmington situation therefore exemplifies the use of a device new to a particular city agency, though not of early use in the field.

Urban Activity Allocation Model. Simulation models developed by planners of urban and regional systems are another type of data analysis innovation. EMPIRIC is one such model designed to assist planners in forecasting long-term population changes and consequent changes in business and service activities. In one case study, the model was applied by the Metropolitan Washington Council of Governments to the Washington, D.C. area.

Formed in 1957 to foster coordinated planning and policymaking, the Council had by the late 1960s recognized that its duties required substantially more information regarding the projected distribution of population, employment, and land use within the metropolitan area than was currently available. Drawing on a data base of demographic, socioeconomic, employment, and accessibility variables, the model offered decisionmakers a capacity to test the likely effect of alternative planning policies on the distribution of metropolitan growth. As in Wilmington, the analysis therefore provided a new framework for decisionmaking by agency officials. Although the analytic techniques were by no means a new invention, this effort constituted the Washington agency's first attempt to use such techniques.

Aggregate Characteristics

Among the 140 case studies that were identified, hardware, computer, and data analysis innovations happened to occur in roughly equal proportions (see Table 3-2). In spite of this approximately even distribution, the three different types of innovations occurred in disproportionate frequency in relation to several characteristics of the innovative situation: the region of the country, median income of the local community, type of service agency, and source and amount of funding.

Table 3-2
Frequency of Three Types of Innovations
(N = 140)

Type of Innovation (Question A-5)	Number of Case Studies
Hardware	54
Computer system	46
Data analysis	40
Total	140

Among the cases identified, significant differences were apparent according to the region of the country in which the innovative effort took place (see Table 3-3). In particular, data analysis was the most frequent subject of studies describing innovative efforts in the New England and Mid-Atlantic states, whereas hardware figured most often in studies covering the North Central and Mountain-Pacific states. In addition to regional location, a number of census characteristics of the specific city, county, or state in which the innovative effort occurred were examined, including the 1970 population, percent population change from 1960 to 1970, median education, and per capita municipal expenditures of the jurisdiction. The type of innovation varied systematically with only one of these characteristics, median income (see Table 3-4). Specifi-

Table 3-3
Relationship Between Region of the Country and Type of Innovation
(N = 140)

	Type of Innovation (Question A-5)		
Region (Question G-7)	Hardware	Computer	Data Analysis
New England and Mid-Atlantic	14	9	20
North Central	17	14	9
South Atlantic and South Central	6	9	7
Mountain-Pacific	16	10	4
Impossible to answer	1	4	0

Note: χ^2 = 12.84, df = 6, $p < 0.05$ (excludes impossible-to-answer cases). Examination of higher quality cases alone significantly supports this relationship.

Table 3-4
Relationship Between Median Income of the Locale and Type of Innovation
(N = 140)

	Type of Innovation (Question A-5)		
Median Income (Question G-5)	Hardware	Computer	Data Analysis
Over $11,000	8	9	5
$10,000 to 10,999	18	6	5
$9,000 to 9,999	14	17	26
Less than $9,000	11	9	4
Impossible to answer	3	5	0

Note: χ^2 = 17.38, df = 6, $p < 0.01$ (excludes impossible-to-answer cases). Examination of higher quality cases alone fails to show any relationship.

cally, communities with high or low median incomes tended to be more involved with hardware innovations, whereas communities with middle-level median incomes tended to be involved with data analysis innovations.

Also, different types of service agencies were associated with different types of innovations (see Table 3-5). The criminal justice and fire, and planning and miscellaneous agencies in our sample used a substantially greater proportion of data analyses than any other group. Health and education agencies, on the other hand, most often worked with computer systems, while hardware innovations constituted the dominant approach of the transportation and public works group.

Finally, the three types of innovations also received their financial support from different sources (see Table 3-6) and in different amounts (see Table 3-7). Data analyses were conducted with no new funds from outside sources far more frequently than were the other innovations. Hardware innovations involved disproportionately more frequent occasions of federal support, and in general, the hardware innovations and computer systems involved larger amounts ($50,000 or more) of financial support than did the data analysis innovations.

Innovation Attributes

Previous research has dealt extensively with the attributes of an innovative device that are related to adoption—i.e., the initial use by an organization of an innovation (Rogers, 1962; Fliegel and Kivlin, 1966; and Zaltman et al., 1973). Although the factors related to adoption may not be the same as those related to implementation, the purpose of the remainder of this chapter is to review the relevant factors identified in the literature, to define the key words or phrases

Table 3-5
Relationship Between Type of Service Agency and Type of Innovation
(N = 140)

	Type of Innovation (Question A-5)		
Type of Service Agency (Question B-2)	Hardware	Computer	Data Analysis
Criminal justice and fire	7	6	13
Health	12	17	2
Education	8	15	0
Transportation and public works	19	1	6
Planning and miscellaneous	8	7	19

Note: $\chi^2 = 57.10$, df = 8, $p < 0.001$. Examination of higher quality cases alone significantly supports this relationship.

Table 3-6

Relationship Between Source of Financial Support and Type of Innovation

(N = 140)

	Type of Innovation (Question A-5)		
Source of Financial Support (Question B-5)	*Hardware*	*Computer*	*Data Analysis*
No new funds	1	3	11
Federal	34	25	20
State or county	6	8	2
Municipal	4	4	5
Private	5	3	2
Impossible to answer	4	3	0

Note: χ^2 = 19.53, df = 8, $p < 0.05$ (excludes impossible-to-answer cases). Examination of higher quality cases alone fails to show any relationship.

Table 3-7

Relationship Between Amount of Financial Support and Type of Innovation

(N = 140)

	Type of Innovation (Question A-5)		
Amount of Financial Support (Question B-6)	*Hardware*	*Computer*	*Data Analysis*
No new funds	1	2	11
Less than $50,000	5	3	6
$50,000 to $250,000	12	6	2
Over $250,000	15	13	3
Impossible to answer	21	22	18

Note: χ^2 = 29.00, df = 6, $p < 0.001$ (excludes impossible-to-answer cases). Examination of higher quality cases alone significantly supports this relationship.

that we looked for in the case studies as indications of the presence or absence of these factors, and to report the relationships between the frequency of occurrence of these key words or phrases and the observation of $success_1$, $success_2$, and failure. The chapter examines only the attributes of the innovative device, whereas the next chapter reviews the background characteristics and implementation factors in the innovative effort and then arrives at overall conclusions comparing the device attributes with these other features. Within the varied array of attributes of the innovative device thought to influence the outcome of an innovative effort, three main clusters may be distinguished:

The intrinsic features of the innovation (e.g., cost and ease of use);

The status of the innovation at the time of proposal (e.g., prior history of use and relevance to the concerns of the organization); and

The potential effects of the device on the local agency and its clients (e.g., immediacy and distribution of benefits).

Intrinsic Features of the Innovation

The existing literature has identified certain intrinsic features of a technological innovation that tend to affect adoption. Previous findings suggest that innovations that are relatively simple to comprehend and use and that are visible, divisible, and reversible are more likely to be adopted than others. At the same time, there is less consensus about such other features as cost.

The related concepts of the *complexity* and *visibility* of an innovation are among the attributes most widely held to influence outcomes. Complex innovations—i.e., those perceived to be difficult to understand and use—have consistently exhibited lower rates of successful adoption than those that are less complex. In their study of farm enterprises, Fliegel and Kivlin (1966) found that the adoption of farm innovations was most strongly related to two attributes of the innovation: complexity and relative advantage. Similarly, Utterback (1974) observed that industrial innovations requiring increased technical skills on the part of users had lower adoption rates than those that did not. As for visibility, the available evidence strongly suggests that innovations that are visible (and hence potentially more easily communicated) are more likely to be adopted than those that are not. Czepiel (1972), for instance, found a particularly strong relation between the visibility and communicability of an innovation and its rate of adoption within the steel industry.

Innovations that are *divisible* into segments and that can be tested on a partial basis—either in relation to a portion of the total target population or in successive stages—are more likely to be adopted than are innovations that are not divisible. In a study of California farmers, Polgar (1963) found that the failure to adopt mosquito extermination was largely a result of the inability to test it on a limited basis. Fliegel and Kivlin's study of farm innovations (1966) produced similar findings. Although the available evidence from empirical studies on the impact of divisibility on adoption in general is somewhat limited, Rogers (1962) has argued strongly for the importance of the concept.

The *reversibility* of an innovation refers to the ease with which an innovation may be terminated and the status quo ante restored once an innovation has been adopted. Lippitt and Havelock (1968) suggested on the basis of their research utilization study that an innovation which can be easily reversed will be more readily adopted than one that cannot be reversed. Taylor (1970) offered additional evidence for the conducive influence of reversibility on adoption.

Central to the question of an innovation's adoption and its subsequent success is its monetary *cost*. The monetary cost may be further subdivided into initial costs and continuing costs. Both Miles (1964) and Gross et al. (1971) concluded from their studies of educational change that innovations that are relatively inexpensive and make use of resources at hand will be more readily adopted than those that are expensive and for which internal resources are unavailable. In further analysis, however, Fliegel and Kivlin (1966) argued on the basis of their study of farm innovations that, when other characteristics of the innovation are held constant, high initial cost is accompanied by an increased likelihood of adoption, whereas high continuing costs exert a weak to moderately negative effect on adoption. Zaltman et al. (1973) also found evidence for this conclusion and suggest that the positive relation between initial cost and adoption may stem from a tendency on the part of adopters to take high cost as an indication of high quality and to prorate the initial costs over the lifetime of the innovation. On the question of the proportion of the total cost borne by the adopter in the presence, for example, of matching funds from external sources for research and demonstration, there has been very little research. It is likely, however, that both the cost actually borne by the adopter and the overall magnitude of the cost of the innovation are relevant items for consideration.

Status of the Innovation at the Time of Proposal

When an innovation is considered for adoption by an organization, both the innovation's past history of accomplishment and its relation to the concerns of the potential adopter may influence the new decision to adopt. At the preliminary stage in the innovative process, the most important attributes of the innovation appear to include: the source of the data for the innovation, the innovation's merit, and its relative advantage, credibility, compatibility, and adaptability to previous practice.

The *source* of an innovation may be potentially significant in two ways. It is possible that the adoption of in-house inventions follows a process substantially different from that of innovations imported from external sources. Further, the adoption of an in-house invention may well be explained by factors very different from innovations that are conceived of elsewhere. It is likely that an innovative idea put forth by personnel within an organization will be viewed as less threatening and as less of an unknown quantity than one proposed by an outsider—particularly if the proponent is viewed as a knowledgeable and trusted staff member.

Merit refers to the demonstrated value of an innovation in previous lab tests or field use. To the extent that a potential adopter is aware of prior successful experience by others with an innovation, adoption appears to be more likely. Related to the concept of merit is the notion of the *relative advantage* of the innovation—that is, the "degree to which an innovation is superior to the ideas it supersedes" (Rogers, 1962). In addition to strictly material gains, advantage is more generally taken to include gains measured in a personal or psychological sense, such as changes in prestige or satisfaction. Innovations perceived to be more advantageous than others will likely be more readily adopted. Tulley et al. (1964) observed that farmers' perceptions of relative advantage substantially influence their decisionmaking with respect to farm problems and innovation. Coe and Barnhill (1967) reported that the failure of an innovative approach to the distribution of medication in a major urban hospital may be traced in large measure to staff feelings that the increase in efficiency to be derived from the innovation was not substantial enough to compensate for the costs of change-over from familiar procedures.

The *credibility* of an innovation is a function of both its espousal by an eminent, authoritative, and respected individual or group and the methods used to evaluate the costs and benefits of early trial use of the innovation. Credible innovations tend to be adopted more readily than those that are less credible. A classic illustration of the effect of an endorsement occurred when Linus Pauling, winner of the Nobel Prize in chemistry, recommended vitamin C as a remedy for the common cold, and there ensued mass purchase of the "cure." Similarly, the communications studies of Hovland et al. (1953) pointed out the strong influence for change exerted by persons regarded as experts in their fields. Coleman et al. (1966) also found that espousal of a new drug by professional respected individuals boosted its acceptance among physicians.

The summary works of Rogers (1962), Zaltman et al. (1973), and Rothman (1974) have emphasized the role of *compatibility*. The available evidence makes a strong case for the fact that an innovation that is compatible with the user's established norms, values, facilities, and practices will be more readily adopted than one that is not. Rogers (1962) has hypothesized that compatibility ensures greater security to the potential adopter and makes the new idea more meaningful to the adopter. Emerson et al. (1968) noted that the practice of birth control is substantially more frequent among families that have already given birth to the number of children they prefer to have. Similarly, Yeracaris (1961) observed that in cases where tuberculosis testing was compatible with health practices, as well as relevant attitudes and values of the population, testing was more readily accepted. Although the circumstances discussed above refer mainly to compatibility with the norms of an individual adopter, the concept may also pertain to organizational practices. Related to the notion of compatibility is that of *adaptability*, but this attribute has been infrequently studied. The major hypothesis is that an innovation that can "be adapted to improvements in technology as opposed to becoming obsolete because of inflexibility [is more likely to be adopted] ... particularly ... where financial investment is high and the ... technology is a rapidly growing one" (Zaltman et al., 1973).

Potential Effects of the Innovation

In addition to the intrinsic features of the innovation and the status of the innovation at its time of proposal, a third set of attributes concerns the potential benefits and effects of the innovation. Among such effects are: the transitivity versus reflexivity of the innovation, and the extent, distribution, immediacy, and regularity of benefits.

The distinction between *transitive* and *reflexive* innovations (Mohr, 1973) is defined by the group of people most affected by the innovation. Innovations adopted by local agencies that directly affect the client served are transitive innovations. Those that bear primarily on operations internal to the agency are reflexive. In some instances, the innovation works toward both of these goals. Although the importance of this distinction to adoption has not been addressed by research to date, one hypothesis is that transitive innovations are more likely to lead to service improvements because client-oriented changes, and not mere administrative changes, are more directly involved.

The importance of the *magnitude, distribution*, and *regularity of benefits* issuing from the innovation has been emphasized by numerous studies to date. The magnitude of benefit is most frequently referred to as the return on investment. In the broadest sense, this term embraces material, social, and psychic benefits. However, this broad usage is beset by a host of definitional and measurement problems, as well as uncertainty regarding the value attributed by an organization to any particular type of return. Zaltman et al. (1973) note that preferred types and schedules of return vary with industry, firm size, and performance motivation. Largely as a result of the measurement problems faced by this broad usage, the narrower concept of financial return or profitability has been more widely cited as a factor impinging on adoption. Fliegel et al. (1968) found that farm innovations with high potential payoffs increased when the statistical effects of other attributes of the innovation were held constant. Similarly, Griliches (1960) found a particularly strong relation between profitability and rate of adoption of hybrid corn in the United States.

The distribution of benefits forthcoming from an innovation may also affect the decision to adopt. The distinction between innovations that confer universal benefits and those that distribute benefits selectively is an important one. Depending on other factors, such as who gets selective benefits, the universality or selectivity of distribution could enhance an innovation's chances of being adopted, although the direction of the relationship to adoption obviously depends on the specific situation. A final issue is the immediacy and regularity of the benefits. Some innovations will produce effects almost immediately after being adopted, while others will require substantial lead time. Those changes producing early results might be expected to be adopted more readily than others (Fliegel and Kivlin, 1966).[a] The regularity of benefits refers to the timing and the certainty with which gains will be observed. Fliegel and Kivlin observed also that innovations characterized by a regular reward schedule were more readily adopted than less regular ones.

Case Survey Findings

Outcomes of the Innovative Efforts

As stated in Chapter 1, our main concern in assessing the outcomes of innovative efforts focused on the joint occurrence of two events: the apparent *incorporation* on an innovation into an agency's routine procedures, and some evidence that the innovation produced a *service improvement*. The combination of these events was used to describe two types of successful outcomes—$success_1$, where incorporation and improvement both occurred, and $success_2$, where neither incorporation nor improvement occurred. The two contrary combinations (incorporation but no improvement, and improvement but no incorporation) were treated as failures.

The determination of these outcomes was based on the answers to two questions in the checklist:

F-1. By the end of the case study, the innovation had been:

(1) Operational and appeared fully incorporated
(2) Operational, but with some doubt about its extent, form, or permanence (e.g., still identified as a special project or supported with special funds)
(3) Discontinued (according to plan) following a period of operation or testing
(4) Discontinued (but not according to plan) following a period of operation or testing
(5) Not operated or tested
(9) Impossible to answer

F-5. The use of the innovation resulted in the following service changes (in service cost, input, output, or effect):

---

[a]Fliegel and Kivlin (1966) conclude from their study of farm innovation that innovations which promise rapid recovery of costs are more likely to be implemented than those which do not. In conflict with those earlier findings, Fliegel et al. (1968) found that rapid cost recovery related negatively to rate of adoption.

(1) Some improvement

(2) Some decline

(3) Both

(4) Evidence showing no change

(5) Question not applicable

(6) Information only

(9) Impossible to answer

For question F-1, the first two alternatives were regarded as a positive outcome—that is, innovative efforts were considered to have been incorporated whether the response was "fully" or "with some doubt." For question F-5, only the first alternative was regarded as a positive outcome. The occurrence of any of the other alternatives for either of the questions was taken to mean that either incorporation or service improvement had not occurred. This definition of the joint occurrence of two events thus created the four possible outcomes (success$_1$, success$_2$, and two types of failure). Table 3-8 shows the definition of the four categories along with the number of case studies that fell into each category. For purposes of analysis, the two types of failure were always lumped together, and thus three categories of outcomes—success$_1$, success$_2$, and failure—defined the dependent variable used throughout the remaining cross-tabulations.

*Relationship of Innovation Attributes
to Successful Efforts*

On the basis of the concepts drawn from the literature, the previously discussed attributes of the innovations were then examined for significant relationships with successful outcomes.[b] Table 3-9 lists all of the attributes that we have

Table 3-8
Outcome Measures of the Innovative Effort
(N = 140)

Incorporation (Question F-1)	Service Improvements (Question F-5)	
	Improvement	*No Improvement*
Incorporated	71 (Success$_1$)	41 (Failure)
Not Incorporated	6 (Failure)	22 (Success$_2$)

[b]It should be remembered that our analysis is based on the occurrence of key words or phrases in the case study, and not the analysis of the case study's own hypotheses.

Table 3-9
Attributes of the Innovative Device

Attribute		Checklist Question
Type of Innovation		
Innovation involved hardware, a computer system, or data analysis	A-5	Innovation mainly involved new machine, artifact, material, or chemical; computer package or system; or analysis using symbolic operations or quantitative data
Intrinsic features of innovation		
Visibility	D-10	Innovation involved concrete artifact
Divisibility for testing purposes	D-9	Innovation testable on portion of target population
Reversibility	D-12	(Obverse of) initial use or testing of innovation said to involve substantial irreversible changes (e.g., employee firing or new facilities)
Cost	B-6	Estimated amount of new funds used to support innovation
Status of innovation at time of proposal		
Source of idea for innovation	D-3	Idea for innovation came from inside agency
Previously demonstrated merit	D-4	Merit had been demonstrated by any one of four criteria (alternatives a, b, c, or d)
Relative advantage	D-4b	Merit had been demonstrated by comparison with existing practice
Credibility	D-4c	Merit had been demonstrated by support or endorsement only
Compatibility	F-9	Case study provides evidence that operation or testing of innovation involved structural or personnel reorganization, permanent addition or reduction of personnel, or changes in procedures within individual jobs
Adaptability	E-16	Case study indicates that innovation had undergone at least one minor modification or been rejected and replaced by other innovation
Potential effects of innovation		
Transitivity	D-6	Innovation's primary intended effect was to create new practices between clients and providers
Immediacy of benefits	D-7	Changes resulting from innovation were expected to be apparent within year of initial use
Frequency and regularity of reward or benefit	D-8	Observable changes could potentially occur more than once

described and the checklist questions on which the attributes were based. Only five of all the usable[c] checklist questions exhibited a significant association with successful innovative efforts: the type of innovation, visibility, divisibility, relative advantage, and transitivity. Appendix E provides the reader with a concrete idea of the nature of the case study evidence; it lists examples of the actual key words or phrases that were coded for some of these items. Reversibility, cost, source of the idea, previous merit, credibility, compatibility, and adaptability were also tested; however, none of them was significantly associated with success.

The three types of innovations (hardware, computers, and data analyses) exhibited significantly different likelihoods of success (see Table 3-10). Of the three types, hardware innovations were most often associated with $success_1$ (service improvement and incorporation), whereas data analytic innovations were most often associated with $success_2$ (no improvement and no incorporation), and computer systems were most often associated with failure. This three-way distinction among $success_1$, $success_2$, and failure should be noted; for the four remaining attributes that were related to successful efforts, there was little distinction between $success_2$ and failure, as the comparisons all tended to show either $success_1$ on the one hand, or $success_2$ and failure on the other.

The concreteness or visibility of an innovation was one significant correlate of the outcome of the innovative effort (see Table 3-11). Those innovations that involved either a concrete object, or both a concrete object and a proper name, tended far more often to be successful than those that had only a name or those that had neither name nor concrete manifestation. The extent to which an innovation was divisible for testing on a limited basis was found to be a second

Table 3-10
Relationship Between Type of Innovation and Successful Efforts
(N = 140)

	Outcome of Innovative Effort		
Type of Innovation (Question A-5)	*Success$_1$*	*Success$_2$*	*Failure*
Hardware	38	5	11
Computer system	23	4	19
Data analysis	10	13	17

Note: $\chi^2 = 23.93$, df = 4, $p < 0.001$. Examination of higher quality cases alone significantly supports this relationship.

---

[c]Before the analysis, two questions were dropped because of a lack of information in the case studies: immediacy and frequency of benefits. In this and all subsequent chapters, we have dropped any checklist questions in which over 50 percent of the responses were in the impossible-to-answer category, or less than 20 percent of the responses were in one of two binary (yes or no) categories.

Table 3-11
Relationship Between Innovation Visibility and Successful Efforts
(N = 140)

	Outcome of Innovative Effort		
Visibility (Question D-10)	*Success$_1$*	*Success$_2$*	*Failure*
Concrete artifact or action	28	8	15
Proper name only	1	3	6
Both	37	5	22
Neither	5	6	4

Note: χ^2 = 16.99, df = 6, $p < 0.01$. Examination of higher quality cases alone fails to show any relationship.

correlate of successful outcomes (see Table 3-12). A higher frequency of success$_1$ was associated with those cases where an innovation either had been or could have been initially tested on a restricted portion of the intended client population.

The relative advantage of an innovation over existing practices was a third important correlate of success (see Table 3-13). The relationship was not as hypothesized, however, inasmuch as those devices that had demonstrated some advantage over existing practices were significantly *less* likely to succeed than were those that had not shown such an advantage. Innovations may be incorporated with some service improvement, in other words, even though the case study showed they had no relative advantage over existing practices. The final innovation attribute found to be significantly associated with success was transitivity (see Table 3-14). Those innovations involving changed practices between clients and service providers, which presumably therefore involved more direct attempts to deal with service outputs than inputs, were more frequently associated with success$_1$ than innovations that did not involve such changed practices.

Table 3-12
Relationship Between Innovation Divisibility and Successful Efforts
(N = 140)

	Outcome of Innovative Effort		
Divisibility (testable on portion of target population–Question D-9)	*Success$_1$*	*Success$_2$*	*Failure*
Yes	40	5	18
No	29	13	24
Impossible to answer	2	4	5

Note: χ^2 = 6.09, df = 2, $p < 0.05$ (excludes impossible-to-answer cases). Examination of higher quality cases alone fails to show any relationship.

Table 3-13
Relationship Between Relative Advantage and Successful Efforts
(N = 140)

Relative Advantage (Question D-4b)	Outcome of Innovative Effort		
	Success₁	*Success₂*	*Failure*
	$Success_1$	$Success_2$	$Failure$
Yes	28	5	25
No	26	13	12
Impossible to answer	17	4	10

Note: $\chi^2 = 7.78$, df = 2, $p < 0.05$ (excludes impossible-to-answer cases). Examination of higher quality cases alone significantly supports this relationship.

Table 3-14
Relationship Between Innovation Transitivity and Successful Efforts
(N = 140)

Transitivity (new practices intended between clients and service providers–Question D-6)	Outcome of Innovative Effort		
	$Success_1$	$Success_2$	$Failure$
Yes	43	5	13
No	28	17	33
Impossible to answer	0	0	1

Note: $\chi^2 = 16.57$, df = 2, $p < 0.001$ (excludes impossible-to-answer case). Examination of higher quality cases alone significantly supports this relationship.

To determine whether the effect of any of these factors was confounded by its interactive relationship with other factors, all of the device factors were then used in a regression analysis.[d] For the purposes of this analysis, the dependent variable had to be modified to exclude the twenty-two $success_2$ cases, so that the remaining cases represented a simple binary variable (success or failure).[e] Wherever necessary, the device factors were also converted to binary categories (usually the presence or absence of the given characteristic).[f] The regression was carried out in stepwise form, so that only the most important factors

[d]Three-way cross-tabulations and other interactive analytic techniques were attempted, but the sample size was too small to draw reliable conclusions from the results.

[e]The exclusion was based on a priori judgment that the $success_2$ outcome was not similar to either $success_1$ or failure, and hence could not be grouped with either category. This hypothesis was partially confirmed by actual analyses that showed the regression results (R^2's) to be lower if the $success_2$ cases were lumped with $success_1$, even though the number of observations increased by twenty-two.

[f]For type of innovation, the variable was defined as either being a hardware innovation or not.

were allowed to enter the regression equation, and the procedure was arbitrarily ended after the sixth step.[g]

The regression analysis was used even though there were coding difficulties. Under a binary scheme (the presence or absence of a given characteristic), cases with impossible-to-answer responses should ideally be eliminated from the analysis because the response is ambiguous. However, such elimination would have reduced the sample size to the point that no analysis could have been conducted, since any case study with an impossible-to-answer response on any of the independent or dependent variables would have been eliminated, and since most case studies had at least one such response. As a partial but not entirely satisfactory remedy, the regression analysis was thus performed twice, the first time with the impossible-to-answer responses coded along with the other responses indicating the absence of a given factor, and the second time along with other responses indicating the presence of a given factor (i.e., coded as "zero" in the first analysis and as "1" in the second).

When this dual analysis was performed, the results showed that it did not much matter how the impossible-to-answer responses had been coded (see Tables 3-15 and 3-16). In both analyses, almost the same six factors appeared, although transitivity and hardware innovations were the only two significant factors, and

Table 3-15

Six Most Important Device Factors Related to Successful Innovative Efforts (A)

(impossible to answer is coded as absence *of factor)*

Attribute (listed in order of stepwise regression analysis)	Regression Results		
	b	Standard Error b	F
Transitivity	0.21	0.11	3.94*
Hardware innovation	0.24	0.11	5.23*
Relative advantage	−0.09	0.09	0.99
Divisibility	0.15	0.10	2.20
Visibility	−0.11	0.09	1.38
Reversibility	−0.07	0.10	0.49
Constant	0.49		

Note: $R^2 = 0.168$, df = 6/111, $F = 3.74$, $p < 0.01$.
*$p < 0.05$.

[g]Subsequent analysis of the factors that did not enter the equation in the first six steps showed that none would have added significantly to the variance explained. An alternative procedure would have been to carry out a non-stepwise regression with all twelve independent variables. However, since there were only 118 tabulations, this would have presented too many variables. As a result, the stepwise regression was used, and the sixth step was chosen as a reasonable stopping point given the number of observations.

Table 3-16

Six Most Important Device Factors Related to Successful Innovative Efforts (B)

(impossible to answer is coded as presence *of factor)*

Attribute (listed in order of stepwise regression analysis)	Regression Results		
	b	Standard Error b	F
Transitivity	0.22	0.10	4.87*
Hardware innovation	0.24	0.10	5.35*
Relative advantage	−0.13	0.09	2.04
Reversibility	−0.12	0.09	1.85
Visibility	−0.09	0.09	1.09
Testability	0.09	0.10	0.86
Constant	0.56		

Note: $R^2 = 0.164$, df $= 6/111$, $F = 3.62$, $p < 0.01$.
*$p < 0.05$.

in both analyses the overall variance explained (R^2) was about 17 percent.

In summary, the results indicate that, if simple pairwise comparisons are made between individual innovation attributes and the outcomes of the innovative effort, successful innovative efforts—defined primarily in terms of success$_1$ —are associated with hardware innovations; transitive innovations in the sense of dealing directly with changes in the way clients use the service and not merely with changes in the administrative procedures internal to the service organization; innovations that have not necessarily demonstrated any relative advantage over existing service practices; visible innovations that involve a concrete object; and divisible innovations in the sense of being testable on a restricted portion of the target population. When the interactive relationships are among the factors taken into account, the only significant relationships are between successful efforts and (1) hardware innovations, and (2) transitivity of the device.

There have been few studies of different innovation characteristics important in local service agencies across a wide variety of innovative devices. If one compares our findings with those of previous research on the adoption of innovations, there are some similarities and differences. Everett Rogers (1962; and with Shoemaker, 1971), who has continually summarized the massive body of research on innovation adoption behavior, has found five attributes that have consistently been important: relative advantage over the ideas being superseded, compatibility with existing practices, simplicity[h] of understanding or use,

[h]*Simplicity* is used instead of the more common term *complexity* in order not to confuse the direction of the relationships.

divisibility, and communicability. Our study had checklist questions that attempted to assess four[i] of these five attributes, as well as many other attributes cited in the literature. Of all the pairwise comparisons, we found four attributes to be significantly related to successful efforts, and of these four, two overlapped with the attributes cited by Rogers—divisibility and visibility (which we have posited as being related to communicability)—whereas one contradicted Rogers' findings (relative advantage and success were *negatively* related). From these results, it may be tentatively concluded that successful innovative devices in local services do not necessarily share the same qualities or attributes that consistently facilitate the adoption of innovations by individuals. In fact, the inconsistent findings suggest that there may be important organizational factors that facilitate the innovative process and that must also be taken into account. The next two chapters attempt to show how an understanding of innovative efforts by local services requires a richer analytic framework than a mere focus on the innovative device alone.

---

[i]Simplicity was the single attribute that was ignored because of a difficulty in developing adequate criteria to be applied to the case studies.

4 Local Organizations and the Innovative Environment

The attributes of the innovation—i.e., the device—are but one set of factors relevant to the innovative process. At least two other sets are also important in influencing the adoption of technological innovations by local service agencies: the attributes of the agency and of the environment within which the agency operates. Our discussion implies a simple conceptual framework for investigating the innovative process. This framework assumes an innovative effort to consist of four elements:

An innovative device (the innovation) and its characteristics;

A background setting, consisting of both organizational and environmental factors (background factors);

The immediate circumstances of the specific innovative effort, also consisting of both organizational and environmental factors (implementation factors); and

The outcomes of the innovative effort (success or failure, based on incorporation and service improvement).

Of particular relevance for the present chapter is the distinction between background and implementation factors. Background factors refer to the steady state of an agency and of its community setting independent of any specific innovative effort, whereas implementation factors refer to the characteristics of a specific innovative effort. Chapter 1 has already indicated that the classic diffusion research has tended to emphasize background factors as more important in the innovative process, while recent research on local organizations has increasingly pointed toward the importance of implementation factors. The present chapter is thus organized to address this issue by separately analyzing background and implementation factors and then comparing their effects with each other and with the attributes of the innovative device.

At the same time, the conceptual framework should not be taken as much more than a way of assessing the case studies. The framework is, for instance, not meant to be the basis for any theorizing about the innovative process or how it works. Such evidence and thoughts are reserved for the next chapter.

The Setting: Background Factors

The background setting for any innovative effort consists of the stable organizational characteristics of the innovating agency and the political, social, and technological climate within which it operates. For instance, there is much research to suggest that larger-sized agencies operating in rapidly changing environments are more likely to innovate. Such characteristics are considered background factors because they are not direct attributes of any specific innovative effort that is undertaken or even any innovative device that is used. We first review the prominent hypotheses about these factors and then present our findings on the relationship between these factors and successful outcomes.

The Innovative Environment

The innovative environment within which an agency operates, independent of any specific innovative effort, includes characteristics of the community and of the technological and economic climates. The local community serves as the broad social context within which innovations occur. Several studies have examined the importance of community characteristics, mainly in relation to nontechnological innovations such as fluoridation, municipal decisions to build public housing, and agency adoptions of new health programs. In general, the studies seem to agree that the more innovative communities or jurisdictions are *large, urbanized, wealthy, of high occupational and educational rank,* and *stable in rate of population turnover* (Aiken and Alford, 1970a and 1970b; Baldridge and Burnham, 1975; Crain, 1966; Mytinger, 1968; and Walker, 1969).

A second set of environmental factors hypothesized to influence innovation is the existence of a *rich technological environment* that presents many opportunities for inventing and adopting innovations (Myers and Marquis, 1969; and Utterback, 1971). The climate thus includes the existence of technological advances as well as the continued adoption of different innovations by other agencies. It also includes the agency's own past experience with innovation. If an agency has a *history of innovative attempts,* this may indicate a work environment predisposed to innovate. As yet another condition of the technological climate, the activities of professional societies and practitioner groups—the American Association of State Highway and Transportation Officials, for example—have recently been found to be associated with positive effects on innovation (Feller et al., 1974). Participation by service practitioners in professional conventions and seminars means exposure to a variety of potentially innovative ideas and reinforces the prestige-generating incentives for engaging in innovative efforts (Hage and Aiken, 1967).

A third set of environmental factors directs attention to national and local *economic conditions.* In the literature, however, the influence of economic factors has been studied mainly in relation to innovations in private firms. These include studies of the roles of market demand and flux, the profitability of investment, and monopolistic power as they affect the processes of invention, innovation, and diffusion (Mansfield, 1961, 1963, 1964; Schmookler, 1966; and Utterback, 1971). Since the parallels between the economics of private and public sector behavior are not obvious, these economic factors as potential influences on innovative behavior in local services will not be pursued further.

The Innovative Organization

Organizational characteristics of local service agencies have long been investigated as potential correlates of the adoption of innovations.[a] The characteristics fall into two groups—the organization's structure and its staff composition. Both of these groups, to emphasize our dichotomy between background and implementation factors, are related to the general condition of the innovating agency, and not to the characteristics of any specific innovative effort.

Structural Factors. Research on the relationship between the structural characteristics of an organization and its innovativeness tends to revolve, explicitly or implicitly, around two polar archetypes. Perhaps the most widely used is the terminology of Burns and Stalker (1961), who distinguish between *organic* and *mechanistic* forms. Organic organizations are highly diverse, but have little formalized task structure, weak communication hierarchies, and greater staff participation in decisionmaking. They are thought to be particularly well suited to the fluid, high information environments in which innovation thrives (Emery and Trist, 1965). Mechanistic organizations, in contrast, are less diverse, have more formalized task structures, more hierarchical control systems, and less participative decisionmaking. They are thought to be better suited to the large-scale processing of routine activities and to the stable, noninnovative environments appropriate for routinized tasks (Thompson, 1965). In sum, the dimensions on which organic and mechanistic organizations differ are diversity, formalization of task structure, centralization, and staff participation in decisionmaking.

Diversity can be defined as the number of different tasks, specialists, technologies, incentives, and rewards employed within the organization. Wilson's (1966) basic thesis is that diversity encourages the initiation of new ideas, but hinders their adoption, and the results from Sapolsky's (1967) study of department stores supports this thesis. Hage and Aiken (1967), however, found a

[a]A number of theorists have distinguished carefully two stages in the innovative process—initiation (invention) and adoption—and contrasted the organizational correlates of success in each stage. Wilson (1966), for example, distinguishes the facilitating effect of organizational diversity during the conception and proposal stage from its inhibiting effect in the adoption stage.

strong positive relationship between diversity in occupational specialties and the rate of adoption of new programs by social welfare and health departments. One possible reconciliation of these contrary findings involves a restatement of Wilson's thesis: Although the proportion of initiated proposals actually adopted by highly diverse organizations is small, the number of proposals initiated will be sufficiently great to ensure a relatively high level of innovative behavior nonetheless. Given this interpretation, our study should find diversity positively related to successful innovative efforts.

Formalization involves the specificity and rigidity with which roles are defined within the organization. A high level of formalization usually ensures the routinization of performance at the expense of individual initiative and organizational innovativeness. *Functional looseness*, a term coined to describe the antithesis of high formalization, is used to characterize a fluid organization in which roles are loosely defined. The presence of ad hoc working groups, task forces, or committees in an organization may be taken as indicators of functional looseness and as a possible explanation of the causal link between that looseness and innovativeness, since the organization's capacity for departures from the standard formal structure may be tied to a general predisposition to adopt new ways of doing things (Bennis, 1966).

Centralization refers primarily to narrowly constricted, hierarchical channels of authority. More centralized organizations tend to prohibit the development of horizontal coalitions in support of an innovation (Thompson, 1965). As a result, structural centralization has been correlated with low innovativeness and decentralization with high innovativeness (Burns and Stalker, 1961; Hage and Aiken, 1967; Kaluzny et al., 1970; and Hage and Dewar, 1973). However, the distinction between initiation and adoption is important. Although decentralization may foster the initiation of new ideas, the more centralized organizations may be more effective at facilitating adoption (Rothman, 1974). Thus Corwin (1972) found that centralization actually fosters the implementation of innovations in schools. In the context of our study—which does not investigate the initiation of innovations but rather their adoption by organizations—we would therefore expect centralization to be positively related to successful innovative efforts.

Substantive *staff participation in decisionmaking* is another organizational characteristic that has been viewed as a correlate of innovativeness, although the link has not been firmly established. Hage and Dewar (1973) suggest that since persons in elite positions have a stake in the status quo and will thus oppose innovations, increased staff participation in decisionmaking may lead to the adoption of more innovations. However, a clearly plausible contrary hypothesis is that high levels of participativeness, while fostering the generation of innovative ideas, may well make their adoption more difficult by diffusing the base of support for the innovation. In short, there are no confident predictions that can be made about the relationship between participation and innovativeness.

In addition to the attributes of the organic and mechanistic archetypes, considerable research has identified two other potentially important organizational characteristics: organizational size and slack. The literature, though rich with illustrative studies, is somewhat ambivalent on the direction of the relationship between *organizational size* and innovativeness (Rothman, 1974). Although Galbraith (1956) and others have suggested that size is highly correlated with innovativeness, Mansfield's (1964) extensive study of industrial firms found no such relationship. In either case, Rogers and Eveland (1975) have noted that size may have little value in explaining the innovative process and that large organizational size probably serves as a proxy for other factors, such as the availability of excess resources, the presence of a more professionalized staff, or the accumulation of a greater range of innovative experience.

As with organizational size, there have been numerous studies of the relationship between *organizational slack* and innovative efforts. Slack may be defined as payments to members of the coalition in excess of what is required to maintain the organization (Cyert and March, 1963) or as a feeling of well-being or perceived success (Knight, 1967). Both definitions suggest that a growing and prospering organization is more likely to have slack than a static one, no matter how large or well established the organization. Under slack conditions, an organization searches for new ideas that enhance subunit goals and prestige without conflicting with the basic structure of the organization. Under nonslack or distress conditions, organizations engage in highly constrained searches to find immediately satisfying (and usually nontechnological) solutions to pressing problems (Cyert and March, 1963).

Of all the concepts related to innovation, slack has been one of the most difficult to measure. Even when organizational records are available, it is hard to identify the precise budgetary or decisionmaking conditions associated with slack. In dealing with existing case studies where access to such records is out of the question, the problem is even more intractable. As a result, our analysis does not attempt to assess slack considerations directly, but instead has identified two signs of *extra resources.* The first is the existence of grants and contracts to the agency from outside sources, since such awards may imply funds beyond operating expenses. The second is the existence of an R&D unit, which might indicate an agency's anticipation of slack conditions and commitment to innovation. However, Thompson (1965) suggests that R&D units, while representing slack, may also hinder innovation. Organizationally segregated, their creativity can become self-contained; unless the entire organization is involved with the R&D unit in the search for innovations, the chances of accepting and implementing the unit's proposals may decrease.

Staff Composition. Although many organization theorists would contend that the composition of an agency's staff—i.e., the professional specialties represented and the relative proportion of professional to nonprofessional workers—is a fundamental structural characteristic, the relationship between *professional-*

ization and innovation occupies such a central a place in the literature that it deserves separate attention. In general, professionalization, defined as an orientation to the norms and values of an extraorganizational professional group, is thought to be highly correlated with innovation.

Because the relevant reference group for professionals is extraorganizational, and because such groups tend to attach occupational status and prestige to innovative activities rather than conformance to intraorganizational norms, professional staff members can be expected to support innovative efforts. By extension, the higher the proportion of professionals on the agency's staff, the more receptive to innovative efforts the agency will be (Thompson, 1965; Blau and Scott, 1962; and Zaltman et al., 1973). In one study, Mohr (1969) found a positive relationship between innovativeness in health departments and the "public health ideology," a measure of acceptance of dominant professional norms by executive officers. Conversely, low educational attainment and the lack of professional education has been an explanation for the resistance to innovative efforts in police departments (Rubenstein, 1973) and fire departments (Archibald and Hoffman, 1969).

A second characteristic of personnel composition that has gained increasing attention in recent years is the extent of *employee unionization*. Basing their arguments largely on the experience of New York City in the late 1960s, where well-publicized innovations attempted by the Lindsay administration appeared to be thwarted by the intransigence of employee unions, commentators have suggested that active employee unions may constitute a significant barrier to innovative efforts. In particular, unionization may play an especially large role in those jurisdictions where prevailing collective bargaining practices appear to impinge on managerial prerogatives (Horton, 1971; and Wellington and Winter, 1971).

Relationship of Background Factors to Successful Outcomes

Table 4-1 presents a summary of the background factors and the relevant checklist questions that were intended to assess each factor. Five of these questions were precluded from any analysis because of a lack of information in the case studies.[b] All the remaining questions were examined for the relationship to success$_1$, success$_2$, and failure in two types of analysis: comparisons in which each question was individually cross-tabulated with the measure of successful

[b]These questions covered association activity, staff participation in decisionmaking, organizational size, staff professionalization, and staff unionization. The criteria for discarding were: over 50 percent of the answers were in the impossible-to-answer category, or less than 20 percent were in one of two binary (yes or no) categories.

Table 4-1
Background Factors

Attribute		Checklist Question
Environmental		
Large community	G-2	1970 census of population
Wealthy community	G-5	1970 median family income
	G-6	1970 local government expenditures per capita
Educated community	G-4	1970 median years of education
Stable community	G-3	Percent population change, 1960-1970
Rich, innovative environment	B-4c	Case study mentions innovations that occurred in other jurisdictions
Agency history of innovation	B-4a	Case study mentions other innovations having occurred in the same agency
Presence of professional activity	B-3	There was a professional association (Question discarded because of insufficient information)
Organizational		
Diversity	C-7a	Case study mentions more than one specialty or profession as routinely belonging to agency
Formalization	H-17	Case study does not mention ad hoc working groups, task forces, or committees, but does mention two or more fixed organizational units in agency
Centralization	C-5	Case study mentions two or more layers of supervisory relationships
Staff participation in decisionmaking	C-7c	Case study mentions participation by service providers in any agency decisionmaking (Question discarded because of insufficient information)
Agency size	C-2	Number of agency employees (Question discarded because of insufficient information)
Extra resources	C-1b or c	Agency had or supported an R&D group or had grants and contracts from outside sources
Professionalization of staff	C-3d	Travel or meetings outside jurisdiction among agency's characteristics (Question discarded because of insufficient information)
Unionization of staff	C-3b	Unions or benevolent associations were mentioned among agency's characteristics (Question discarded because of insufficient information)

outcomes; and multivariate regression analysis in which all the questions were regressed against the same dependent measure. The analytic procedures, in other words, were identical to those discussed in Chapter 3.

Of the ten background factors that were thus included in the cross-tabulations, only two were statistically correlated with successful outcomes. The two factors were centralization and one of the components of extra resources—the presence of an R&D group within the organization. The results for centralization (as measured by a proxy—the mention of two or more layers of supervisory relationships in the agency) are consistent with Corwin's (1972) finding in centralized school systems—i.e., that concentration of decisionmaking in a hierarchical authority structure is positively correlated with successful innovative efforts (see Table 4-2). Close examination of this finding indicates that this relationship is strong for *both* $success_1$ and $success_2$, suggesting that centralization may be a particularly important characteristic of agencies that successfully reject an innovation that fails to demonstrate service improvements ($success_2$). Similarly, whether the agency has or supports an R&D or analysis group was also positively related to successful outcomes, but most conspicuously related to $success_2$. Table 4-3 shows that agencies making appropriate rejections were more likely to have an R&D or analysis group, while agencies failing to incorporate or reject appropriately were more likely not to have one. This result is probably related to the fact that (as shown in Chapter 3) the type of innovation most frequently associated with $success_2$ outcomes was the data analysis innovation, and the presence of an R&D group was correlated with an attempt to use such innovations. None of the other background factors was significantly related to successful outcomes.

To determine whether the effect of either of these factors was confounded by its interactive relationship with other factors, all of the background factors were then used in a stepwise regression analysis, ending at the sixth step. The analysis followed the procedure outlined in Chapter 3, with the dependent variable modified to exclude the twenty-two $success_2$ cases and the background

Table 4-2
Relationship Between Centralization and Successful Efforts
(N = 140)

Layers of Supervisory Relationships (Question C-5)	Outcome of Innovative Effort		
	$Success_1$	$Success_2$	Failure
Two or more (centralized)	30	12	11
None or one (not as centralized)	15	1	15
Impossible to answer	26	9	21

Note: $\chi^2 = 9.84$, df = 2, $p < 0.01$ (excludes impossible-to-answer cases). Examination of higher quality cases alone significantly supports this relationship.

Table 4-3

Relationship Between the Existence of an Agency R&D Group and Successful Efforts

(N = 140)

Existence of R&D Group *(Question C-1b)*	*Outcome of Innovative Effort*		
	Success$_1$	*Success$_2$*	*Failure*
Yes	21	13	12
No	21	4	19
Impossible to answer	28	5	16

Note: χ^2 = 6.27, df = 2, $p < 0.05$ (excludes impossible-to-answer cases). Examination of higher quality cases alone significantly supports this relationship.

factors represented by binary categories (usually involving the presence or absence of the given characteristic). Similarly, the regression was carried out twice, with the impossible-to-answer cases coded in the first analysis along with the absence of a characteristic, and in the second analysis with the presence of the characteristic.

The two analyses produced nonconflicting results, with centralization being the most important factor when all factors were taken into account, and with the presence of an R&D group not appearing in the regression equation. Table 4-4 shows the results when the impossible-to-answer cases are coded along with other responses indicating the absence of the given characteristic.[c] Overall, the top six background factors accounted for only 14 percent of the variance in the dependent variable—that is, with a modified definition of successful efforts in which the success$_2$ cases were dropped from the analysis, the total R^2 was 0.142.

In summary, the background factors appear related to successful outcomes in the following manner. When success$_1$ is the main criterion for assessing outcomes, successful innovative efforts occur more frequently when agencies are *centralized.* This result is obtained in a cross-tabular analysis and does not change when a multivariate analysis is used to control for the interactive effects of the other variables. The background factors as a group, however, account for only a small proportion (14 percent) of the total variance in the dependent variable.

The Immediate Circumstances: Implementation Factors

Whereas background factors represent the environmental or organizational characteristics that constitute the general setting in which an innovative effort

---

[c]While centralization appears in the second regression equation, its coefficient, as well as the coefficients of all the other variables and the R^2 for the entire equation, were not significant. Therefore, although the second equation does not support the results of the first, it also does not contradict those results.

Table 4-4

Six Most Important Background Factors Related to Successful Innovative Efforts

(impossible to answer is coded as absence of factor)

Attribute (listed in order of stepwise regression analysis)	Regression Results		
	b	Standard Error b	F
Centralization	0.20	0.09	4.72*
Rich innovative environment	−0.19	0.09	4.16*
Large community	−0.09	0.04	5.40*
Agency history of innovation	−0.19	0.10	3.74
Formalization	−0.16	0.11	2.21
Wealthy community	−0.06	0.05	1.62
Constant	1.06		

Note: $R^2 = 0.142$, df = $6/111$, $F = 3.50$, $p < 0.01$.
*$p < 0.05$.

occurs, implementation factors represent environmental or organizational characteristics that are the immediate ingredients in a specific innovative effort. Once again, we first review the prominent hypotheses about these implementation factors and then present our findings.

Environmental Factors

Several environmental factors have been considered important for the success of specific innovative efforts. Numerous studies of innovations in the private sector have suggested the hypothesis that market demand, or the existence of a *prior need* for specific change, is a common prelude to the adoption of technological innovations. Indeed, in a summary review of the literature on numerous cases of innovations in the private sector, Utterback (1974) found that prior need was the most important correlate of the adoption of innovations. This has led to the notion that "demand-pull" rather than "technology-push" is one of the early environmental conditions to appear in relation to innovative efforts.

Other environmental factors have mainly to do with the amount and nature of political and administrative support that is generated for the innovative effort. Such support can be critical, because government agencies, unlike private firms, are simultaneously autonomous organizations and subunits of a larger organization—the local governmental jurisdiction. Thus, although it is generally useful to analyze the activities of a police department or a public health agency as an autonomous organization, such an agency is highly dependent on the general jurisdiction and its "overhead" agencies and executives—e.g., the local legislative body, the chief executive of the jurisdiction, and such related staff offices as the budget bureau. Since specific innovative efforts usually do not come to the attention of the legislative body but may be the explicit focus of an administrative decision, it is the *chief executive's support* that in particular may make a difference. Besides the support of officials, *client participation* can also influence the outcome of specific innovative efforts. Although there has been little research on whether such participation facilitates or retards innovation, Brager (cited in Rothman, 1974) found that the employment of indigenous paraprofessionals increased the organization's effectiveness in activating a new program.

Organizational Factors

Three sets of organizational factors appear to be relevant to any innovative effort. First, there is the planning, training, and monitoring process, especially in relation to the service officials responsible for implementing or using the innovation. The extent and nature of these activities, including the occurrence of any unforeseen delays, may influence the outcome of the innovative effort. Second, there are the characteristics and background of the major actors in the effort, be they innovators, implementers, or advocates. Their positions, power, and status in the organization and among their peers can often affect the outcomes. Third, there is the potential effect of the innovative effort on the organization itself, which again may create resistance to or facilitate the innovative effort.

Planning, Training, Monitoring, and Delays. Every innovative effort must ultimately be concerned with how the service practitioners in the agency are brought into the innovative process. If there is adequate allowance for *practitioner participation* in the planning phase, the practitioners may get an opportunity for orientation and *training*, the innovation may be better tailored to existing practices, and, as a result, any potential resistance to change by the practitioners may be reduced. Gross et al. (1971), for instance, found that the major barriers to implementation of an educational innovation were that teachers had no clear understanding of what was expected of them and that they lacked the skills and knowledge needed to perform their new role. Similarly, the implementation of innovations requires continued *monitoring* by those who decided to try the innovation in the first place. Such monitoring may be needed to enforce the changes to be carried out as well as to surmount any unforeseen problems. Again, evidence for the importance of such monitoring comes mostly from experiences in the education sector (Gross et al., 1971; and House, 1974). As an overall element in the support for the innovative effort, and especially in relation to these planning and monitoring efforts, the *support of the agency* *head* has been found to reduce resistance to an innovation and thereby to increase the chances of its adoption (Zaltman et al., 1973). Finally, *implementation delays* in the innovative process may reduce the chances of adoption. These delays may be due to events within the agency, typically related to resistance to the innovation during planning or training, but they can also be due to events external to the agency—e.g., strikes affecting the production of the device, client protests over the importance of the expenditure, or delays created by funding difficulties from outside sources. Such delays can impede the progress of the innovative effort, but can also reduce the confidence or enthusiasm of its advocates.

Characteristics of Major Actors. In traditional studies of technological innovations, the main change agent has usually been defined as either the inventor or adopter of the innovation. With innovative efforts in local organizations, however, the major actors are not easy to identify. Indeed, the innovator need not be an individual, but may be a small group either inside or outside the innovating organization. The alternative functions fulfilled by the major actors may be:

To introduce the innovation to the organization;

To marshal the appropriate resources and implementation plans;

To test the innovation in the organization;

To use the innovation on a permanent basis; or

Any combination of the above.

For instance, innovation in a fire department may depend upon the fire chief, mayor or mayoral aide, and analyst or technician. All three may be involved and may collectively form an innovative group. In a partial attempt to deal with this problem, we shall be concerned with three potential actors in any innovative effort: the person or group that first proposes the innovation to the agency (the innovator); the person or group that decides to implement or operate the innovation (the implementer); and the person or group most identified with the advocacy or support for the innovation (the advocate).

The first important attribute of these actors is the extent to which they are *members of the innovating agency.* In a series of studies to identify the source of the idea for different innovations in the private sector, most of the successfully developed and implemented ideas came from outside the innovative firm (Utterback, 1974). On the other hand, in local organizations, the threat of outsiders may increase staff resistance to externally produced ideas (Zaltman et al., 1973), so that the direction of the relationship between inside membership and successful outcomes cannot be predicted.

The other relevant attributes covered by previous research pertain mainly to the innovator. Innovators have typically demonstrated a *cosmopolite career pattern* (Rogers and Shoemaker, 1971); they are usually well educated and use their training and experience to seek innovative solutions (Utterback, 1971). They are also younger, of higher social status, and of higher income than noninnovators, and they may travel more widely and be more knowledgeable about other innovative efforts (Carter and Williams, 1957).

Innovators can also be perceived as being *veterans* or opinion leaders in their fields (Marsh and Coleman, 1954). Related to this may be a greater sense of professionalism, which has been frequently found to be characteristic of innovators. The professionalism links innovators to a network that provides an alternative reference group to the organization that employs them. Carlson (1961), for instance, describes innovators as "career-bound" workers, in the sense that the professional group serves as a support system that makes risk-taking possible. As one potential by-product, Utterback (1971), Rogers and Shoemaker (1971), Shepard (1967), Schoenberg (1973), and Carlson (1961) all point out that the innovator occupies a marginal role in his or her organization, in the sense that the organization does not monopolize the loyalty of the innovator.

Finally, Corwin (1972), Hawkes (1961), and Knight (1967) all emphasize the position of the innovator in the organization. Knight differentiates among three levels of organization related to the *power to innovate.* The highest level (policymaking and planning roles) has the greatest effect on product, process, structural, and personnel innovation; midlevel staff (e.g., market researchers or design engineers) have less effect, particularly in structural and personnel categories; and production workers have the least effect on all categories of possible change.

Potential Effect on Organization. Two potential effects of the innovation on the organization may have opposing influences on adoption. The *pervasiveness of the innovation* in affecting large numbers of agency units has been frequently held to be a negative factor for adoption. Both Menzel (1960) and Barnett (1953) have pointed out that innovations which affect and necessitate adjustment by many elements of the adopting organization will be more slowly adopted than those which are less pervasive. The existence of direct *service output goals* of the innovation,[d] in contrast, may have positive effects on adoption. The literature usually distinguishes a production versus service orientation of an organization; within this framework, emphasis on production or cost

---

[d]As described, this attribute is similar to transitivity as defined in Chapter 3. However, transitivity was based on the notion of effecting a change in the actual practices between clients and providers and was thus distinguished from innovative devices that did not directly affect clients. The service output attribute, on the other hand, was based on the distinction between a stated goal of actually increasing service outputs as opposed to increasing cost savings or improving information for decisionmaking.

efficiency instead of on direct improvements in services results in less innovation (Rosner, 1968; Thompson, 1965; and Rothman, 1974).

Relationship of Implementation Factors to Successful Outcomes

Table 4-5 lists all of these implementation factors, along with the relevant checklist questions. Of the fourteen relevant questions, none had to be excluded from analysis because of lack of information in the case studies. Therefore, all the questions were examined first for their simple relationship to $success_1$, $success_2$, and failure, and then for their relationship to the modified success measure (i.e., excluding the twenty-two $success_2$ cases) as part of a regression analysis.

In the cross-tabulations, only one environmental variable—client participation—was significantly related to successful innovative efforts. Table 4-6 indicates that when clients were involved in the innovative effort or even mentioned in the decisionmaking, the effort was *more* likely to be associated with $success_1$, but when no client participation was in evidence, there were no differences between the outcomes of $success_1$ and failure.

Among the organizational variables, two showed a significant positive association with success: the presence of a service output goal and of practitioner training in the use of the innovation. As Table 4-7 shows, when improved service output was the primary stated goal, $success_1$ was twice as likely to occur as failure, whereas failure was the more frequent end when another goal (or vaguely stated goal) was mentioned in relation to the innovation. As for practitioner training, Table 4-8 shows that where training or instruction of any sort was mentioned as part of the innovative process, $success_1$ was three times as likely to occur as failure, whereas failure was somewhat more likely when no such training was mentioned. With both the service output goal and practitioner training factors, there was little distinction between $success_2$ and failure.

As in the analysis of the device and background factors, a stepwise regression analysis was again carried out, but in this instance the results differed, depending upon whether the impossible-to-answer responses were coded along with the presence or absence of a given characteristic. In both analyses, client participation was a significant variable; but practitioner training was significant in one analysis but not the other, and the presence of a service output goal was not significant in either analysis.[e] Because of these differing results, it is difficult to draw any conclusions from the interactive analysis.

In summary, the most important implementation factors appeared to be related to successful efforts in the following manner. In simple pairwise comparisons, successful innovative efforts occurred more frequently when agencies provided for client participation and practitioner training, and when the intended goal was to improve service outputs rather than merely to reduce costs or increase information for decisionmaking. In the interactive analysis, the only conclusive result was that client participation was a significant variable.

---

[e]The overall R^2 was 0.204 for the first equation and 0.145 for the second.

Table 4-5
Implementation Factors

Attribute		Checklist Question
Environmental		
Prior need	B-1	Case study mentions need to meet service demands or reduce costs among existing conditions
Chief executive support	E-13a	Case study mentions supportive role of chief executive
Client participation	B-7	Innovative effort involved participatory process during implementation
Organizational		
Practitioner participation	E-10	Service practitioners first mentioned at time of innovation planning
Practitioner training	E-11	Service practitioners had training or practice with innovation
Implementer monitoring	E-12	Implementer last mentioned along with evaluation or final summary
Implementation delays	H-9	Unexpected delay within or outside agency
Agency head support	E-13e	Case study mentions supportive role of innovating agency head
Main actors are within agency	H-16	Innovator, implementer, and advocate of innovation were all from inside agency
Cosmopolite innovator	H-5	Innovator had more education, meetings, or contacts outside agency than other officials
Innovator is a veteran in agency	H-6	Innovator had been employed in more than one positive in agency, had over five years of employment in agency, had report or product associated with his name, or had acknowledged role as veteran or opinion leader
Innovator has power to innovate	H-7	Innovator had a decisionmaking role in agency, had access to slack resources, or had contacts with clients
Pervasiveness	D-13	Full use of innovation could potentially affect a line unit of agency or people throughout agency
Service output goal	D-5	Primary stated goal of innovation was service improvements or additions

Summary Analysis: Comparison of Device, Background, and Implementation Factors

The preceding sections have identified several device, background, and implementation variables that appear to be significant correlates of successful innovative efforts. To determine the amount of variance explained by all three sets of factors, as well as to determine the most important individual attributes

Table 4-6
Relationship Between Client Participation and Successful Efforts
(N = 140)

Client Participation (Question B-7)	Outcome of Innovative Effort		
	Success₁	*Success₂*	*Failure*
Some participatory process	26	5	9
No process, but client mentioned	25	8	10
No participation	20	9	26
Impossible to answer	0	0	2

Note: $\chi^2 = 10.76$, df = 4, $p < 0.05$ (excludes impossible-to-answer cases). Examination of higher quality cases alone significantly supports this relationship.

Table 4-7
Relationship Between Innovation Goal and Successful Efforts
(N = 140)

Innovation Goal (Question D-5)	Outcome of Innovative Effort		
	Success₁	*Success₂*	*Failure*
Improve service outputs	54	11	25
All other	17	11	22

Note: $\chi^2 = 8.76$, df = 2, $p < 0.05$. Examination of higher quality cases alone significantly supports this relationship.

Table 4-8
Relationship Between Practitioner Training and Successful Efforts
(N = 140)

Practitioner Training (Question E-11)	Outcome of Innovative Effort		
	Success₁	*Success₂*	*Failure*
Some	46	10	14
None	25	12	33

Note: $\chi^2 = 14.08$, df = 2, $p < 0.001$. Examination of higher quality cases alone significantly supports this relationship.

when all others are also taken into account, another pair of stepwise regressions was performed, in which the top six device, background, and implementation attributes from the previous regressions were considered together. (The pair of regressions again reflected the alternative coding of the impossible-to-answer responses.) In these regressions, eighteen variables were thus made available, and the stepwise procedure was arbitrarily ended after the tenth step.[f] Table 4-9 presents the results when the impossible-to-answer responses were coded along with the absence of a given factor.[g] The table indicates that the ten variables account for a significant 35 percent of the variance in the dependent variable.[h]

Among the individual variables, although our first major hypothesis had been that the implementation factors might play a more important role in this

Table 4-9

Ten Most Important Background, Implementation, and Device Factors Related to Successful Innovative Efforts

(impossible to answer is coded as absence of factor)

Attribute (listed in order of stepwise regression analysis)	Regression Results		
	b	Standard Error b	F
Practitioner training	0.31	0.08	14.81[c]
Transitivity of device	0.18	0.09	3.87
Rich, innovative environment	−0.25	0.09	7.93[b]
Agency history of innovation	−0.18	0.08	4.69[a]
Centralization	0.13	0.08	2.36
Hardware innovation	0.18	0.09	3.87
Wealthy community	−0.06	0.04	1.80
Formalization	−0.17	0.09	3.40
Large community	−0.06	0.04	2.36
Prior need	0.10	0.08	1.37
Constant	0.66		

Note: $R^2 = 0.350$, df = 10/107, $F = 5.76$, $p < 0.01$.
[a]$p < 0.05$.
[b]$p < 0.01$.
[c]$p < 0.001$.

[f]The procedure represents a departure from our previous use of the regression technique. In the preceding sections, the technique was used to confirm the results of simple pairwise cross-tabulations. In the present section, the technique is offered as the only way of comparing the importance of different sets of variables. Thus, whereas the results in the previous sections were based on both cross-tabulations and regression analysis, the present section is based only on the latter; the results should be interpreted cautiously.

[g]Only one question is presented, because the two regressions differed in the order of significance of individual variables, but not in the overall listing of the variables or the overall variance explained.

[h]For purposes of comparing the overall result with the previous regressions, if the stepwise procedure had been stopped after the sixth step, the amount of variance explained would have been 30 percent ($R^2 = 0.301$)–an amount still substantially larger than those of the previous regressions.

overall regression, in fact the ten variables that appeared included a fairly even distribution of device, background, and implementation factors. This mixture suggests that successful innovative efforts cannot be determined solely on the basis of one set of factors, but that *successful efforts consist of a complex situation in which the nature of the innovation, the background, and the implementation factors must all be considered.* This finding is therefore contrary to our hypothesis.

The overall results, as well as the previous analyses of the background, implementation, and device factors, lead to the following conclusions:

1. When the setting (background factors) is considered alone, the most important correlate of successful innovative efforts is that the innovating agency is centralized. This factor was significantly correlated with success in a cross-tabular analysis, and the relationship was still significant following a regression analysis in which the statistical interactions with the other background factors were taken into account.

2. When the immediate circumstances (implementation factors) are considered alone, the most important correlates of success are client participation, the provision of practitioner training, and an innovative effort that is intended to create improvements in service outputs. Only the importance of client participation, however, was consistently confirmed by the regression analysis, although there was some support for the importance of practitioner training.

3. When the characteristics of the innovative device are considered alone (Chapter 3), the most important correlates of success are hardware innovations and transitive innovations. Both characteristics were significant in both cross-tabular and regression analyses.

4. When the most important variables from the setting, the implementation factors, and the characteristics of the innovative device are all compared, the result is that the top ten variables can account for a fairly high 35 percent of the variance for successful innovative efforts ($success_1$). This proportion suggests that, since no single type of factor dominates the final list of the ten most important variables, we must conclude that successful innovative efforts in local organizations are a function of a complex array of factors, some related to the background or setting, some to the immediate circumstances (implementation factors), and some to the nature of the innovative device. This conclusion is contrary to our initial hypothesis that implementation factors alone would be the most important.

5. Throughout the cross-tabular analyses, only three correlates of $success_2$ were found: a centralized agency, the presence of an R&D staff group in the agency, and a data analysis type of innovation.

The observation of these statistical relationships has indicated the major correlates of successful innovative efforts in our 140 case studies of technological innovations in state and local governments. The findings should be interpreted with care, since they are based on the analysis of the verbal content of the case study, rather than on any collection of data directly from the field. However, one implication from the findings is that the factors for which no significant relationships were found have not been considered important in the case study literature. These factors for which no correlations were found may be less likely to have played a causal role in producing successful innovative efforts.

To develop some understanding of the actual organizational process at work during an innovative effort, we now attempt to analyze our evidence in a slightly different manner and to piece the factors together in a more theoretically meaningful fashion.

5 Implementing New Technology: Two Processes?

Introduction

The previous chapters have identified various factors associated with successful innovative efforts. Although such factors are of interest in helping to identify the important conditions under which success may occur, the factors do not necessarily lead to a better understanding of why success occurs. The present chapter begins with a brief discussion of the implementation problem in state and local services. It then attempts to build an argument for two separate innovative processes, with the implication that successful efforts are the result of both processes at work.

The Implementation Problem: Clues for Two Processes

How public organizations implement programmatic changes have become a topic of major policy concern. Where analysts may have simply focused on the assessment of policy outcomes during the 1960s, the last few years have produced a sobering reexamination of the need to investigate the steps that occur between new policy initiatives and the occurrence of outcomes (e.g., Pressman and Wildavsky, 1973; Berman and McLaughlin, 1974; Williams, 1975; and Hargrove, 1975). Instead of a mechanistic input-output paradigm, the new analytic concern has raised such questions as:

Whether a new program had sufficient support and time to get started properly in the first place;

Whether the program deviated in actual practice from what was initially planned;

Whether the behavior of service practitioners changed as anticipated; and

Whether the initial changes eventually became a permanent, routinized function within the organization.

In short, the concern with implementation is that if the "treatment" did not really occur as was expected, then a simple examination of outcomes will always be disappointing and misleading. In this sense, the implementation problem extends beyond the mere adoption or first use of innovations. Successful implementation must ultimately be defined as the incorporation or routine use of innovations on a permanent basis by an organization. Furthermore, the failure to understand the implementation process is viewed by some as the major current impediment to improving public programs (McLaughlin and Berman, 1975; and Williams, 1975).

The implementation issue has typically arisen in relation to federally supported service programs. In education, the massive aid-to-education programs legislated in the 1960s were aimed at reforming the education of children in low-income families. When these programs were started, the initial expectations were merely that the children's educational performance could be assessed and, it was hoped, would show some improvement as a result of a particular program. Only after the individual projects began to be operated at the school level, however, was it realized that the implementation process had frequently changed the nature of the programs and hence the nature of the expected outcomes. New projects varied particularly in the degree to which they provided teachers with initial training, allowed for adequate staff meetings, and monitored changes in teaching practices (Berman and Pauly, 1975). In a few cases, projects changed so much during implementation that the children of low-income families were no longer even the actual beneficiaries. Similar adaptations took place in other federal programs. One study found that paraprofessional jobs aimed at reducing unemployment among neighborhood residents were mostly filled by residents from outside the neighborhood and sometimes even from outside the city (Harrison, 1973). Another study found that state governments made little attempt to use highway safety funds for the projects that would most reduce existing hazards, but merely supported the most convenient projects (Comptroller General of the United States, 1972).

The lessons from the federal experiences coincided with lessons from municipal services. Management scientists, brought into situations where quantitative analysis could potentially produce guidelines for improving police, fire, sanitation, and other services, were learning that their analysis could be technically sound but totally unused if, for example, the analysis was done for a decisionmaker who ultimately had no power to implement the results, the decisionmaker had a political timetable that precluded sufficient time to test and implement the results, or the service practitioners were uninformed of the innovation until its design had become permanently cast (Rosenbloom and Russell, 1971; and Szanton, 1972). To improve the chances that an analysis would have an effect, not only were these conditions to be avoided, but the analysis had to have stemmed from a clear prior need, dealt with as well-defined a problem as possible, and involved an issue that could not be deferred (Radnor et al., 1970; and Burt et al., 1972). Once an innovative analysis was tried, there still remained the problem of determining precisely what changes had occurred and how these changes related to the intended ones. The main ingredient for success was often a decisionmaker who was skilled enough to understand the analysis (Ernst, 1972). But in addition, if the analytic group that had originally designed the analysis was not the one that monitored its implementation, the use of the analysis was almost certain to change, with consequently major implications for the outcomes that could be expected (Radnor et al., 1970; Ernst, 1972; and United States Department of Justice, 1973a and b).

These and other experiences with public programs have resulted in the present concern with the implementation process. The essential point is that implementation cannot be taken for granted, but must be monitored and measured along with any outcomes. This means assessing the activities associated with the installation of a new set of policies and procedures—e.g., the changed functions of personnel, formal reorganizations, and the marshaling of adequate resources (Gross et al., 1971). A second point is that the permanence of any change must be scrutinized before any conclusions may be drawn as to whether a new policy or procedure has become routinized. Routinization may be reflected in the development of formal bureaucratic procedures, in the ability of new functions to survive the turnover of specific personnel, in the standard appearance of a new program as a line item in the budget, or in the development of training and socialization procedures for new personnel (Hage and Aiken, 1970). The fact that implementation has been a problem, however, suggests that any understanding of innovative efforts must discriminate between at least two outcomes—actual service improvements (which may occur in the short run even though the innovation is not implemented in the long run) and routinization of use (which may occur in the long run independent of whether service improvements occurred).

Incorporation versus Service Improvements as Outcomes

In the previous chapters, we have defined successful innovative efforts as those efforts that: (1) both produced service improvements and appeared to have been incorporated by the service organization (success$_1$), and (2) showed no service improvements and appeared to have been rejected by the service organization (success$_2$). Innovative efforts that failed were defined as those that: (1) appeared to produce no service improvements but nevertheless had been incorporated, or (2) produced a service improvement but appeared to have been rejected. Thus success and failure were defined as the combined occurrence of two conditions, or outcomes.

The present chapter deals with the implementation issue by teasing apart these two outcomes and examining separately those factors related to incorporation and those related to service improvements. Our understanding of the implementation process in public organizations could be enhanced to the extent that we find different factors related to those two outcomes. The underlying theory for positing such differences is based on the premise that public organizations, as opposed to profit-making ones, may pursue goals that do not necessarily coincide solely with the achievement of greater service efficiency or effectiveness. Innovations may be adopted because they serve the self-interest of the organization—its growth, increase in hierarchical status, or likelihood of survival. For public—unlike profit-making—organizations, attainment of self-interest goals of ten depends less upon market performance (and hence the service efficiency or effectiveness) than upon bureaucratic and political factors. Furthermore, although an innovation that is adopted by a public organization may also produce service improvements, the problems of defining and measuring the appropriate service outputs of public organizations may help to keep improved service efficiency only secondary to the self-interest goal.

These differences do not mean that incorporation and service improvement are mutually exclusive outcomes. On the contrary, there is a strong positive association between the two. Table 5-1 shows this association and also defines the incorporation and service improvement outcomes in a slightly more discriminating manner than in previous discussions.[a] The key point is that the incorporation and service improvement outcomes, although correlated, may represent the results of two independent organizational processes at work. Our

Table 5-1
Relationship Between Incorporation and Service Improvement
(N = 140)

	Service Improvement (Question F-5)			
Incorporation (Question F-1)	*Yes*	*No*	*Information Only*	*Impossible to Answer*
Full	39	6	13	2
Partial (some doubt)	33	10	8	1
Discontinued or not ' operated	6	16	3	3

Note: χ^2 = 29.18, df = 4, $p < 0.001$ (excludes impossible-to-answer cases). Examination of higher quality cases alone significantly supports this relationship.

---

[a]Incorporation has been broken down into those innovations that appeared fully incorporated by the end of the case study, those that appeared partially incorporated as a result of some continuing special project or other status associated with nonpermanence, and those that were discontinued or not operated and hence not incorporated; service improvement has been broken down into those innovations that produced some improvement, those that produced no change or a negative change, and those that produced useful information for decisionmaking purposes—but no concrete service improvement. The categories are all based on questions F-1 and F-5 in the checklist. In the previous chapters, these separate categories were clustered so that an innovation was considered either incorporated (whether fully or partially) or not, and either producing a service improvement or not (the information-only outcome did not count as a service improvement).

hypothesis, therefore, is that, despite the strong relationship between the two outcomes, different factors concerning the innovative situation will be related to one outcome but not the other, and that in general those factors dealing with *bureaucratic self-interest* will more frequently be related to the occurrence of incorporation, whereas those factors dealing with *production efficiency* will more frequently be related to the occurrence of service improvements.

Some sense of which factors fall into the bureaucratic self-interest versus production efficiency categories can be developed if we consider two stereotypes of the innovative process in public organizations. The stereotypes have been purposely drawn in contrasting and hence exaggerated form for analytic reasons, representing an ideal dichotomy that is not likely to be found in a real organization. Since the production efficiency stereotype has been more frequently documented by the existing organizational literature, we deal with it first.

Two Innovative Processes

Production Efficiency

One traditional interpretation of innovative behavior in public organizations is that it stems from a rational, problem-solving approach. Havelock (1969) has reviewed much of the research that supports this approach, which we also discussed briefly in Chapter 1. In this approach, a problem or need arises in some aspect of the agency's operations, and this leads sequentially to a number of steps:

Some analysis of the specific attributes of the problem;

A search for alternative solutions;

The identification of resources required to support an innovative effort;

The actual application and testing of an innovative device or plan; and

The evaluation and eventual rejection or adoption of the innovation on a permanent basis (for an example of this problem-solving framework, see Robbins et al., 1973).

The use of the terms *rational* and *problem solving* to describe this approach, however, is misleading because of the implication that other approaches—especially the bureaucratic self-interest stereotype (which is described in the next section)—are irrational and not oriented toward problems. We consider production efficiency to be a more accurate label, since the essence of the stereotype is not that it is rational or problem solving, but that it regards organizational innovation as originating predominantly from the motive of improving the goods or services provided by the organization.

For production efficiency, the presence or occurrence of several attributes in an innovative situation may be considered to increase the probability of organizational change. These attributes relate to the external environment of the innovating agency, the agency itself, the desired characteristics of the innovative device, and the specific innovative effort. Many of these attributes have been examined in a different context in the previous chapter, but it is worth briefly reviewing them here.

Among the attributes of the external environment, one of the most important conditions is the existence of a prior need or demand for improved performance. This need may be created by a rich external environment in which other agencies are innovating, or it may be created by demands for specific improvements in agency services. The focus on prior need derives in part from experiences with the adoption of technological innovations by private organizations (e.g., Utterback, 1971 and 1974; Lambright and Teich, 1974; Schultz and Slevin, 1975; and Kelly et al., 1975), where most innovations appear to result from the existence of a market need (demand-pull) rather than a technological breakthrough (technology-push). Downs (1967) coined the term "performance gap" to describe this condition, but he has used it mainly in relation to the bureaucratic self-interest stereotype; according to our interpretation, the performance gap is more appropriate to the production efficiency stereotype, since the gap is defined in terms of service performance.

Among the attributes of the agency itself, those most frequently cited as important for facilitating organizational change are (1) the existence of adequate resources and (2) the use of flexible and task-oriented mechanisms, such as ad hoc groups or committees. The resources may be both organizational and information, helping the agency to identify the alternative solutions and to muster the necessary support for the innovative effort. The availability of excess resources—frequently labeled *slack* resources (Cyert and March, 1963)—has usually been considered a critical aspect of any organizational effort to innovate. Although the existence of slack resources is difficult to measure, studies of both private and public organizations have shown that other conditions, such as the size of the agency's budget (Mohr, 1969), the size of the agency (Carroll, 1967), or even the existence of the agency within a wealthier community of high social rank (Scott, 1968; Walker, 1969; and Corwin, 1975) can serve as indicators of extra resources and appear important to the innovative process (for a contrary finding, see Rosner, 1968). In addition, the presence of federal funds to support the innovative effort may also be considered an excess resource. Informational resources are produced by the agency's participation in a communications network involving other agencies as well as intermediary institutions such as professional associations (Feller et al., 1974) and research organizations (Hayes and Rasmussen, 1972; and Crawford, 1973). Evidence for the importance of these informational resources in the innovative process has been found in both private (Utterback, 1971) and public (Corwin, 1972; and Cohn and Manning, 1974) organizations.

The third group of attributes concerns the characteristics of the innovative device. To improve production efficiency, an innovative device must clearly have some merit or relative advantage over existing practices. The device is also more likely to lead to improvements if it is transitive (i.e., designed to change practices between providers and clients and not merely to change administrative procedures), if it is divisible (i.e., can first be tested on a restricted portion of the whole target population), if it is visible and hence more easily communicated, and if the effects of testing are reversible (i.e., the agency can return to its prior state if the device is not adopted). This emphasis on the need for meritorious and testable innovations has been reflected in several studies of technological innovation in local agencies, with the usual finding being that most local agencies are unable to carry out testing properly. The studies typically recommend that federal agencies or some independent research organizations be assigned the responsibility for testing and then even for endorsing meritorious devices (e.g., The Urban Institute, 1971; Frohman et al., 1972; Feild, 1972; and Cohn and Manning, 1974).

The fourth and last group of attributes has to do with the innovative effort. For instance, the characteristics of the personnel involved in the effort are very important. On the one hand, the presence of a cosmopolite innovator—one who by dint of having richer experiences, more formal training, or a larger set of informal contacts in other jurisdictions is more change oriented—can facilitate organizational change (Mytinger, 1968). On the other hand, resistance to change on the part of agency service practitioners—who may be acting realistically since the innovation may in the long run constitute a threat to their jobs (The Urban Institute, 1971)—can serve as the main barrier to innovation (e.g., Mohr, 1969; Rosenbloom and Russell, 1971; and United States Department of Justice, 1973a). In fact, the production efficiency view has traditionally glossed over all implementation problems by ascribing them to resistance to change on the part of service practitioners. Although the situation is clearly more complex, recent studies have emphasized the need for participatory opportunities and formal training for service practitioners in relation to the innovative effort (Richland, 1965; Hatry, 1971; Frohman et al., 1972; Utech and Utech, 1973; and House, 1974). Such participation and training is assumed to remove much of the resistance to change. Two other characteristics of the innovative effort are considered to play a negative role in facilitating innovation: any unexpected delay in the implementation process, and client participation in the process.

Table 5-2 summarizes the attributes that are important to a production

94

Table 5-2
Attributes of Production Efficiency

Attribute		Checklist Question
External environment		
Rich, innovative environment	B-4c	Case study mentions innovations that occurred in other jurisdictions
Prior need	B-1	Case study mentions, among preexisting conditions, need to meet service demands or reduce costs
Agency characteristics		
Task-oriented structures	H-17	Study mentions ad hoc working groups or committees
Availability of extra resources	H-14	Agency either had R&D group, outside grants or contracts, or
	G-6	Locale had high local government expenditures per capita
Federal support	B-5	Innovative effort was mainly supported by federal funds
Large agency size	C-2	Number of agency employees (Question discarded because of insufficient information)
Wealthy community	G-5	High 1970 median family income
Part of professional information network	B-3	There was a professional association (Question discarded because of insufficient information)
Innovative device		
Relative advantage	D-4b	Merit had been demonstrated by comparison with existing practice
Transitivity	D-6	Innovation's primary intended effect was to create new practices between clients and providers
Divisibility for testing purposes	D-9	Innovation testable on portion of target population
Visibility	D-10	Innovation involved concrete artifact
Reversibility	D-12	(Obverse of) initial use or testing of innovation said to involve substantial irreversible changes (e.g., employee firing or new facilities)
Innovative effort		
Cosmopolite innovator	H-5	Innovator had more education, meetings, or contacts outside agency than other officials
Practitioner participation	E-10	Service practitioners first mentioned at time of innovation planning
Practitioner training	E-11	Service practitioners had training or practice with innovation
No implementation delay	H-9	(Obverse of) unexpected delay within or outside agency
No client participation	B-7	(Obverse of) innovative effort involved participatory process during implementation

efficiency explanation of organizational innovation.[b] The table also refers to the specific questions developed for our checklist to assess the case studies for the presence or absence of these attributes. Such attributes, however, are hypothesized to be mainly related to the service improvement outcome but not to the incorporation of an innovation on a permanent basis. As recent research has increasingly suggested (e.g., Berman and McLaughlin, 1974), other factors may be more influential in determining whether an innovation will be fully incorporated. Innovations that do produce initial service improvements, in other words, sometimes fail to be incorporated, and sometimes an innovation may be incorporated even though there are no clear service improvements. To understand the other factors that may be more important in determining whether an innovation is incorporated, we turn to the bureaucratic self-interest stereotype, remembering again that the stereotype is purposely exaggerated to contrast with production efficiency.

Bureaucratic Self-Interest

The features of bureaucratic self-interest can be derived from the unwritten rules of organizational survival and competition in public bureaucracies. Some of these rules are commonly accepted as part of our working knowledge of bureaucratic behavior, but there has been little empirical research, especially related to innovations, to test the important hypotheses. The self-interest is that of the individual bureaucrat who may act in a rational, problem-solving manner to fulfill his self-interest. The main goal from his standpoint is to survive new elections or organizational changes, and the most assured way of surviving is to encourage organizational growth in power and status. Naturally, this does not mean the pursuit of power and status to the exclusion of the public interest. It means only that changes that lead to organizational survival, all other things being equal, are more likely to be incorporated on a permanent basis.

Some of the reasons for the relationship between bureaucratic growth and survival have been described by Downs (1967). First, rapidly growing bureaus tend to attract more capable personnel because of the high rates of promotions that are likely to exist. Second, rapid growth reduces internal conflict by creating new opportunities for the majority of officials within the organization, rather than making them compete for scarce resources. Third, very large bureaus can actually begin to "impose a certain degree of stability upon their external environment" (p. 17). Taken together, all of these conditions will put a bureau in a better position to survive the threats occurring as a result of external reorganizations—threats that can lead to the abolishment of the bureau. An important corollary of the growth-survival link is that a bureau is less vulnerable to dissolution the older it becomes.

---

[b]Of the eighteen such attributes, further analysis with two of them—agency size and professional activity—was precluded because of a lack of information in the case studies. The criteria for discarding were: over 50 percent of the answers were in the impossible-to-answer category, or less than 20 percent were in one of two binary (yes or no) categories.

The tendency toward bureaucratic growth can also be explained in economic terms, if one accepts changes in an agency's budget as the appropriate instrument of growth (Niskanen, 1968 and 1971). Because bureaus exchange their output for a total budget, but not at a per unit rate (i.e., the review process in the annual budget cycle), they operate in essence as if they were private monopolies. Since larger budgets, with their attendant increases in salaries, provide the only rewards comparable to higher profits in the private sector, bureaus are constantly striving to maximize their budgets (Niskanen, 1968; and Ahlbrandt, 1974). Budget maximization becomes the means for increasing organizational power, prestige, and patronage. Once again, this does not mean that the bureau will pursue budget maximization at the expense of the public interest and meaningful service improvements, but only that the potential for budget increases will make a specific proposal more attractive.

From the standpoint of bureaucratic survival and growth, the presence or occurrence of several attributes in an innovative situation may be considered as likely to increase the probability of organizational change. In general, these attributes are related to growth maximization at the least probable risk of failure (Alesch, 1971). In some instances the attributes are the same as those that are important from the production efficiency standpoint. In some instances, however, they are different. Whichever the case, we can consider the attributes in the same four categories of the external environment, the agency, the innovative device, and the specific innovative effort.

The attributes of the external environment that lead to innovation are similar to those considered from the production efficiency standpoint—that is, the agency is often stimulated to innovate by innovations in other jurisdictions (Downs, 1967, p. 263; and Pincus, 1974). However, the changes need not result from the creation of specific performance gaps, if such gaps are defined (as they usually are) in terms of the production of goods or services.

It is among the remaining three groups of attributes that the strongest contrast between the production efficiency and bureaucratic self-interest stereotypes occurs. Among the agency characteristics, the most important from the bureaucratic self-interest standpoint are those that deal with the potential effect of the innovation on the agency. First and most critical, the agency is more likely to innovate if the innovative effort entails increases in agency budget or staff. Second, because of the desire to minimize the disruptions associated with any organizational change, an innovation that affects the fewest number of people within the agency or that causes the least amount of formal reorganization is more likely to be incorporated (Downs, 1967, pp. 174, 196). Third, following Down's reasoning, a young agency is more likely to innovate.

The important attributes of the innovative device are those that minimize the risks of failure, since bureaucratic organizations often produce more punishment for failure than reward for innovation (Gordon, 1973). From this perspective, a device that has previously demonstrated some relative advantage will, as in the production efficiency stereotype, be more likely to be incorporated. However, in direct contrast to the production efficiency stereotype, the device is also more likely to be incorporated if it is less testable, less visible, and less reversible. The ideal innovative device, in other words, is one whose merit may have been previously demonstrated, but whose performance in the agency is difficult to assess and to communicate. The resulting ambiguity can be used by the ambitious bureaucrat as the basis for claimed improvements that are difficult to disprove. Moreover, if the device fails, the ambiguity may also make the failure less obvious to the other members of the agency.

Finally, the most important attributes of the innovative effort have to do with the degree of internal organizational support for the innovation. The relevant characteristics of the major actors (the innovator, implementer, or advocate) involved in the innovation, for instance, are not so much those related to cosmopolitanism, but rather to their position within the agency. The more that the actors are within rather than from outside the agency, the more they have some leverage to implement; and the more that they are accepted as veterans in the service, the more likely the innovative effort will succeed. As a particularly important addition, if the chief executive (e.g., mayor) supports the innovative effort, the effort is also more likely to be incorporated (Radnor et al., 1970; and Rosenbloom and Russell, 1971). In the implementation process itself, the facilitating conditions are that the service practitioners participate in the planning and have some training and practice with the innovation (House, 1974), that those responsible for implementation monitor the process throughout its later stages and not merely at the initial planning stage (Gross et al., 1971, pp. 195-216), and that delays in implementation be avoided.

Table 5-3 summarizes the important attributes of the bureaucratic self-interest stereotype.[c] The table also indicates the checklist questions that were designed to assess the presence or absence of these attributes.

Case Survey Findings

*Evidence for Two Processes: Pairwise Comparisons
of Attributes to Outcomes*

The initial analysis focused on the pairwise relationships between the variables for each stereotype and the two outcomes of service improvement and incorporation. All the attributes listed in Tables 5-2 and 5-3, in other words, were examined for their individual association with each of these two outcomes.

Of the attributes that were predicted to be associated with service improvement because they were production efficiency attributes, five were found to be significantly associated:[d]

---

[c]Further analysis on one attribute—the age of the agency—was precluded because of a lack of information in the case studies.

[d]Where they do not appear in the text, the contingency tables for the cited relationships are presented in Appendix D.

Table 5-3
Attributes of Bureaucratic Self-Interest

Attribute		Checklist Question
External environment		
Rich, innovative environment	B-4c	Case study mentions innovations that occurred in other jurisdictions
Agency characteristics		
Innovation involves increases in agency staff	H-18	Innovative effort involved hiring new personnel
Innovation affects few staff members	D-13	(Obverse of) full use of innovation could potentially affect agency line unit or people throughout agency
Innovation involves little reorganization	F-9	(Obverse of) innovation involved new unit or switches in personnel assignments
Agency is young	C-1	Agency created in past five years (Question discarded because of insufficient information tion)
Innovative device		
Relative advantage	D-4b	Merit had been demonstrated by comparison with existing practice
Not easily divisble for testing purposes	D-9	(Obverse of) innovation testable on portion of target population
Not visible	D-10	(Obverse of) innovation involved concrete artifact
Not reversible	D-12	Initial use or testing of innovation said to involve substantial irreversible changes (e.g., employee firing or new facilities)
Innovative effort		
Main actors within agency	H-16	Innovator, implementer, and advocate of innovation were all from inside agency
Innovator has power to implement	H-7	Innovator had decisionmaking role in agency, had access to slack resources, or had contacts with clients
Innovator is veteran in agency	H-6	Innovator had been employed in more than one position in agency, had over five years of employment in agency, had report or product associated with his name, or had acknowledged role as veteran or opinion leader
Chief executive support	E-13a	Case study mentions supporting role of chief executive
Practitioner participation	E-10	Service practitioners first mentioned at time of innovation planning
Practitioner training	E-11	Service practitioners had training or practice with innovation
Implementer monitoring	E-12	Implementer last mentioned along with evaluation or final summary
No implementation delay	H-9	(Obverse of) unexpected delay within or outside agency

The innovation was transitive—i.e., designed to create new practices between service providers and clients (χ^2 = 23.38, df = 4, $p < 0.001$);

The innovation was divisible (χ^2 = 11.32, df = 2, $p < 0.01$);

The innovative effort involved practitioner training (χ^2 = 11.93, df = 2, $p < 0.01$);

There was no implementation delay (χ^2 = 14.99, df = 2, $p < 0.001$); and

There was client participation (χ^2 = 13.83, df = 4, $p < 0.05$).

Of these five, note that the presence of client participation was *positively* related with the occurrence of service improvements (see Table 5-4), rather than negatively as had been expected. This joint occurrence of client participation and service improvement appears similar to previous findings about innovative efforts to decentralize urban services (Yin and Yates, 1975). The relationship may be due to the fact that client involvement creates external pressure to seek improvements in a serious manner, since more people are aware of the innovative effort. Some support for this hypothesis may be the observation that the occurrence of any publicity about an innovative effort was also positively related to the occurrence of service improvement.

Of the attributes that were predicted to be associated with incorporation because they were bureaucratic self-interest attributes, four were found to be significantly associated:

The innovation did not involve the hiring of new personnel (χ^2 = 12.46, df = 2, $p < 0.01$);

The innovation had the support of the chief executive (χ^2 = 11.09, df = 4, $p < 0.05$);

The main actors (advocate, implementer, and innovator) were inside the agency (χ^2 = 17.98, df = 6, $p < 0.01$); and

Table 5-4
Relationship Between Client Participation and Service Improvement

Client Participation (Question B-7)	Service Improvement (Question F-5)			
	Yes	*No*	*Information Only*	*Impossible to Answer*
Some participation	28	8	3	1
No participation, but client mentioned	28	9	4	2
Neither of above	22	15	17	3

Note: χ^2 = 13.83, df = 4, $p < 0.05$ (excludes impossible-to-answer cases). Examination of higher quality cases alone significantly supports this relationship.

There was no implementation delay ($\chi^2 = 8.03$, df = 2, $p < 0.05$).

Of these four, note that the hiring of new personnel was *negatively* related to incorporation (see Table 5-5), contrary to the prediction that had been made for a positive association. This negative relationship is difficult to explain. One possibility follows the observation that most of the hiring of new personnel in the case studies has been associated with innovations that have been federally funded. These new personnel were therefore not necessarily real additions to the service practitioner staff, but may have been employees in special categories that could later be eliminated and hence would not add to the permanent growth of the agency. Another possibility, however, is that bureaucratic growth is not such a simple element of the bureaucratic self-interest process. More mature bureaus, for instance, may promote their self-interests in other ways, and our case studies may have included a larger proportion of such mature bureaus.

As important as the finding of these relationships was another finding: Except for one instance, none of the attributes predicted to be related to only one of the outcomes was unexpectedly found to be related to the other outcome. In other words, with one exception, none of the production efficiency attributes was significantly related to incorporation, and none of the bureaucratic self-interest attributes was significantly related to service improvement. The lack of association is reinforced by the fact that in most instances the corresponding chi-square values were very low and did not even approach statistical significance.

The single exception to this pattern concerned the availability of federal funds to support the innovative effort, and this attribute was unexpectedly related to incorporation. However, the relationship was in a *negative* direction, so that the result does not contradict the notion of the two stereotypes. Table 5-6 shows that federal support was most frequently associated with innovations that had been partially incorporated, and it was least frequently associated with innovations that had been fully incorporated. Although one explanation of this

Table 5-5
Relationship Between New Hiring and Incorporation

Hiring of New Personnel (Question H-18)	Incorporation (Question F-1)		
	Full	Partial (some doubt)	Discontinued or not Operated
Yes	13	28	10
No	47	24	18

Note: $\chi^2 = 12.46$, df = 2, $p < 0.01$. Examination of higher quality cases alone significantly supports this relationship.

Table 5-6

Relationship Between Federal Support for the Innovation and Incorporation

(N = 140)

	Incorporation (Question F-1)		
Support for the Innovative Effort *(Question B-5)*	*Full*	*Partial (some doubt)*	*Discontinued or not Operated*
Funds from a federal agency	26	36	17
No funds or funds from other sources	34	16	11

Note: $\chi^2 = 7.86$, df = 2, $p < 0.05$. Examination of higher quality cases alone significantly supports this relationship.

finding is the potential coding circularity that the innovation was judged not fully incorporated in part because federal funds were mentioned, such an explanation does not account for the fact that the federal funds were also more frequently associated with innovations that were discontinued or not operated.

In summary, the analysis of the pairwise relationships tentatively supports the notion of two different processes leading to the occurrence of service improvement and incorporation. Of the attributes hypothesized to be related to one outcome but not the other, a handful were found to be significantly related to the appropriate outcome, and none was found to be related to the inappropriate one.

Further Evidence for Two Processes: Regression Analysis

Although the pairwise comparisons support the notion of two innovative processes, the analysis does not address the problem of the interactive relationships among the independent variables. Such relationships may be complex and may be obscured by simple pairwise comparisons. To attempt to deal with the problem, we again employed a regression analysis. To use this procedure, wherever necessary we redefined all of the attributes of interest, as well as in the service improvement and incorporation outcomes, into binary categories to satisfy the requirement that regression analysis only be performed on interval or binary data. Thus, for instance, the service improvement outcome was collapsed so that improvements counted in one category, and the "no improvements" and "useful information" responses were combined into the other category. Similarly, fully incorporated outcomes were in one category and the two other incorporation outcomes (partial and discontinued or not operated) were in the other. For all the attributes, the binary coding ultimately meant either the presence or absence of the given characteristic.

To test the notion of the two innovative processes, two regressions were carried out—one in which the dependent variable was service improvement, and the other in which it was full incorporation. For both dependent variables, all of the production efficiency and bureaucratic self-interest attributes were made available for a stepwise regression procedure in which the ten independent variables most closely related to each dependent variable were allowed to enter the final equation. The same procedure, a stepwise regression making available all the attributes from Tables 5-2 and 5-3 and concluding at the end of the tenth step, was in other words identical for each dependent variable.[e] The test was thus to see the extent to which (1) the ten independent variables for each regression were the ones hypothesized to be important for the particular dependent variable, and (2) the total regression equation explained a significant portion of the variation for each dependent variable.

The results tend to confirm the two innovative processes.[f] Tables 5-7 and 5-8 list the ten attributes most related to service improvement and incorporation. For service improvement (Table 5-7), the first observation is that all ten of the variables were those hypothesized to be important to service improvement, and none were those hypothesized to be important to incorporation. The most significant attributes were that (1) the innovation was designed to create new practices between service providers and clients, (2) innovative efforts had *not* occurred in other jurisdictions, and (3) service practitioners received some training or practice in the use of the innovation. At the same time, the regression variables did not include the attribute of "no implementation delay" and gave only minor importance to client participation and divisibility—three attributes that were originally significant in the pairwise correlations—suggesting that these attributes are not as important when the others are taken into account. Overall, the ten variables accounted for a statistically significant 29 percent of the variation in the dependent variable.

For incorporation (Table 5-8), the initial observation is that six of the ten attributes were those hypothesized to be important to incorporation. However, of the inappropriate variables, three (federal support, cosmopolite innovator, and extra resources) had a negative relationship, so that they do not contradict the notion of two innovative processes. Only the last variable (divisibility) actually contradicted the notion; but it was not statistically significant, and the size of its standard error suggests that little confidence can be placed even in the direction of the relationship. The most significant attributes were that: (1) the

[e]An alternative procedure would have been to carry out a non-stepwise regression with all the independent variables. However, since there were only 140 observations, this would have presented too many variables. As a result, the stepwise regression was used, and the tenth step was chosen as a reasonable stopping point, given the number of observations. Subsequent analysis also showed that of the remaining independent variables that did not enter the equation, none would have added significantly to the variance explained.

[f]The results were similar whether or not the impossible-to-answer responses were coded along with the presence or absence of a characteristic.

Table 5-7
Ten Most Important Attributes Related to Service Improvement
(impossible to answer coded as absence of factor)

Attribute *(listed in order of stepwise regression analysis)*	Regression Results		
	b	*Standard Error b*	*F*
Transitivity	0.38	0.08	20.55[b]
Practitioner training	0.18	0.08	5.32[a]
Rich, innovative environment	−0.18	0.08	5.52[a]
Relative advantage	0.13	0.08	2.55
Client participation	0.08	0.05	2.67
Visibility	0.11	0.08	2.01
Practitioner participation	−0.10	0.08	1.82
Task-oriented structures	0.12	0.09	1.90
Extra resources	−0.05	0.03	2.01
Divisibility	0.10	0.09	1.18
Constant	0.47		

Note: $R^2 = 0.293$, df = $10/129$, $F = 5.35$, $p < 0.001$.
[a] $p < 0.05$.
[b] $p < 0.001$.

chief executive supported the innovative effort, (2) the main actors were from within the agency, (3) there was no federal support, (4) there was no implementation delay, and (5) the innovator did *not* exhibit cosmopolite characteristics. Of less importance, but still statistically significant, were that: (6) there were no increases in agency staff, (7) there were no extra resources, and (8) service practitioners received some training or practice in the use of the innovation. Of all the significant attributes, the one again not easily explained is the negative relationship to increases in agency staff. Overall, the ten variables accounted for a statistically significant 36 percent of the variation in the dependent variable.

The regression results, especially when interpreted in conjunction with the pairwise comparisons, provide strong support for the two processes. Not only do different factors appear to be related to the two outcomes, but the regression equations account for substantial portions of the variance in the dependent variable.

Type of Innovation: A Speculative Example
of the Two Processes at Work

The innovative devices in the 140 case studies fell into three categories (as described in Chapter 3): hardware, computer systems, and data analytic

Table 5-8

Ten Most Important Attributes Related to Incorporation

(impossible to answer is coded as absence of factor)

Attribute (listed in order of stepwise regression analysis)	Regression Results		
	b	Standard Error b	F
Increases in agency staff	−0.22	0.08	7.38[b]
Chief executive support	0.42	0.09	23.05[c]
No implementation delay	0.21	0.08	7.87[b]
Practitioner training	0.17	0.07	5.22[a]
Federal support	−0.21	0.07	7.93[b]
Main actors within agency	0.17	0.04	17.57[c]
Cosmopolite innovator	−0.24	0.09	7.60[b]
Extra resources	−0.20	0.07	7.36[b]
Implementer monitoring	−0.17	0.09	3.73
Divisibility	0.11	0.08	1.81
Constant	0.58		

Note: R^2 = 0.356, df = 10/129, F = 7.14, $p < 0.001$.

[a]$p < 0.05$.

[b]$p < 0.01$.

[c]$p < 0.001$.

innovations. These three categories were differentially related to service improvement and incorporation, suggesting the possibility that one type of innovation—hardware devices—may be best suited for supporting the production efficiency process, whereas a second type—computer systems—may be best suited for supporting the bureaucratic self-interest process. However, the evidence is not as clear-cut as it is suggestive. First, Table 5-9 shows that innovative efforts involving hardware devices were more frequently associated with service improvement than were computer systems or data analytic innovations. Second Table 5-10 shows that computer systems, in contrast, were more frequently associated with full incorporation than were hardware devices or data analytic innovations. These relationships mean that, as compared with computer systems, hardware devices were less likely to be fully incorporated, despite the fact that they showed a high rate of service improvement.

A somewhat speculative explanation for these relationships is that hardware devices may not entail too great a risk of failure, may be too divisible and visible, and may lead to eventual reductions (rather than additions) in staff. Most typically, the hardware device may be the object of a short-term demonstration project that appears to meet a prior need for improved services, but the use of the device may not sufficiently change bureaucratic behavior to become a

Table 5-9
Relationship Between Type of Innovation and Service Improvement
(N = 140)

Type of Innovation (Question A-5)	Service Improvement (Question F-5)			
	Yes	*No*	*Information Only*	*Impossible to Answer*
Hardware device	43	8	0	3
Computer system	24	12	8	2
Data analysis	11	12	16	1

Note: $\chi^2 = 35.26$, df = 4, $p < 0.001$ (excludes impossible-to-answer cases). Examination of higher quality cases alone significantly supports this relationship.

Table 5-10
Relationship Between Type of Innovation and Incorporation
(N = 140)

Type of Innovation (Question A-5)	Incorporation (Question F-1)		
	Full	*Partial (some doubt)*	*Discontinued or not Operated*
Hardware device	18	27	9
Computer system	27	14	5
Data analysis	15	11	14

Note: $\chi^2 = 14.79$, df = 4, $p < 0.01$. Examination of higher quality cases alone fails to show any relationship.

permanent practice once the initial group of innovators has left, or once the initial financial support has ceased. In contrast, computer systems may not present as high a risk of failure and may be less divisible and visible; unless the computer system is actually not working (or down) for substantial periods of time, the value of the computer system may be difficult to assess in terms of service improvement and hence less liable to the accusation that the system has failed (if there are any complaints, a working computer system can always be made to appear responsive to these complaints through continued reprogramming efforts). Most typically, the installation of a computer system may become an acceptable and desirable technological innovation that does not necessarily stem from a prior need, but usually entails permanent additions to staff and budget.

These characteristics lead to certain hypotheses about the relationship between the type of innovation and the other attributes of the innovative effort—hardware devices should be more divisible, visible, and reversible than computer systems, and they should also be more frequently associated with a prior need for service improvement, but less frequently associated with a permanent increase in staff. (See Appendix D for the contingency tables.) The evidence from the case studies gave only partial support for these hypotheses. Significantly more hardware devices were associated with divisibility than were computer systems ($\chi^2 = 26.40$, df = 2, $p < 0.001$), but significantly *fewer* were more visible ($\chi^2 = 50.46$, df = 6, $p < 0.001$) or reversible ($\chi^2 = 9.15$, df = 2, $p < 0.02$). Fewer computer systems were associated with the existence of a prior need as hypothesized ($\chi^2 = 7.82$, df = 2, $p < 0.05$), but there was no significant relationship between the type of innovation and increases in staff. The results are thus equivocal with regard to the characterizations, but it may be that, although the precise characterizations are incorrect, the main distinction between the role of hardware devices and computer systems in the innovative process deserves further research.

Summary Discussion

The aggregate evidence from the case studies suggests that successful innovative efforts by local services may entail two distinct but interrelated processes. One process is associated with production efficiency and results in service improvement; the other is associated with the fulfillment of bureaucratic self-interest and results in incorporation. There is some overlap between the two processes in that they share a few common attributes such as the occurrence of practitioner training and the absence of implementation delay, but in general the characteristics of each process are different.

The production efficiency process emphasizes problem solving for making service improvements. Some of the relevant factors include the existence of a prior need and extra resources, the availability of an innovative device that is divisible, visible, reversible, and that affects practices between service providers and clients, and the presence of a cosmopolite innovator. The bureaucratic self-interest process emphasizes organizational survival and self-interest. Some of the relevant characteristics are: an innovation that affects few staff members, is not visible, divisible, or reversible; an innovative effort in which there is support by the mayor or chief executive and by major actors within the innovating agency; and an effort that has no federal support. Our main evidence for these two processes draws from cross-tabular and regression analyses. Both analyses showed that, where correlations were found, factors hypothesized to be important to one process but not the other did tend to be correlated with the appropriate outcome (i.e., either service improvement or incorporation) but not with the inappropriate one. We have further speculated that among the different types of innovations, computer systems as innovative devices may suit the bureaucratic self-interest conditions better than do hardware devices, and hardware devices may suit the production efficiency conditions better than do computer systems.

The possible existence of these two processes has some important implications. First, it may be that most change agents external to a local agency—consultants, other local officials, or federal bureaucrats—have implicitly attempted to promote innovations that improve production efficiency but that do not serve the bureaucratic self-interest of the innovating agency. The change agents may thus be pursuing an ineffective strategy for creating enduring changes, and this might explain the frequently reported frustrations of external change agents.

Second, it would be important to develop innovation strategies that can both improve production efficiency and serve bureaucratic self-interest. This may imply the need to investigate the peculiar administrative and political constraints and incentives of a local agency along with the potential costs and benefits from a given innovation. The most viable strategy ought to be the one that, for each local setting and innovative opportunity, accounts for both sets of conditions. For instance, local decisionmakers, when considering an innovation, may use some criteria that appear to be task oriented (e.g., the need for the innovation and the potential service benefits to be derived from it) and other criteria that appear to be process-oriented (e.g., the likely reaction of organizational personnel or higher officials to the innovation). These joint considerations might be one manifestation of the simultaneous relevance of the production efficiency and bureaucratic self-interest processes.

Third, nontechnological innovations (e.g., program budgeting, management by objectives, or improved information systems that are not computer based) may also need to be interpreted from the vantage point of both processes. Most innovations—technological and nontechnological—are claimed to be undertaken with a production efficiency orientation. Yet the innovations all have clear consequences for bureaucratic self-interests, and in some cases these consequences may inadvertently undermine any production efficiency goals. The redistribution of bureaucratic power created by an innovation, for instance, may thus be more crucial to the ultimate incorporation of an innovation than the demonstration of a specific service improvement.

These implications alone warrant further research into the distinctiveness of the two processes. The evidence provided by our study derives solely from existing case studies. As such, it requires corroboration by other investigators (using different sources of information and methods of analysis) that focuses on both technological and nontechnological innovations. One major contribution that new investigations could make would be to identify in greater detail the organizational conditions of incorporation or routinization. These conditions might include the following:

Personnel qualifications for using the innovation are included in job descriptions or hiring criteria for staff;

Standard procedures exist for repair and maintenance—e.g., maintenance contracts are routinely administered;

Supplies of material output (e.g., paper, punch cards, gasoline) are smoothly linked to the operational use of the innovation; and

All vital components of the innovation, such as special staff, supplies, parts, etc., are visible in the agency's budget, as opposed to being charged against some undesignated administrative account.

6

Role of the Federal Government

The immediate policy concern of this study was to identify those actions by which the federal government could facilitate the use of new technology in local services. The actions need not automatically lead to the adoption and incorporation of new technology, but could also lead to the improved ability of local agencies to assess and reject inappropriate technology. Moreover, the actions need not necessarily imply the sponsorship by federal agencies of specific innovation projects, but could also include policies that improve the setting of standards, the provision of technical consultation, or other regulatory activities by the federal government.

Background for the Federal Role

Historically, the interest in having the federal government play a role in such technological development has stemmed on the one hand from the accomplishments of the space program and the subsequent aspiration that local services could be another logical target for new technology (Feldman et al., 1965; Rogers and Carton, 1968; and Committee on Science and Astronautics, 1969). As a result, NASA, the National Science Foundation, and other federal science agencies initiated a wide variety of programs aimed at state and local utilization of new technology (Doctors, 1969; Crawford, 1973; and Anuskiewicz, 1973). Some programs involved the support of demonstration projects such as the California Four Cities project (Comptroller General of the United States, 1975). Other programs emphasized information dissemination and the coordination of science and technology activities at the state level. The policy initiatives appeared to reach one milestone with the President's Message on Science and Technology in March 1972. Not only did that message restate the national priority for what has since become known as *public technology*, but by that time there were also several technology-transfer institutions successfully underway: Public Technology, Inc., The New York City-Rand Institute, The Urban Institute, and the Urban Observatories, to name just a few.[a]

---

[a]The whole issue of new institutions to serve in analytic and brokerage capacities as advisors to state and local governments has received considerable treatment. From the social science perspective, see Special Commission on the Social Sciences (1969). For a comparison of over a dozen local policy analysis institutions, not including Public Technology, Inc. (PTI), see Hayes and Rasmussen (1972). On the evolution of PTI, or a technology broker operating on a national scale, voices of support for such an organization can be found in several places—for instance, Haire (1969); The Urban Institute (1971); Council of State Governments (1972); and Federal Council for Science and Technology (1972). The precursor to PTI was the International City Management Association's Technology Application Program (TAP).

109

On the other hand, a second motivating force has been the growing federal role in civilian (as opposed to military or space) R&D. This role has primarily taken the form of federal involvement in different sectors—e.g., agriculture, health, transportation, housing, and education—with the appropriate federal agency setting the policies and intimately engaged in the R&D activities in each sector, often with little regard for the activities in other sectors. All together, civilian R&D supported by the federal government has grown rapidly in absolute as well as relative terms (see Figure 6-1). For the fiscal year 1976, for instance, federally supported civilian R&D obligations are estimated to be $7.3 billion and 34 percent of the total federal R&D dollar, compared with $3.9 billion and 24 percent in 1970. Although most of the civilian R&D expenditures are aimed at

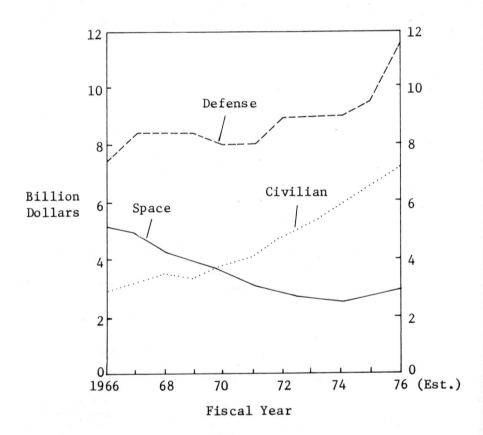

Source: Federal Council for Science and Technology, *Report on the Federal R&D Program, FY 1976* (Washington, D.C., 1975).

Figure 6-1. Research and Development Obligations, 1966-1976

private industry, a substantial portion nevertheless either directly or indirectly affects state and local agencies.

These two somewhat separate developments—the emergence of interest in public technology stemming from the space program and the growth of federal support for civilian R&D activities—have helped to set the stage for some of the major disappointments and dilemmas in federal policymaking. A major disappointment has been that, unlike the space program, public technology has yet to have had a substantial effect on the cities' housing, transportation, public safety, or educational problems. Furthermore, most local services such as fire and police protection, sanitation and public works, mass transit, and public education are still organized much as they were decades ago. A major dilemma has been the difficulty of developing federal policies that are consistent within the various functional sectors. Because of the traditional organization of federal agencies by functional sector, there are different policies in different sectors. The local police department, for instance, works with the Department of Justice with one set of regulations, while the local welfare or drug agencies work with the Department of Health, Education, and Welfare with another set of rules. For dealing with a common problem—e.g., a youthful drug offender—this fractionated arrangement presents administrative inconsistencies that are at once inequitable and inefficient.

In spite of these conditions, the hope continues that more effective federal programs can be created in the future. With state and local governments increasingly suffering from budgetary problems, the installation of technological innovations that can improve service efficiencies would presumably remain high on the list of local priorities. With continuing support for federal laboratories and new technological development, the invention of new devices to deal with local service problems would seem to be a realistic expectation. One theoretically desirable situation would thus be where federal resources are used to support the high front-end costs of developing and installing technological innovations, while local agencies are subsequently able to reap the benefits of the long-term cost savings. To achieve this or a similarly beneficial situation, it is worth summarizing the range of federal policy alternatives and examining the implications for these alternatives on the basis of the evidence from our study.

Alternative Federal Policies

The design of effective federal R&D strategies must be based on an understanding of the overall process by which new technological goods are introduced into the marketplace. For any local service, the creation of technological innovations not only involves the relevant local agency, but usually also requires the participation of a research or other organization that invents the innovation, a goods manufacturer that produces it, and a communications network that distributes information about it from one locale to another. In some cases, a federal agency may serve directly in one or more of these capacities. In other cases, however, federal policies can have a varied and less direct effect on the private institutions that are involved. Whichever the situation, the insights for developing the most effective federal R&D strategies are likely to come from an understanding of the incentive and institutional structures found in the technological innovation process. A useful term for describing the components of this process is the *Technology Delivery System* (TDS).[b]

The major components of a TDS are:

Organizations that act as sources of funding for R&D and related activities;

R&D performers, or the creators of the technological innovations that may be converted by manufacturers into new or improved goods;

Producers or manufacturers of the goods; and

Purchasers of the goods, or the ultimate users of products delivered by the system.

Each TDS component can consist of a number of organizations. For example, R&D may be supported by both federal agencies and private firms, as in the case of health care computer systems. As another example, the producers' component usually contains both factor input and final producers. Factor input producers are firms that supply final producers with the intermediate products needed in the manufacture of goods sold to local agencies or consumers. In the public safety sector, semiconductor manufacturers, who in turn produce the goods ultimately purchased by police departments.

The notion of a TDS also includes the environment within which the component institutions are linked or regulated. Intermediary institutions such as Public Technology, Inc., for example, provide links between goods manufacturers in the fire services and local agency consumers. Lending institutions also serve a regulatory function as they may be called upon for funds to finance the capital projects related to technological innovations. Finally, direct regulation by federal or state government agencies is increasingly an important factor for technological innovations, as with federal pollution standards and the encouragement of pollution-reducing efforts.

One potentially useful principle for policymaking purposes is that the more a single organization appears to perform the different roles associated with each component, the more the TDS is likely to be able to produce and implement

---

[b]The TDS concept was introduced by Edward Wenk in 1970 and has subsequently been developed by Wenk and others. See Wenk (1970 and 1975); and Committee on Public Engineering Policy (1973, p. 2). The TDS concept is applied to the solar energy sector in an excellent recent article by Ezra (1975).

technological innovations.[c] An industrial firm that both performs R&D and then produces the new products resulting from the R&D has strong incentives to develop internal links and feedback mechanisms among marketing, manufacturing, and R&D. One thus might describe the "industrial paradigm" as a TDS in which a single firm funds and performs R&D and then produces goods for sale to the ultimate user. This TDS usually exhibits strong links—including distributors and financial intermediaries—between the goods producers and consumers. The typical TDS in the sectors involving local services such as public safety, education, and health, however, are much less integrated than the industrial paradigm. Most commonly, a federal agency is the source of R&D funding, a nonprofit or profit-making organization is the R&D performer, a private manufacturer is the goods producer, and the local agency is the goods consumer. All are separate entities.

As a result, federal agencies may suboptimize their performance in supporting R&D by not having adequate concern for the coupling to goods producers, purchasers, or even to the actions of federal agencies in other sectors. For example, an R&D contract may be awarded solely on the basis of cost and the R&D performer's technical competence without consideration of its utilization plans or marketing capability. One goal for future federal policies might be to improve the integration of the various TDS components in each local service sector.

The TDS framework helps to identify and enumerate the different classes of federal policies that can influence technological innovations by state and local agencies. If each local service sector consists of the four poorly integrated TDS components as well as an external environment that links these components, then the federal policies can be categorized according to which of these components is most affected. Thus, for each case study under analysis, a series of policy-related questions may be asked. In relation to the first component (source of funding), the basic issue of whether the federal government had any funding role in the innovative effort can be raised. This means identifying whether federal resources of any kind were associated with any aspect of the innovative effort. In relation to the second component (R&D performer), the relevant questions are whether there was any federal support either: (1) during the early R&D of the innovation or (2) for work done by a research organization or university. As for the third component (goods manufacturer), the question is whether there was any federal support for product development or evaluation— i.e., the testing of the innovation in some artificial environment. Similarly, for the fourth component (the local agency acting as the goods purchaser or consumer), federal resources may have been used to support the implementation effort in general, to train local personnel, or to carry out evaluations. Finally,

[c]We are grateful to Walter Baer of The Rand Corporation for suggesting this and other ideas about the usefulness of the TDS as a heuristic device for understanding technological innovation.

the potential policies affecting the external environment include whether there was a law or regulation related to the innovative effort, whether there was any federal support for conferences, clearinghouses, or other information-disseminating activities, or whether federal officials provided technical assistance or consultation services (and presumably served some integrating function). Table 6-1 summarizes all of these classes of policies and matches them with the ten checklist questions that were intended to probe for the evidence of such policies.

Because our 140 case studies covered a full range of local services, these questions regarding federal policies have necessarily been cast in general terms—that is, our questions only deal with basic classes of federal policies and not with the specific circumstances of individual policy. As such, the findings may be more useful to the Office of Management and Budget, the National Science Foundation, and other agencies concerned with setting policies across functional service sectors rather than the line agencies. However, even though our study may uncover certain distinctions in this manner, many federal policies are not set according to such general categories. In particular, many policies are made by the various federal agencies that dominate different local service sectors: the Department of Housing and Urban Development, National Bureau of Standards, and the Department of Justice for public safety and fire protection services; the Department of Transportation and the Environmental Protection Agency for transportation and public works services; the Department of Health, Education, and Welfare for health services; the Office of Education for education services; and the Department of Housing and Urban Development and other agencies for planning, coordinative, and miscellaneous services. Thus to the extent that our study also uncovers systematic service differences among the innovative experiences, there may be policy implications for these different sectors and their respective agencies. In theory, one desirable analysis would

Table 6-1
Classes of Federal Policies Related to Technological Innovations in Local Services

Federal Support Activity	Checklist Question
Any support for any innovative effort	B-5
Support for R&D for work of research organization or university	D-14a, D-14g
Support for product development	D-14b
Support for implementation effort, local personnel training, or evaluation	D-14d, D-14f, D-14h
Existence of law or regulation, support for information dissemination, or technical assistance	B-3, D-14c, D-14e

have been to examine each class of policies in each service sector. The small number of case studies, however, precluded this fine an analysis; hence, the following section deals first with the general classes of policies and then with differences among service sectors, but does not systematically consider the interaction between the two.

Case Survey Findings

General Classes of Federal Policies

As with the previous chapters, the main task was to identify factors related to successful innovative efforts, defined both as innovations that led to improvements and were incorporated ($success_1$) and as innovations that did not lead to improvements and were not incorporated ($success_2$). Of secondary concern was to identify factors related either to incorporation or service improvement but not both, with the supposition that federal policies might play different roles in t e production efficiency and bureaucratic self-interest processes. The relationships to three types of policies, however, could not be examined at all because they occurred in the case studies with such low frequency as to make further analysis difficult to interpret: support for product development (only 9.3 percent of the cases indicated the presence of such support), the presence of a law or regulation (only 7.8 percent), and support for information-disseminating activities (only 15.0 percent).[d]

The analysis of the pairwise relationships between the seven remaining questions on federal policies and the success outcome showed that *none* of the federal policies bore a statistically significant relationship to successful innovative efforts. Table 6-2 shows a typical result—that federal support of any sort in relation to the innovative effort did not occur with differential frequency, whether the effort succeeded or failed. The relationship is so weak that it does not even approach statistical significance, and this was the situation for the other policy variables as well. The observation of a lack of relationship between federal policies and success was also confirmed by regression analysis. When all seven questions were used as independent variables and the modified success outcome was used as the dependent variable (discarding the twenty-two no-improvement-no-incorporation cases and categorizing all remaining cases into a binary success-failure scheme), the total equation yielded an R^2 of 0.090 (F not significant), indicating that the federal factors as a group accounted for less than 10 percent of the variance. (Again, the regression analysis did not differ whether the impossible-to-answer responses were coded along with the presence or

[d]The criteria for discarding questions were: over 50 percent of the answers were in the impossible-to-answer category, or less than 20 percent were in one of two binary (yes or no) categories.

Table 6-2
Relationship Between Overall Federal Support and Successful Efforts
(N = 140)

| | Any Federal Support for Any Innovative Effort (Question B-5) | |
Outcome of Innovative Effort	Yes	No
Success$_1$	40	31
Success$_2$	12	10
Failure	27	20

Note: χ^2 = not significant. Examination of higher quality cases alone also supports this lack of relationship.

absence of a factor.) The main conclusion simply appears to be that federal factors were unrelated to the success outcome.

Generally similar results were found for the relationships of the federal policies to service improvement and incorporation. There were *no* significant relationships between any of the policies and service improvement. For incorporation, there were two significant relationships, but both were in a *negative* direction. One of these was noted in the last chapter—overall federal support for the innovative effort occurred less frequently with efforts that became fully incorporated. The other involved the provision of technical assistance, which also occurred less frequently in relation to efforts that became fully incorporated (see Table 6-3). The negative relationships both lead to the possibility that the presence of federal support is somehow associated with conditions that are not conducive to incorporation. Regression analysis, first using service improvement and then incorporation as the dependent variable, and in each case allowing the independent variables to enter into the equation in stepwise

Table 6-3
Relationship Between Federal Technical Assistance and Incorporation
(N = 140)

| | Incorporation (Question F-1) | | |
Federal Support for Technical Assistance (Question D-14e)	Full	Partial (some doubt)	Discontinued or Not Operated
Yes	8	19	13
No	51	31	15
Impossible to answer	1	2	0

Note: χ^2 = 12.87, df = 2, $p < 0.01$ (excludes impossible-to-answer cases). Examination of high quality cases alone significantly supports this relationship.

fashion, confirmed the analysis of the pairwise relations. For service improvement, the federal factors as a group accounted for a statistically insignificant portion of the variance ($R^2 = 0.076$, F not significant). For incorporation, only five independent variables entered the equation and accounted for a significant but still low portion of the variance, with the only significant single relationship being a negative one between technical assistance and incorporation (see Table 6-4). The main conclusion appears to be that, except for the negative relationships as noted, federal factors were generally not important in accounting for the variance in the service improvement and incorporation outcomes.

The failure to find any positive, significant relationships between federal policies and any of the three outcomes may be interpreted in two ways. First, there is always the possibility that the specific variables were improperly chosen or defined, and that the lack of positive relationships was attributable to measurement error. Alternatively, the results may be taken as adding to a growing body of evidence that, for innovative efforts in local services, federal support or participation in project-specific activities may not be a determining or even contributing factor for the outcome of those projects. Previous evidence to this effect has come from an analysis of urban decentralization efforts (Yin and Yates, 1975) and of a variety of innovative programs in local public schools (Berman and Pauly, 1975). In both studies, factors other than federal ones were found to be related to outcomes when individual projects were studied.

Our findings do not necessarily mean that federal support is unimportant for technological innovation. They may mean that project-specific activities are not the best level of analysis for identifying the results of federal support, and that the effects of federal policies may be more appropriately sought by assessing, for example, the regional or statewide standardization of programs as a

Table 6-4
Federal Factors Related to Incorporation

(impossible to answer is coded as absence of factor)

Attribute *(listed in order of stepwise regression analysis)*	Regression Results		
	b	*Standard Error b*	*F*
Federal technical assistance	−0.27	0.10	6.76*
Federal support of any innovative effort	−0.16	0.11	2.29
Federal training of local personnel	−0.04	0.11	0.17
Federal support for implementation effort	0.03	0.11	0.06
Federal support for evaluation	0.02	0.10	0.05
Constant	0.58		

Note: $R^2 = 0.109$, df $= 5/134$, $F = 3.27$, $p < 0.01$
*$p < 0.05$.

result of federal regulations, or by assessing changes in local services in general rather than for specific projects. Certain local agencies may establish innovative programs because of the availability of federal funds over a period of time for a series of projects that are not necessarily related; although no single project may be able to link its success to the availability of the federal funds, the agency as a whole may operate in a more innovative environment and successfully use new technologies.

Service Sector Differences

Another way of identifying potential federal policy implications is to examine differences among service sectors. Each case study was categorized by the type of local agency in which the innovative effort took place, and the types were clustered (because of the small number of case studies for most of the types) into five sectors: police and fire, transportation (including traffic police) and public works, health, education, and planning and miscellaneous. To the extent that there were differences in innovative experiences among these sectors, these may have policy implications for the federal agencies dominant in each sector.

In relation to successful outcomes, the most noteworthy findings were a high rate of successful rejections ($success_2$) in the planning and miscellaneous sector and a high rate of failures in the police and fire category (see Table 6-5). Both findings appear to reflect the fact that these two sectors were the ones which most frequently attempted data analytic innovations, and such innovations (as pointed out in Chapter 3) were more prone to either successful rejection or failure than were the hardware or computer system innovations. As for service improvements, there was again a significant relationship between sectors and this outcome (see Table 6-6). Again, the major differences were in

Table 6-5
Relationship Between Service Sectors and Successful Efforts
(N = 140)

	Outcome of Innovative Effort		
Service Sector (Question B-2)	*Success₁*	*Success₂*	*Failure*
Police and fire	11	2	13
Transportation and public works	16	3	7
Health	18	5	8
Education	16	2	5
Planning and miscellaneous	10	10	14

Note: $\chi^2 = 16.64$, df = 8, $p < 0.05$. Examination of higher quality cases alone significantly supports this relationship.

Table 6-6
Relationship Between Service Sectors and Service Improvement
(N = 140)

| Service Sector (Question B-2) | Service Improvement (Question F-5) | | | |
	Yes	No	Information Only	Impossible to Answer
Police and fire	12	5	8	1
Transportation and public works	20	3	2	1
Health	19	7	4	1
Education	16	5	0	2
Planning and miscellaneous	11	12	10	1

Note: χ^2 = 22.17, df = 8, $p < 0.01$ (excludes impossible-to-answer cases). Examination of higher quality cases alone significantly supports this relationship.

the planning and miscellaneous sector and the police and fire sector: since both sectors had attempted more data analytic innovations, both had a higher frequency of "useful information only" or "no service improvement" outcomes. As for incorporation, there was no significant association with sectors, although there was a tendency for education to be different from the other sectors in that a disproportionately large number of education cases were only partially incorporated. In summary, however, the main sector differences related to the three outcomes were mainly attributable to differences in the type of innovations attempted in each sector; in other respects, the sector experiences were similar and therefore did not suggest any implications for federal policy.

The Federal Role: An Alternative Approach

This chapter has attempted to analyze the potential federal policy implications of our study and to present the relevant case survey findings. In almost every analysis, there was no relationship found between the outcomes of the innovative effort and the presence of federal support for such diverse activities as technical assistance, implementation, and training of local personnel. The only significant findings were of negative relationships between incorporation and either the presence of any federal support or the presence of support for technical assistance.

The fact that federal factors appear not to be related to most of the outcomes in our 140 case studies should be interpreted with caution, but it should also not be taken lightly. It should be interpreted with caution because the analysis only covers the potential effect of federal policies at the project-specific level, and because several important policy alternatives (e.g., support for product development and the role of federal laws and regulations) were not explored because the case studies lacked the necessary information. It should also be interpreted with caution because the federal role may be important, but not on a project-by-project basis. For instance, in service areas such as highways and transportation, other investigations (Feller et al., 1974) have suggested that federal activities can be extremely important in developing a general R&D capability in a service sector over a long period of time, both by stimulating technological development and by supporting a network of communications activities in the sector. Our findings do not in any way contradict these results, nor do they rule out the possibility that other federal policies measured by other variables might not be related to project-specific outcomes.

The results of the case survey should not be taken lightly, however, because other nonfederal factors, as shown in the previous chapters, do appear to be closely related to project-specific outcomes. It is the strength of these nonfederal relationships, combined with the failure to find significant evidence about the effect of federal policies on project-specific outcomes, that raises the possibility of reconsidering the direction of federal policies. One problem may be that too much attention has been given in the past to specific projects or innovations. The implementation of federal policies has generally involved proposing, testing, and evaluating a specific innovation. Moreover, to carry out the testing, federal funds have often been used to support a special organizational unit (e.g., project team) within a local agency. Yet such discrete projects may be highly transient. Project personnel may be hired or specially assigned only for the duration of external or federal support, and after the additional funding ceases, the project may end and the project team disbanded. This can occur even when the team is composed of agency personnel, who may have to return to their original preinnovation assignments or who may even turn to new assignments that are part of yet another new project. In short, the day-to-day routine of the agency's work may have changed little even though many specific projects or innovations have been tried.

If, as the previous chapter has indicated, the incorporation of innovations in local agencies is partially the result of a bureaucratic self-interest process, federal policies must be designed to coincide with such interests to be effective. One alternative might be to reconsider entirely the project-specific approach. For instance, consider the characteristic world of a person in state or local service practice, whether the person is a police officer, judge, teacher, social worker, or other type of practitioner. First, such a person receives highly specialized, formal training that takes place in law schools, police academies, and other professional schools. Second, even with such training, the person usually cannot become a practitioner without some certification procedure that may call for a formal examination (e.g., the bar exam or a civil service entrance exam). Third, the person generally advances his/her career through on-the-job performance, political and personal ties,[e] and further testing and certification (as in promotion

---

[e]This should not be taken as a pejorative point. Many positions are filled on the basis of appointments by chief executives and approval by legislatures. In addition, opportunities for

examinations for fire and police personnel). Fourth, the person as a practitioner usually belongs to two important groups: a professional peer group that is organized around professional associations (local and national) and, in some cases, public service unions; and a bureaucratic organization or local agency that is part of a state or local government. Fifth, the person's everyday routine mainly involves interactions within these two important groups but also with one other group: clients or service users. In most local services, the server-served relationship (e.g., police officer-citizen; lawyer-client; teacher-student or parent; doctor—patient) is one of the most important aspects of daily operations.

From the point of view of this characteristic world, how is traditional practice as well as new practice learned? We believe this is an important issue for further research on innovative efforts. Our tentative hypothesis, however, would be as follows: The initial training and certification, as well as further study for civil service promotions, certainly provide formal tools and skills. The early on-the-job experience serves as a critical socialization process that is probably most important in determining the nature of subsequent practice. Finally, the information communicated through formal and informal channels as part of the professional or bureaucratic organization will also influence the nature of service practice. Beyond these major sources of influence, most other new information may have little effect on practice.

To the extent that this scenario is valid, it can be seen that project-specific federal strategies tend to rely on the less important aspects of the practitioner's world. The formation of special project teams and the dissemination of final reports from specific projects are relatively peripheral to the work of the practitioner. Not surprisingly, these approaches to implementation may have little long-term effect in transforming R&D knowledge into practice. An alternative approach would therefore be to identify and utilize the "natural points" for changing practices. Four such points that ought to be examined in future research are: curriculum development in the basic training institutions, curriculum development in the certification procedures, the activities of professional societies, and specific cyclical functions that affect the local service organization (e.g., the passage of new legislation, the procurement of supplies and equipment, and even collective bargaining negotiations). Innovative practices, in other words, may not result mainly from specific innovative efforts; what may be required is the application of a much longer-term view of the implementation process in which new R&D knowledge is converted into practice as part of the normal training and career development of service practitioners.

The overall approach of identifying and using natural points of entry is but one new approach to R&D utilization that deserves further consideration.[f] For precise comparison purposes, evaluative research should be designed to compare such an approach with the traditional federal implementation strategies. The im-

advancement (in any employment) are often communicated through collegial and friendship networks.

[f]This approach, as well as an elaboration of the points made here, is described in Yin (1976).

plications of such a new approach, however, are already evident and should be made clear.

First, the new approach deemphasizes any direct link between a specific research project culminating in a specific innovative practice. The use of natural points of entry implies that new technology may be translated into new practices only through a series of intermediate steps, including the sufficient replication of results, the publication of the results in practitioner textbooks, or the use of the results in organizational procedures such as the purchasing process. This may be contrasted with the traditional implementation strategies, where it has been assumed that a specific problem can be addressed by a specific research project, leading to policy-relevant conclusions that are worthy of immediate field testing or implementation.

Second, the new approach implies a much longer time lag between an R&D activity and the eventual installation of new practices. This will mean a reduction in expectations, at least at the outset, concerning the ability of R&D to address crisis problems such as the urban disorders of the 1960s or a sudden crime wave in a given city. However, such a reduction in expectations may indeed be a major lesson to be derived from the events of the last decade. In retrospect, where R&D has been most successful in providing guidelines for new practices—e.g., national defense, agriculture, highways, and medical care—the successes appear to have resulted from (1) long-standing investments in R&D, and (2) implementation strategies that have been nurtured over a period of at least several decades. The expectations, such as the effort to land a man on the moon, appear to occur when there is a specific, concrete, and possibly nonsocial mission, and where the required R&D activity is largely an engineering effort that can take advantage of a reservoir of basic research that already exists. Thus the implementation of new technology must be considered a process that will mainly occur (if there is to be any success at all) over a long period of time.

Third, the new approach places increased demands on the aggregation of research results than is presently the case. Soundly based R&D knowledge is the outcome of an incremental and cumulative process. Steps can and should be taken to facilitate this process, such as the encouragement of research assessments and inventories. This also means that research investigators must adequately communicate with each other (and be given the time to consider the relationship of their findings to those of other studies), that data collection procedures and measures must be standardized so that different studies can be compared, and that new or existing third-party institutions, such as the National Bureau of Standards, must play a stronger role in deciding the new technology which should be incorporated at the natural points of entry—e.g., new curricula, certification procedures, or purchasing standards. In other words, most individual research projects will probably not lead to implementation (and should not be judged heavily in terms of their utilization); those that do will do so only after an additional period of time is allowed for the reanalysis process.

7

Conclusions

Summary of Findings

The preceding chapters have examined technological innovations in state and local governments by analyzing the evidence from 140 case studies. Our analysis has been based, in other words, on a review of existing literature—studies that have reported on individual innovative experiences by a specific local service organization in a specific locale and during a specific time period. Although these case studies represent a major part of the empirical literature on technological innovation in state and local governments, our findings should nevertheless be treated as but one of several sources of information.

The review process has been facilitated by the use of a case survey method that is replicable and allows the case studies to be analyzed in a rigorous manner. To this extent, the method of analysis has been more scientifically based than the traditional procedure for reviewing the literature. The analytic focus has been to identify the characteristics most frequently correlated with successful innovative efforts—i.e., efforts that produced some service improvement and were incorporated ($success_1$) or ones that produced no improvement and were not incorporated ($success_2$). The analysis covered a variety of innovations and local agencies.

The initial analysis, based on both pairwise cross-tabulations and regression techniques, examined the attributes of the innovative device that were associated with successful efforts. Even though the 140 case studies included a varied array of hardware innovations, computer systems, and data analysis innovations, the results showed that there existed a few common characteristics that were correlated with successful efforts. The two most important characteristics were that an innovative device be (1) a *hardware* device and (2) a *transitive* device—aimed at creating changes in service practices with clients (and not mere administrative or internal changes). Overall, however, the findings are different from those of previous studies of attributes found to be related to the adoption of technological innovations by individual farmers, doctors, consumers, and the like (Rogers, 1962; and Rogers and Shoemaker, 1971). Our results suggest instead that organizational, implementation, and other factors may also be relevant in accounting for innovative outcomes in local service organizations where innovation is not a unitary act by a single adopting individual.

Our analysis thus went on to examine successful efforts as a function of two other groups of attributes: the setting (background factors) and the immediate

123

circumstances for any given innovative effort (implementation factors). The most important background factor was the presence of an agency whose decisionmaking structure was *centralized*; the most important implementation factor was the presence of *client participation*, though some evidence was found that practitioner training was also important.

Of the device, background, and implementation factors that appeared important, two therefore dealt with client aspects of service delivery and deserve further comment. The first was considered a characteristic of the device: transitive innovations that aim at establishing new practices between service providers and clients were found to be significant correlates of successful outcomes. Second, the existence of some sort of client participation in the implementation process was also a significant correlate. These results suggest that client involvement—in the form of either an intended service change or actual participation—may provide external pressure that is beneficial to the innovative process. Agency managers may act with greater care and with somewhat more perseverance when clients are even potentially involved, and under such circumstances, the innovative effort is more likely to succeed. The results thus provide another example of the potentially beneficial effects of client participation, even where the innovation is a technological rather than purely client-oriented one.

When the device, background, and implementation factors were compared simultaneously, the overall combination accounted for much more of the variance than any group alone. The best explanation for the occurrence of successful efforts was not just built around device attributes alone ($R^2 = 0.168$), or even around background ($R^2 = 0.140$) or implementation attributes alone ($R^2 = 0.204$), but around all three ($R^2 = 0.350$). Moreover, the significant individual factors were not dominantly of one of the three types, but again represented all three. In terms of the first major hypothesis posed in Chapter 1, we were therefore surprised to find that implementation factors as a group did not play a more dominant role than the other two groups. The main conclusion is, on the contrary, that successful innovative efforts involve a variety of conditions, some related to the nature of the innovative device, some related to background factors, and others related to implementation factors.

A more focused examination of the implementation process alone, however, provided the most theoretically significant aspect of our findings. This was a comparison of the correlates of the two components of successful efforts—service improvement and incorporation. Even though these two components were highly correlated with each other, there were nevertheless two different sets of attributes related to each. These two different sets were described as part of two potentially different innovative processes, one involving *production efficiency* and leading mainly to service improvement, and the other involving *bureaucratic self-interest* and leading mainly to incorporation.

The basis for having postulated two innovative processes is that public bureaucracies are continually innovating and changing, but they appear to do so more as a function of the opportunities for bureaucratic growth, status, and power than merely as a function of the need to improve services (Downs, 1967). Thus, even though a particular innovation can improve services, if it does not serve bureaucratic goals, it is not likely to be incorporated. Similarly, some innovations may be incorporated because they serve these goals, even though little service improvement has been produced. In essence, because of the way in which public bureaucracies gain their income (i.e., through the annual budget review process, rather than through market mechanisms) and because of the general difficulty in measuring and assessing the services that public bureaucracies deliver, innovative efforts in public agencies appear to involve a different set of circumstances from those involved in the adoption of innovations by individuals or private firms.

The results support the notion of two innovative processes by showing that the attributes significantly related to service improvements were not correlated with incorporation, and vice versa. Service improvement most often occurred in the presence of a transitive device and innovative efforts that included opportunities for practitioner training. Incorporation, in contrast, most often occurred when: the chief executive supported the effort; the innovator, implementer, and advocate for the effort were located within rather than outside the agency; there was no federal support or implementation delay; and there were no increases in agency staff. Thus, in relation to the second major hypothesis in Chapter 1, our findings most certainly support the idea of two innovative processes, and both processes may be important to the successful use of new technology.

Finally, the analysis focused on the potential role of federal policies. This was done by examining successful efforts as a function of the presence of federal support for any number of activities—e.g., technical assistance, overall support for implementation, or support for the early R&D involving the innovative device. The main finding was that no federal factors were associated with successful innovative efforts. As a group, the seven federal factors accounted for less of the variance ($R^2 = 0.090$) in our measure of success than the most important device factors, the most important background factors, the most important implementation factors, or the most important device, background, and implementation factors combined. Moreover, among the federal policies, the provision of technical assistance was the single most significant *negative* correlate of incorporation. The findings therefore support the third major hypothesis in Chapter 1. If successful efforts are assessed on a case-specific basis at the local level, federal policies appear not to play a direct role, although subsequent research could show that federal actions are important in some more complex fashion. One suggestion is that federal factors may still play an important role in a capacity-building function; federal support of the activities of professional associations over an extended period of time, for example, may result in more innovative behavior by local organizations, even though the outcomes for any specific innovative effort can be related directly to any federal action.

These overall results are in some ways similar and in other ways somewhat different from those of previous studies in which one or more types of innovations were also examined at more than one site. (Appendix F summarizes seventeen such studies; they differ from the 140 original case studies in that they cover the experiences at more than one site.) The result concerning the importance of centralization, for instance, parallels that of Corwin (1972). Similarly, the results concerning the negative relationship of federal technical assistance has also been reported elsewhere (Frohman et al., 1972). However, our findings differ from those of previous studies in that many of the earlier studies emphasized other characteristics—e.g., the size of the innovating agency as a correlate of successful innovative efforts (e.g., Mohr, 1969; Hage and Aiken, 1967; Mytinger, 1968; Deal et al., 1975; Baldridge, 1975; and Corwin, 1975).

One possible reason for the differences between our results and those of previous studies may simply be a lack of information in the 140 case studies. A second reason, however, may be the less conventional research design followed by our study. Whereas previous studies have tended to focus on single types of innovations across many different sites (e.g., the jet-axe, the adoption of new instructional programs, the use of hospital discharge data systems, or the adoption of new health programs), our findings are based on the aggregate experience of many different types of innovations in many different sites. For this reason, our analysis has been able to compare the importance of a variety of attributes of the innovative device with other attributes of the innovative situation. Few of the other studies have been able to make such comparisons, and therefore our results cannot really be discussed in relation to most of them. Furthermore, our research design has also allowed us to examine the effects of different types of federal policies; again, such an examination might have been difficult if the type of innovation were the same across sites and if the federal role therefore did not vary across the sites.

Conclusions: The Local Theme

Another distinctive characteristic of our research design can serve as the basis for drawing together the main implications of our study. Unlike most studies, our investigation covered not only a diverse array of innovative devices, but also a wide range of service agencies—police departments, schools, hospitals, public works departments, planning agencies, and the like. Almost every one of the seventeen multisite studies summarized in Appendix F, in contrast, focused on only one type of service agency. Our study design thus enabled us to make comparisons among different types of agencies—comparisons that the other studies could not make.

In examining our evidence for differences among service agencies, we found that certain types of agencies (planning and public safety) were more frequently associated with certain types of innovations (data analysis) and that the occurrence of service improvements therefore differed among the agencies. However, in spite of these differences, there was no relationship between the type of agency and the occurrence of incorporation. In other words, differences in service functions apparently did not affect the extent to which innovations were incorporated. This finding contrasts sharply with a previous study of client-oriented innovations (Yin and Yates, 1975), where the strong differences in the traditional relationships between service providers and clients in education, health, and public safety, for instance, produced considerably different patterns of implementation. The fact that such service differences did not appear in relation to technological innovations suggests that certain bureaucratic factors may transcend service differences and represent a *common condition* of local service organizations.

The apparent universality of this common condition in relation to technological innovations should not be underestimated. One of the most remarkable features of state and local agencies has been their ability to grow rapidly without changing their essential technical nature. The growth over the last two decades has been significant in absolute and relative terms, with many state and local governments now even playing an important role as components of the local economy and employment market. Yet, except possibly for the diversification in social services, the basic types of services offered—from public works to sanitation to education to public safety—have not changed much, nor has the way in which these services are delivered—how garbagemen collect the garbage, how teachers teach, how firemen or policemen deal with emergencies, or even how planners plan.

The appearance of a technological innovation has usually occurred as a small incident or diversion within this context of common conditions, as few single innovations have dramatically affected the totality of the local system. What may be more important for increasing the impact of innovations in local organizations in the future is not the promotion of specific innovations, but the modification of the organizational incentives and self-interests for successfully incorporating an innovation. Here, our identification of a set of bureaucratic self-interest factors may be extremely important. Such factors have not received adequate empirical attention in the past, and yet these factors may be an important predictor of successful innovative efforts.

The main policy implication of this point is this: If federal policies focus only on promoting specific innovations, then the effect of federal policies may also have a minimal effect on the functions of state and local agencies. Our evidence showed no relationships between federal policies and the outcomes of specific innovative efforts. This suggests that successful innovations in local services in the future may not follow the federal support of specific efforts or even of new technological devices. Instead, federal policies may have to aim at changing some of the common conditions of local service organizations. Thus our suggestion is that federal support be undertaken with a capacity-building rather than case-specific objective. Policies may be important, for instance, in creating an innovative environment by influencing such conditions as:

The curriculum development process in basic practitioner training and certification procedures;

The social network of service professionals, including the activities of practitioner associations or unions in increasing practitioner communication about innovations;

The organizational context within which the agency operates and its relations to overhead agencies in the same jurisdictions, including the passage of new legislation and collective bargaining procedures; and

The internal bureaucratic context in which the agency itself is organized and operates, including the procurement of supplies and equipment.

The present study has provided suggestions about the last two of these conditions. We identified the key role of hardware innovations, transitive innovations, centralized agencies, and client participation as correlates of successful innovative efforts; as correlates of incorporation, we identified the importance of chief executive support and of the presence within the innovating agency of the major innovative actors. These factors appear to be important in the innovative process in local organizations, independent of the specific innovative device, site, or type of service agency involved. If these findings are corroborated in future research, then they may represent the beginning of a theoretical base for designing the policies to influence the common conditions of local service organizations.

Research may have failed to develop such a theoretical base in the past because the research has overemphasized the implementation of federally designed and mandated programs. One study, for instance, has suggested that local implementation is but the microlevel phase of the macrolevel problem of implementing federal programs (McLaughlin and Berman, 1975). Another study describes the implementation problem as consisting mainly of guidelines development (based on new legislation), resource allocation by a support agency, monitoring by the support agency of a local performer, auditing, and evaluation—a framework that was also developed to reflect implementation as seen from a federal perspective (Rein and Rabinovitz, 1974). Similarly, many of the other prominent works on implementing public policy have been concerned with federal programs (e.g., Allison, 1971; Pressman and Wildavsky, 1973; Hargrove, 1975; and Williams, 1975).

In relation to the implementation of change in local services, the federal perspective is likely to be misleading for several reasons. First, the local system is part of a social system, whereas the federal one is not. Fire, health, police, education, and other local services developed as part of the social fabric of the local community. This history included the development of services around neighborly as well as patronage relations. In contrast to the importance of the social norms of this system at the local level, the federal programs and federal perspective revolve mainly around administrative issues. Innovative changes in local services may thus require modifications in social structures and different implementation strategies from those developed from a federal perspective. For instance, although local civil servants may no longer live in the neighborhoods or central cities in which they work, they may nevertheless share a strong localist orientation that is reinforced by the absence of lateral entry to most civil service jobs. The orientation might include predispositions to resist innovations on historic and sentimental grounds that may be less important in considering, for example, the reorganization of federal agencies.

Second, local jurisdictions have always had constitutionally delegated responsibility for educational, police, fire, sanitation, and other such services. The jurisdictions have developed a set of traditions in which federal programs may be seen as only one component, rather than vice versa. The design and provision of local services, for instance, is part of a process that has relied on volunteer support (many local officeholders still receive only nominal salaries), private services (e.g., private schools, hospitals, and trash collection), contractual arrangements for services from private companies, or the direct services of local government agencies. Federal support has only become prominent in the last two decades, and from the local perspective, the use of federal resources represents only one of many alternatives. This view of the delivery of local services cannot be appreciated from the federal perspective.

Third and most important, the federal perspective leads somewhat incorrectly to an overemphasis on the *differences* among local services. In contrast, we have suggested that an understanding of innovative changes is more likely to follow from an appreciation of the *similarities* or common conditions in local services. Typically, the federal perspective begins with a single federal program (e.g., Model Cities, school lunch program, or law enforcement training) that is to be implemented by local agencies. Because there is a standard set of federal regulations for this program, any deviations from site to site are quite prominent and receive undue attention because of the concern with gaining uniform acceptance and allowing uniform evaluation of the federal program. The result is the development of a picture of local service organizations that is incorrectly dominated by regional differences, discrepancies among state (and local) laws, personnel and budgetary differences from one locale to another, and other fine distinctions in bureaucratic procedure from one agency to another. Such differences do exist, but there may be many more similarities than differences across sites and types of agencies. One does not learn much about what different police departments share in common, much less about what schools and police might have in common. Yet in the final analysis such departments might share many important commonalities, and only an understanding of the commonalities may lead to advances in the implementation of innovations, especially technological ones.

The main research implication from our findings is that the instigation of successful innovative efforts will depend upon further knowledge of the common features shared by local service organizations. To the extent that this is true, it is essential that future research develop a comparative perspective. Especially with regard to new case studies of innovative efforts, such case studies should not be built solely around single site-specific experiences. There should be at a minimum two experiences—preferably in different agencies or locales—being studied within the same research design. The pairing of the cases would not preclude the use of special questions to investigate more closely each of the two innovative situations, but the comparative framework would encourage the use of some common set of questions through which different innovations and different agencies could be contrasted and any similarities (as well as differences) could be drawn. Naturally, if more than two experiences, or if case studies conducted by different investigators could be coordinated in this fashion, the results would be even better and more susceptible to comparative statistical anlysis. In the long run, a standardized case study procedure, which included questions concerning the innovative device, background factors, implementation factors, and outcomes, would facilitate the development of new knowledge of innovations across sites and across agencies by providing the basis for checking the completeness of proposed case studies as well as a common fieldwork strategy.

All agencies operate within some network of service professionals and within some community and regulatory context, and all share certain organizational and bureaucratic rules. A plausible assumption is that we need to know more about these conditions to implement any substantial technological innovation.

Appendixes

Appendix A:
List of Sources

Bibliographic Sources Consulted

Bibliographic Index
Bibliographies from the Diffusion Documents Center
    University of Michigan
Bibliography on Productivity in Service Industries
    York College, CUNY
Educational Resources Information Center (ERIC)
George Washington University Library
Gutman Library, Harvard University
Innovation Information Center
    George Washington University
MEDLARS
MIT Library
Municipal Assessment Series of Policy-Related Studies, sponsored
    by the National Science Foundation
National Criminal Justice Reference Service
National League of Cities Library
National Library of Medicine
National Technical Information Service (NTIS)
Rand Corporation Library, Santa Monica
Sociological Abstracts
Sociology of Education Abstracts
UCLA Library
Urban Institute Library
Urban Problems: A Catalog of Dissertations
    University Microfilms
U.S. Department of Health, Education, and Welfare Library
U.S. Department of Housing and Urban Development Library
U.S. Office of Education Library

Journals Searched

Administrative Science Quarterly
American Behavioral Scientist
American Journal of Political Science
American Journal of Sociology
American Political Science Review

American Sociological Review
Bureaucrat
Journal of Applied Behavioral Science
Journal of Politics
Journal of the American Institute of Planners
Journal of Urban Analysis
Management Science
Nation's Cities
Operations Research
Policy Sciences
Policy Studies Journal
Public Administration Review
Public Interest
Public Policy
Social Forces
Social Problems
Social Science Quarterly
Socio-Economic Planning Sciences
Urban Affairs Quarterly
Urban Studies

Federal, Local, and National Association Officials Contacted

Fire and Criminal Justice

Barra, Ralph, NBS
Crites, Laura, ICMA
Heaphy, John, Police Foundation
Knight, Fred, ICMA
Levin, Bud, Commerce
Lyons, John, NBS
Pazour, John, ICMA

Health

Gardell, Gerald, RMPS-HEW
Rockoff, Maxine, HRA—HEW
Waxman, Bruce, HRA-HEW
Weissman, Norman, HRA-HEW
Yedinak, Stephen, HUD

Education

Cooley, William, University of Pittsburgh Learning and Development Center
Fogelstrom, Clarence, OE-HEW
Mays, John, NIE
Melmed, Arthur, NIE
Narayanan, Jean, OE-HEW
Nebens, Michael, OE-HEW
Timpane, Michael, Rand (formerly OASPW, HEW)
Wallington, Jim, Association for Educational Communication and Technology

Transportation, Public Works, and Sanitation

Frisby, Harry, Sanitation Superintendent, Inglewood, California
Johnson, Lyle, Governmental Refuse Collection and Disposal Association
Linhares, Al, DOT
Shuster, Ken, EPA

Planning and Administration

Crawford, Robert, NSF
Griffith, Owen, Anaheim, California
Hardy, Tom, Scottsdale, Arizona
Hayward, Nancy, Productivity Commission
Hersman, Frank, NSF
King, W. Matt, Huntington Beach, California
Licciardello, Mike, Fresno, California
Meisner, Robert, GAO
Mock, John, NSF
Ottwell, Ron, Sanitation Department, Phoenix, Arizona
Seidman, David, NSF
Siegel, Alan, HUD
Singleton, Harvey, Tacoma, Washington
Warren, Forrest, Pasadena, California
Weiss, Jerry, San Jose, California

Research Investigators Contacted

Bingham, Richard, Marquette University
Bodoff, Joan, York College, CUNY

Carey, William, A.D. Little
Corwin, Ronald, Ohio State University
DelaBarre, Dell, California Innovation Group
Feiner, Albert, Practical Concepts, Inc.
Feller, Irwin, Pennsylvania State University
Fritz, Elaine, University of Pittsburgh
Gray, Justin, Justin Gray Associates
Greenberger, Martin, Johns Hopkins University
Halbower, Charles, A.D. Little
Hatry, Harry, The Urban Institute
Herriott, Robert, Abt Associates
Hurley, David, A.D. Little
Knox, Wendell, Abt Associates
Light, Richard, Harvard University
Limstead, George, Naval Weapons Center
Macomber, H.L., California Institute of Technology
Mohr, Lawrence, University of Michigan
Mulloy, Angela, Alan M. Voorhees & Associates, Inc.
Pack, Janet, University of Pennsylvania
Rettig, Richard, Ohio State University
Robbins, Martin, University of Denver
Schroeder, Walter, Massachusetts Institute of Technology
Schwartz, Judah, Massachusetts Institute of Technology
Spuck, Dennis, University of Pittsburgh
Stearns, Robert, Stearns, Conrad, and Schmidt Engineers
Stragier, Marc, Government Innovators
Tanner, Chuck, University of Pittsburgh
Terry, Robert, A.D. Little

Appendix B:
List of Studies

Criminal Justice and Fire

Applied Technology, "Automated Status Reporting Police Communications Study: Final Report," Costa Mesa, California (August 1971, NTIS PB 204 538).

Burt, Marvin, et al., "Fire Station Location Analysis," in "Factors Affecting the Impact of Urban Policy Analysis: Ten Case Histories," working paper, The Urban Institute, Washington, D.C. (July 1972), pp. 42-55.

Burt, Marvin, et al., "Fireboat Analysis: City A," in "Factors Affecting the Impact of Urban Policy Analysis: Ten Case Histories," working paper, The Urban Institute, Washington, D.C. (July 1972), pp. 22-31.

Burt, Marvin, et al., "Fireboat Analysis: City B," in "Factors Affecting the Impact of Urban Policy Analysis: Ten Case Histories," working paper, The Urban Institute, Washington, D.C. (July 1972), pp. 32-41.

District of Columbia Metropolitan Police Department, "Crime Reduction through Aerial Patrol," (1973, NTIS PB 215 711).

Fath, A. Frederick, "Scheduling Techniques for Municipal Court Traffic Sessions," Boeing Aerospace Company, Seattle (April 1973, NTIS PB 222 368).

Frohman, Alan, et al., "Case Study of an Innovation: Rapid Water," in "Factors Affecting Innovation in the Fire Services," Pugh-Roberts Associates, Inc., Cambridge, Massachusetts (March 1972).

Greenberger, Martin, "Rand Studies the Fire Department," in "Models in the Policy Process," unpublished manuscript, Johns Hopkins University, Baltimore (1975), pp. VIII-1-VIII-53.

Heller, N.B., and J.T. McEwen, "Computerized Scheduling of Police Manpower," 2 vol., St. Louis Police Department (March 1973, NTIS PB 232 017 and PB 232 072).

Hendrick, Thomas E., and Donald R. Plane, "An Analysis of the Development of Fire-Fighting Resources in Denver, Colorado," R-1566/3-HUD, The New York City-Rand Institute (May 1975).

Ignall, Edward J., et al., "Improving the Deployment of New York City Fire Companies," The Rand Corporation, P-5280, Santa Monica (July 1974).

Illinois Institute of Technology, "Superbeat: A System for the Effective Distribution of Police Patrol Units," Chicago (October 1973).

Kolesar, Peter, and Warren E. Walker, "An Algorithm for the Dynamic Relocation of Fire Companies," *Operations Research* 22 (March/April 1974):249-274.

Lambright, W. Henry, and Albert H. Teich, "Rapid Water," in "Federal Laboratories and Technology Transfer," Syracuse University Research Corporation (March 1974), pp. 141-166.

Larson, Richard C., "Improving the Effectiveness of New York City's 911," in Alvin W. Drake et al., eds., *Analysis of Public Systems* (Cambridge, Massachusetts: MIT Press, 1972), pp. 151-180.

Laudon, Kenneth C., "A Police Regional Information System," in *Computers and Bureaucratic Reform: The Political Functions of Urban Information Systems* (New York: John Wiley and Sons, 1974), pp. 174-221.

Laudon, Kenneth C., "An Emerging State Department of Justice," in *Computers and Bureaucratic Reform: The Political Functions of Urban Information Systems* (New York: John Wiley and Sons, 1974), pp. 222-275.

Madrazo, Frank G., "Pilot Computerized Infrared Data File for Forensic Science Laboratories: An Evaluation Study," New York State Division of Criminal Justice Services, Criminalistics Research Bureau, Albany (November 1972, NTIS PB 220 206).

Moore, Mark H., et al., "The Case of the Fourth Platoon," *Urban Analysis* 3 (1974):207-258.

Pasadena Police Department, "Improving the Effectiveness of Police Helicopter Patrol Operations," Pasadena, California (March 1972).

Russell, John R., "Fire House Location in East Lansing," in Richard S. Rosenbloom and John R. Russell, *New Tools for Urban Management* (Boston: Graduate School of Business Administration, Harvard University, 1971), pp. 60-67.

Shamblin, James E., et al., "Application of University Resources to Local Government Problems," Oklahoma State University, Stillwater (November 1972, NTIS PB 222 393).

United States Department of Justice, Law Enforcement Assistance Administration, "Dade County Public Safety Department-STOL " Washington, D.C. (1973).

The Urban Institute and The International City Management Association, "Police Case: Manpower Resource Allocation—Kansas City, Missouri Police Department," in "The Challenge of Productivity Diversity: Improving Local Government Productivity Measurement and Evaluation. Part IV: Procedures for Identifying and Evaluating Innovations—Six Case Studies," Washington, D.C. (June 1972), pp. 102-112.

Walker, Warren, et al., "An Analysis of the Deployment of Fire-Fighting Resources in Wilmington, Delaware," R-1566/5-HUD, The New York City-Rand Institute (July 1975).

Whisenand, Paul M., et al., "Project ACE (Aerial Crime Enforcement), Riverside Police Department, Final Report," Institute for Police Studies, California State University, Long Beach (June 1972).

Health

Arthur D. Little, Inc., "Appendix A: A Review of the Medlab System in the Surgical Intensive Care Unit at the Massachusetts General Hospital," Cambridge, Massachusetts (March 1973).

Arthur D. Little, Inc., "Appendix B: A Review of the Automated Medical Systems Computer at the University of Minnesota Hospital," Cambridge, Massachusetts (March 1973).

Ayers, W.R., et al., "Mobilizing the Emergency Room Record: A Case Study in the Capture of Technology Developed Elsewhere for Use in Health Care Delivery," *Computers in Biology and Medicine* 3 (1973):153-163.

Battelle Memorial Institute, "Evaluation of the Implementation of a Medical Information System in a General Community Hospital. Volume I: Summary and Study Structure and Methodology"; and "Volume II: Evaluation Studies and Analyses," Columbus, Ohio (September 1973, NTIS PB 232 784 and PB 232 785).

Bodin, Lawrence D., et al., "Financing Mental-Health Services in the State of New York," *Operations Research* 20 (September/October 1972):942-954.

Boyd, D.R., et al., "Computerized Trauma Registry: A New Method for Categorizing Physical Injuries," *Aerospace Medicine* (June 1971):607-615.

Coe, Rodney M., and Elizabeth A. Barnhill, "Experiment in a System of Medications," in Rodney M. Coe, ed., *Planned Change in the Hospital: Case Studies of Organizational Innovation* (New York: Praeger Publishers, 1970), pp. 101-121.

Coe, Rodney M., and Elizabeth A. Barnhill, "Social Dimensions of Failure in Innovation," *Human Organization* 26 (Fall 1967):149-156.

Conover, Christopher, and Walter S. Baer, "Demonstration Project Case Study: Computer-Assisted Electrocardiogram Analysis," unpublished manuscript, The Rand Corporation, Santa Monica (November 1974).

Dobrow, Robert J., et al., "Transmission of Electrocardiograms from a Community Hospital for Remote Computer Analysis," *American Journal of Cardiology* 21 (May 1968):687-698.

Dwyer, Thomas F., "Telepsychiatry: Psychiatric Consultation by Interactive Television," *American Journal of Psychiatry* 130 (August 1973):865-869.

Elliott, Robert V., "Demonstration and Evaluation of Computer-Assisted Analysis and Interpretation of the Electrocardiogram: A State-of-the-Art Report," St. Luke's Hospital, Denver, Colorado (September 1972, NTIS PB 218 976).

Farlee, Coralie, "Failure of an Innovation: Computer-Generated Medication Schedules," *Hospital Administration* (Fall 1972):43-51.

Finley, Paul R., et al., "Electronic Data Processing in a Private Hospital Laboratory," *American Journal of Clinical Pathology* 48 (December 1967):575-589.

Gee, David A., "Innovation in Patient Food Service," in Rodney M. Coe, ed., *Planned Change in the Hospital: Case Studies of Organizational Innovation* (New York: Praeger Publishers, 1970), pp. 23-44.

Gordon, Diana R., "Getting the Lead out," in *City Limits* (New York: Charterhouse, 1973), pp. 17-62.

Greenberger, Martin, "The Rand Hospital Bed Utilization Study," in "Models in the Policy Process," unpublished manuscript, Johns Hopkins University, Baltimore (1975), pp. IX-1-IX-47.

Grossman, Jerome H., et al., "Evaluation of Computer-Acquired Patient Histories," *Journal of the American Medical Association* 215 (February 1971):1286-1291.

Hammond, William E., et al., "GEMISCH—A Minicomputer Information Support System," *Proceedings of the Institute of Electrical and Electronics Engineers* 61 (November 1973):1575-1583.

Hirsch, Robert L., and Julian B. Schorr, "A Computerized Blood Inventory System in the Service of the Community, the Blood Donor and the Patient-Recipient," Community Blood Council of Greater New York City (July 1970, NTIS PB 217 526).

Lehr, James L., et al., "Experience with MARS (Missouri Automated Radiology System)," *Diagnostic Radiology* 106 (February 1973):289-294.

Littauer, David, et al., "Evaluating Change in Systems of Infant Feeding," in Rodney M. Coe, ed., *Planned Change in the Hospital: Case Studies of Organizational Innovation* (New York: Praeger Publishers, 1970), pp. 45-100.

Menolascino, Frank J., and Robert G. Osborne, "Psychiatric Television Consultation for the Mentally Retarded," *American Journal of Psychiatry* 127 (October 1970):515-520.

Nelkin, Dorothy, *Methadone Maintenance: A Technological Fix* (New York: George Braziller, 1973).

Penterman, Donald G., "Vital Function Telemetry," in "Consolidated Systems of Emergency Services (Project 20/20)," Nebraska State Office of the Adjutant General (March 1971, NTIS PB 217 108).

Pincus, Steven B., et al., "A Study of Selected Innovative Hospital Programs in Ambulatory Care," Bio-Dynamics, Inc., Burlington, Massachusetts (May 1974, NTIS PB 233 921).

Russell, John R., "Addiction Control in New York City (B)," in *Cases in Urban Management* (Cambridge, Massachusetts: MIT Press, 1974), pp. 247-282.

Serway, Gay D., and Gustave J. Rath, "Computerized Project Cash Flow Statement to Plan Hospital Expansion," *Inquiry* IX (December 1972): 59-63.

Solow, Charles, et al., "24-Hour Psychiatric Consultation Via TV," *American Journal of Psychiatry* 127 (June 1971): 1684-1687.

Wallace, Keene M., "Computerized Dosimetry for Cancer Patients Now Available in South Carolina," *Journal of the South Carolina Medical Association* 67 (August 1971): 353-354.

Wittson, Cecil L., and Reba Benschoter, "Two-Way Television: Helping the Medical Center Reach Out," *American Journal of Psychiatry* 129 (November 1972): 624-627.

Education

Anselm, Karl R., "The Dynamics of a Major Technological Innovation in a Public Elementary School," Ed.D. dissertation, University of California, Berkeley (1969).

Artunian, Carol Ann, "Case Studies in Practical Career Guidance, Number 5: Computerized Vocational Information System, Willowbrook High School, Villa Park, Illinois," American Institutes for Research, Palo Alto, California (June 1973, ERIC ED 078 334).

Block, Karen K., et al., "A Computer Resource for the Elementary School: Progress Report, 1971-1972," Pennsylvania Learning Research and Development Center, Pittsburgh University (1972, ERIC ED 076 304).

Board of Education of the City School District of the City of Cincinnati [Ohio], "School Management and Evaluation System: Project Termination Report" (ERIC ED 084 718). (No date.)

Campbell, Vincent N., "The Televote System for Civic Communication," American Institutes for Research, Palo Alto, California (September 1974).

Cincinnati [Ohio] Board of Education, "Computer-Assisted Instruction for the Blind and Deaf" (October 1974).

Dunn, Alex, and Jean Wastler, "Computer-Assisted Instruction Project: Project REFLECT—Final Report," Board of Education of Montgomery County, Rockville, Maryland (1972, ERIC ED 066 876).

Easter, John, et al., "Comprehensive Achievement Monitoring in the Sequoia Union High School District," Educational Services Division, Sequoia Union High School District, Redwood City, California (December 1973, ERIC ED 087 472).

Gebolys, Suzette, "Evaluation Report: Planning for the Utilization of the Texas Telecomputer Grid in Elementary and Secondary Schools," Dallas Independent School District (1974).

Horry County Board of Education, Conway, South Carolina, "Improved Mathematics Curriculum Through Computer Time-Sharing—End of Project Report for Title III, ESEA" (June 1973, ERIC ED 085 263).

Lambright, W. Henry, and Albert H. Teich, "Silent Communication Alarm Network (SCAN)," in "Federal Laboratories and Technology Transfer," Syracuse University Research Corporation (March 1974), pp. 75-104.

McKinlay, Bruce, and Daniel Adams, "Evaluation on the Occupational Information Access System as Used at Churchill High School: A Project Report," Bureau of Governmental Research and Service, University of Oregon (October 1971, ERIC ED 084 435).

Milne, Bruce G., and Wilfred W. Richter, "Evaluation Report for Library Demonstration—Dial Access Retrieval System," Mitchell Independent School District #45, Mitchell, South Dakota (March 1973, ERIC ED 007 465).

"Oregon Total Information System, Title III, ESEA Evaluation," Oregon Total Information System, Eugene (May 1971 ERIC ED 088 416).

Palmer, Richard Phillips, "Brockton High School Automated Circulation System," in *Case Studies in Library Computer Systems* (New York: R.R. Bowker Company, 1973), pp. 6-12.

School District of the City of Lincoln [Nebraska], "Project ADMIRE: Assistance for Decision Making Through Information Retrieval in Education. End of Budget Period Report" (June 1970, ERIC ED 066 820).

Smith, Barry D., and Mildred F. Cooper, "Instructional Television Program: An Evaluation," Office of Planning, Research, and Evaluation, District of Columbia Schools (1974, ERIC ED 088 475).

Street, W. Paul, ed., "Computerized Instruction in Mathematics Versus Other Methods of Mathematics Instruction Under ESEA Title I Programs in Kentucky," Bureau of School Service, University of Kentucky (June 1972, ERIC ED 068 354).

Teague, Helen, *The Multi-Sensory Aids Demonstration Program in the Nashville, Tennessee Education Improvement Project, 1965-1969*, Ed.D. dissertation, Indiana University (Ann Arbor, Michigan: University Microfilms, 1969).

Utah State Board of Education, "Planning and Implementing an Integrated Media Program in Utah Public Schools," (Jordan School District) (February 1972, ERIC ED 070 298).

Utah State Board of Education, "Planning and Implementing an Integrated Media Program in Utah Public Schools," (Provo School District) (February 1972, ERIC ED 070 298).

WCET-TV, Cincinnati, Ohio, "Report of Television Multi-Channel System in Lincoln Heights Elementary School—Progress Report" (September 1973).

Public Works and Transportation

American Academy of Transportation, "Flint Transportation Authority Demonstration Project: Maxi-Cab Commuter Club," Ann Arbor, Michigan (May 1972, NTIS PB 220-903).

Bacalis, George, et al., "Ann Arbor Dial-a-Ride Pilot Project, Final Report," Ann Arbor Transportation Authority, Ann Arbor, Michigan (April 1973).

Bergmann, Dietrich R., "Issues in Urban Bus System Schedule Optimization," Bureau of Transportation of the State of Michigan (May 1972, NTIS PB 214 473).

Carcich, Italo G., et al., "A Pressure Sewer System Demonstration," New York State Department of Environmental Conservation (November 1972, NTIS PB 214 409).

DaVee, William, and Marc G. Stragier, "Mechanized, Non-Stop Residential Solid Waste Collection," Tolleson, Arizona (August 1973).

de Neufville, Richard, "Cost-Effectiveness Analysis of Civil Engineering Systems: New York City's Primary Water Supply," *Operations Research* 18 (September/October 1970):785-804.

Dewey, Michael and Betty Mikkelsen, "Grand Rapids Model Cities Dial-a-Ride: Summary Report on Design and Implementation, December 1972-August 1973," Ford Motor Company, Dearborn, Michigan (October 1973).

Fleischauer, Patricia D., "Godzilla and Friends: A Federally Funded Demonstration Project," unpublished manuscript, The Rand Corporation, Santa Monica (November 1974).

Goeller, Bruce, and Patricia Fleischauer, "The Haddonfield Dial-a-Ride Demonstration," unpublished manuscript, The Rand Corporation, Santa Monica (August 1975).

Gordon, Diana R., "The Science of Tunneling Through," in *City Limits* (New York: Charterhouse, 1973), pp. 167-207.

Gwynn, D.W., and Anthony U. Simpson, "Dial-a-Ride Demonstration in Haddonfield," in Highway Research Board, National Academy of Sciences, *Demand-Responsive Transportation Systems*, Washington, D.C., (1973), pp. 38-43.

Jones, Ralph K., and Kent B. Joscelyn, "Computerized Allocation of Police Traffic Services: A Demonstration Study," Indiana University, Bloomington (March 1972, NTIS PB 213 025).

LEX Systems, Inc., and DAVE Systems, Inc., "Implementation and Operation of a Demand Responsive Public Transportation System (Haddonfield Dial-a-Ride," State of New Jersey Department of Transportation (March 1974, NTIS UMTA-NJ-06-0002-74-3).

Malo, Alger F., et al., "An Innovative Pedestrian Crosswalk Safety Device Demonstration," City of Detroit Department of Streets and Traffic and the University of Michigan Highway Safety Research Institute (1971, NTIS PB 213 106).

Mechling, Jerry E., "A Successful Innovation: Manpower Scheduling," *Urban Analysis* 1974):259-313.

Notess, Charles B., and Robert E. Paaswell, "Demand Activated Transportation for the Elderly," *Transportation Engineering Journal* 98 (November 1972):807-821.

Pazour, John, "Nashville-ICMA Productivity Improvement Project—Project Report No. 1: Water Meter Maintenance and Repair," International City Management Association, Washington, D.C. (1974).

Pazour, John, "Nashville-ICMA Productivity Improvement Project—Project Report No. 2: Water Meter Reader Routing," International City Management Association, Washington, D.C. (1974).

Peat, Marwick, Mitchell and Company, "A Review of Some Anticipated and Observed Impacts of the Bay Area Rapid Transit System," Washington, D.C. (May 1974).

Penterman, Donald G., "One Country Road Equipment Test," in "Consolidated Systems of Emergency Services (Project 20/20)," Nebraska State Office of the Adjutant General (March 1971, NTIS PB 217 108).

Stragier, Marc G., "Mechanized Residential Solid Waste Collection," Department of Public Works, Scottsdale, Arizona (February 1973).

The Urban Institute and The International City Management Association, "Solid Waste Collection Case: One-Man Refuse Collection, Non-Mechanized, Inglewood, California," in "The Challenge of Productivity Diversity: Improving Local Government Productivity Measurement and Evaluation. Part IV: Procedures for Identifying and Evaluating Innovations—Six Case Studies," Washington, D.C. (June 1972), pp. 14-28.

The Urban Institute and The International City Management Association, "Solid Waste Collection Case: One-Man Refuse Collection Systems—The Barrel Snatcher and the Mechanical Bag Retriever, Bellaire, Texas," in "The Challenge of Productivity Diversity: Improving Local Government Productivity Measurement and Evaluation. Part IV: Procedures for Identifying and Evaluating Innovations—Six Case Studies," Washington, D.C. (June 1972), pp. 29-51.

The Urban Institute and The International City Management Association, "Solid Waste Collection Case: One-Man Refuse Collection Systems—The Barrel Snatcher and the Mechanical Bag Retriever, Scottsdale, Arizona," in "The Challenge of Productivity Diversity: Improving Local Government Productivity Measurement and Evaluation. Part IV: Procedures for Identifying and Evaluating Innovations—Six Case Studies," Washington, D.C. (June 1974), pp. 29-51.

Urbanik II, Thomas, "Dial-a-Ride Project in Ann Arbor: Description and Operation," in Highway Research Board, National Academy of Sciences, *Demand-Responsive Transportation Systems*, Washington, D.C. (1973), pp. 53-60.

Wright, Roger, et al., "The Impact of Street Lighting on Crime," The University of Michigan, Ann Arbor (May 1974).

Planning and Other

Altman, Stanley M., and Robert Nathans, "The University and Approaches to Problems of State and Local Governments," *Policy Sciences* 3 (September 1972):339-347.

Bretz, Rudy, "Two-Way TV Teleconferencing for Government: The MRC-TV System," The Rand Corporation, R-1489-MRC, Santa Monica (April 1974).

Brewer, Garry, "Pittsburgh," in *Politicians, Bureaucrats, and the Consultant* (New York: Basic Books, 1973), pp. 169-215.

Brewer, Garry, "San Francisco," in *Politicians, Bureaucrats, and the Consultant* (New York: Basic Books, 1973), pp. 114-168.

Brounstein, Sidney, et al., "Evaluation of USAC Project," Peat, Marwick, Mitchell and Company, Washington, D.C. (June 1973, NTIS PB 222 202).

Burkholz, Leonora, "City of New York Emergency Ambulance Service Demonstration Project," New York City Office of the Mayor (April 1970, NTIS PB 195 053).

Burt, Marvin, et al., "Analysis of Swimming Opportunities in the Model City Neighborhood," in "Factors Affecting the Impact of Urban Policy Analysis: Ten Case Histories," working paper, The Urban Institute, Washington, D.C. (July 1972), pp. 92-98.

Burt, Marvin, et al., "Emergency Ambulance Service Analysis," in "Factors Affecting the Impact of Urban Policy Analysis: Ten Case Histories," working paper, The Urban Institute, Washington, D.C. (July 1972), pp. 56-63.

Burt, Marvin, et al., "Mechanical Street Sweeping Analysis," in "Factors Affecting the Impact of Urban Policy Analysis: Ten Case Histories," working paper, The Urban Institute, Washington, D.C. (July 1972), pp. 73-84.

Burt, Marvin, et al., "On-Site Incineration Analysis," in "Factors Affecting the Impact of Urban Policy Analysis: Ten Case Histories," working paper, The Urban Institute, Washington, D.C. (July 1972), pp. 73-84.

Burt, Marvin, et al., "Solid Waste Collection and Disposal Analysis," in "Factors Affecting the Impact of Urban Policy Analysis: Ten Case Histories," working paper, The Urban Institute, Washington, D.C. (July 1972), pp. 85-91.

Burt, Marvin, et al., "Subemployment Analysis," in "Factors Affecting the Impact of Urban Policy Analysis: Ten Case Histories," working paper, The Urban Institute, Washington, D.C. (July 1972), pp. 99-110.

Burt, Marvin, et al., "Venereal Disease Control Program Analysis," in "Factors Affecting the Impact of Urban Policy Analysis: Ten Case Histories," working paper, The Urban Institute, Washington, D.C. (July 1972), pp. 111-118.

Ermer, Virginia B., "The Effect of Computerization on Housing Inspection," in "Street Level Bureaucrats and Urban Reform," paper presented at the 1972 Meeting of the American Political Science Association, Washington, D.C.

Habig, William C., "Model Cities Dial-a-Ride System in Columbus, Ohio," in Highway Research Board, National Academy of Sciences, *Demand-Responsive Transportation Systems*, Washington, D.C. (1973), pp. 27-30.

Hack, Gary, et al., "Improving City Streets for Use at Night: The Norfolk Experiment," Department of Urban Studies and Planning, Massachusetts Institute of Technology, Cambridge (June 1974).

International City Management Association, "Applying Systems Analysis in Urban Government: Three Case Studies," Washington, D.C. (March 1972), pp. 11-18.

International City Management Association, "Applying Systems Analysis in Urban Government: Three Case Studies," Washington, D.C. (March 1972), pp. 21-26.

Laudon, Kenneth C., "Total Efficiency in Western County," in *Computers and Bureaucratic Reform: The Political Functions of Urban Information Systems* (New York: John Wiley and Sons, 1974), pp. 101-173.

Medak, George M., "A Shared System: The Solution in Long Beach, California," *Bureaucrat* 1 (Winter 1972):331-338.

MIT Urban Dynamics Group, "Urban Dynamics in Lowell," Massachusetts Institute of Technology, Cambridge (September 1974).

O'Block, Robert P., "New Jersey Housing Finance Agency," in Richard S. Rosenbloom and John R. Russell, *New Tools for Urban Management* (Boston: Graduate School of Business Administration, Harvard University, 1971), pp. 109-153.

Pack, Janet R., "The Use of Urban Models in Urban Policy Making: Washington, D.C. Council of Governments and EMPIRIC Activity Allocation Model," Fels Center, University of Pennsylvania (January 1974).

Palmer, Richard Phillips, "Cleveland Public Library Automated Acquisition System," in *Case Studies in Library Computer Systems* (New York: R.R. Bowker Company, 1973), pp. 177-187.

Palmer, Richard Phillips, "San Francisco Public Library Automated Serials System," in *Case Studies in Library Computer Systems* (New York: R.R. Bowker Company, 1973), pp. 74-80.

Peat, Marwick, Mitchell and Company, "EMPIRIC Activity Allocation Model: Application to the Washington Metropolitan Region," Washington, D.C. (December 1972, NTIS PB 220 835).

Penterman, Donald G., "Computer Assisted Information Systems," in "Consolidated Systems of Emergency Services (Project 20/20)," Nebraska State Office of the Adjutant General (March 1971, NTIS PB 217 108).

Penterman, Donald G., "Notification," in "Consolidated Systems of Emergency Services (Project 20/20)," Nebraska State Office of the Adjutant General (March 1971, NTIS PB 217 108).

Russell, John R., "Background to the Dayton Analysis," in Richard S. Rosenbloom and John R. Russell, *New Tools for Urban Management* (Boston: Graduate School of Business Administration, Harvard University, 1971), pp. 29-60.

Russell, John R., "New York City Housing Authority Incinerator Air Pollution Abatement Project," in *Cases in Urban Management* (Cambridge, Massachusetts: MIT Press, 1974), pp. 459-493.

San Francisco Department of City Planning, "The San Francisco Community Simulation Model," in Ira M. Robinson, ed., *Decisionmaking in Urban Planning* (Beverly Hills: Sage, 1972), pp. 555-595.

Savas E.S., "A Computer-Based System for Forming Efficient Election Districts," *Operations Research* 19 (January/February 1971):135-155.

Savas, E.S., "The Political Properties of Crystalline H_2O: Planning for Snow Emergencies in New York," *Management Science* 20 (October 1973): 137-145.

Scientific Analysis Corporation, "California Steam Bus Project Final Report—Surveys," San Francisco (1973, NTIS PB 217 511).

Yedidia, Avram, et al., "Mobile Multiphasic Screening in an Industrial Setting," *Journal of Occupational Medicine* 11 (November 1969): 601-662.

Studies Not Meeting Criteria

Allen, W. Bruce, and Richard R. Mudge, "The Impact of Rapid Transit on Urban Development: The Case of the Philadelphia-Lindenwold High Speed Line," The New York City-Rand Institute, P-5246 (August 1974).

American Justice Institute, "CAPER: Crime Analysis—Project Evaluation—Research," San Jose, California (March 1972, NTIS PB 213 661).

Andrews, Janet T., and Byrdine Tuthill, "Computer-Based Management of Dietary Departments," *Hospitals* 42 (July 1968):117-123.

Annett, Hugh Hunter, *The Adaptability of the NASA Planning Process to Planning for Urban Systems: A Case Study of Planning for a Low and Moderate Income Housing Program in New Castle County, Delaware* (High Wycomb, England: University Microfilms Limited, 1972).

Applied Management Sciences, Inc., "San Jose's Municipal Solid Waste System: A Case Study," Silver Spring, Maryland (1973, NTIS PB 240 395).

Arnold, Arthur A., "Educational Automation: A Supplementary Center for Northeast Louisiana. End of Project Report," Concordia Parish School Board, Vidalia, Louisiana (February 1972, ERIC ED 078 870).

Arthur D. Little, Inc., "Evaluation of Computer-Based Patient Monitoring Systems," Cambridge, Massachusetts (March 1973).

Arthur D. Little, Inc., "A Review of the Patient Monitoring System at the University of Alabama Medical Center," Cambridge, Massachusetts (March 1973).

Atlanta [Georgia] Public Schools, "The MUST Project: Final Report" (1972, ERIC ED 075 977).

Ayers, William R., et al., "Description of an On-Line Information System for Pediatric Pulmonary Patients: Operational Experience in the Emergency Rooms of Three Hospitals," *American Review of Respiratory Disease* 105 (1972):914-918.

Bauer, Herbert J., "A Case Study of a Demand-Responsive Transportation System," Research Laboratories, General Motors Corporation, Warren, Michigan (September 10, 1970).

Benschoter, Reba Ann, "CCTV-Pioneering Nebraska Medical Center," *Educational Broadcasting* (October 1971).

Brennand, J.R., "Demonstration Plan for a Dynamically Routed Transit Feeder System," General Research Corporation, Report IMR-695, Santa Barbara (August 1967).

Brown, F.R., et al., "Automatic Vehicle Monitoring System," Cubic Corporation, San Diego (October 1972, NTIS PB 221 046).

Cadwell, G. Mason, "Intervention into a Turbulent Urban Situation: A Case Study," Drexel University, Philadelphia (June 1973).

Campbell, Gregory L., "A Spatially Distributed Queuing Model for Police Patrol Sector Design," Massachusetts Institute of Technology, Cambridge (June 1972, NTIS PB 226 133).

Chandler, Charles S., "Establishing an Operations Research Program in a State Vocational Rehabilitation Agency," South Carolina Vocational Rehabilitation Department, Columbia (March 1972).

Cobb, Charles W., "A Management Information System for Mental Health Planning and Program Evaluation: A Developing Model," *Community Mental Health Journal* 7 (1971):280-286.

DeMarco, James P., and Shirley A. Snavely, "Nurse Staffing with a Data Processing System," *American Journal of Nursing* 63 (October 1963):122-125.

Dunwell, Stephen, et al., "Report on WRITE: A Computer-Assisted Instruction Course in Written English Usage," Shared Educational Computer System, Inc., Poughkeepsie, New York (January 1972, ERIC ED 083 816).

Dyer, R. Scott, et al., "A Computerized Data Management System for a Regional Clinical Virology Laboratory," *Computers in Biology and Medicine* 4 (1974):223-227.

Farnam, William F., and Harry M. Frisby, "One-Man Operated Collection Vehicles," City of Inglewood, California. (No date.)

Fath, A. Frederick, et al., "Callboxes to Computers—A Computerized Emergency Dispatch System Specification for the Tacoma-Pierce County Law Enforcement Communications Center," Boeing Aerospace Company, Seattle (September 1973, NTIS PB 224 073).

Fox, Herbert, *Urban Technology: A Primer on Problems* (New York: Marcel Dekker, Inc., 1973).

"Geoplanning Research Program, Systems Analysis Task 1 Report," USAC-Des Moines Geoplanning Demonstration Project, Des Moines (November 1972, NTIS PB 223 187).

Goeller, Bruce F., et al., "San Diego Clean Air Project: Summary Report," The Rand Corporation, R-1362-SD, Santa Monica (December 1973).

Gordon, Theodore J. and The Futures Group, "The Electric Power Research Institute: A Potential Case Study in Institutional Innovation," working paper, Industrial Economics Division, Denver Research Institute, University of Denver, Denver (September 1973).

Greenes, R.A., et al., "Design and Implementaion of a Clinical Data Management System," *Computers and Biomedical Research* 2 (1969):469-485.

Hall, Keith A., and Harold E. Mitzel, "A Pilot Program of High School Computer-Assisted Instruction Mathematics Courses," *Journal of Educational Technology Systems* 2 (Winter 1974):157-175.

Hamilton, William F., and Samual Raymond, "A System of Computer-Generated Laboratory Reports for Clinical Use," *Computers in Biology and Medicine* 3 (1973):141-151.

Hausner, Jack, and Warren Walker, "An Analysis of the Deployment of Fire-Fighting Resources in Trenton, New Jersey," The New York City-Rand Institute, R-1566/1-TRNTN (February 1975).

Hausner, Jack, et al., "An Analysis of the Deployment of Fire-Fighting Resources in Yonkers, New York," The New York City-Rand Institute, R-1566/2-HUD/CY (October 1974).

Hendrick, Thomas, E., et al., "Policy Analysis for Urban Fire Stations: How Many and Where," The Denver Urban Observatory, Denver (November 1974, NTIS PB 239 711).

Hicks, G. Phillip, et al., "Routine Use of a Small Digital Computer in the Clinical Laboratory," *Journal of the American Medical Association* 196 (June 1966):155-160.

Huntington Beach, California Police Department, "Automated Traffic Records System: Phase 2, Message Switching," Huntington Beach, California (1972, NTIS PB 225 392/0).

The Institute of Criminal Justice and Criminology, University of Maryland, "Criminal Justice Monograph: Innovation in Law Enforcement," U.S. Department of Justice, Law Enforcement Assistance Administration, National Institute of Law Enforcement and Criminal Justice, Washington, D.C. (June 1973).

"Integrated Municipal Information System Project, Charlotte, North Carolina: Task 2 Summary Report," City of Charlotte, North Carolina, USAC Project (June 1973, NTIS PB 223 415).

"Integrated Municipal Information System Project, Dayton, Ohio: Purchasing Component, Volume 5," City of Dayton, Ohio, USAC Project (July 1, 1973, NTIS PB 223 561).

Kohn, Sherwood D., "Experiment in Planning an Urban High School: The Baltimore Charette," Educational Facilities Laboratories, New York (November 1969).

Kolesar, Peter, and Warren E. Walker, "A Simulation Model of Police Patrol Operations: Program Description," The New York City-Rand Institute, R-1625/2-HUD/NYC (February 1975).

Koltnow, Peter, "Successful Cities: Six Case Studies in Transportation Progress," Highway Users Federation for Safety and Mobility, Washington, D.C. (1971).

Kravetz, Nathan, "The Intermediate School with Windows," *Urban Review* 2 (June 1967):3-5.

"Laboratory Data Handling System Is Automatic," *Hospital Management* (June 1965):84-88.

Lambright, W. Henry, "Government and Technological Innovation: Weather Modification as a Case in Point," *Public Administration Review* (January/ February 1972):1-10.

LeMenager, Charles, et al., "Low Cost Housing—Demonstration Project," California Department of Housing and Community Development, Sacramento (June 1970, NTIS PB 194 757).

Lukoff, Irving, et al., "Heroin Use and Crime in a Methadone Maintenance Program," Vera Institute of Justice, New York (February 1973, NTIS PB 219 650).

Mathis, Ronnie R., "An Evaluation of the Effectiveness of the 4-H TV Science Project in Jackson County," College of Agriculture, University of Georgia, Athens (1971, ERIC ED 067 553).

McGown, Helyn L., and Gerald W. Faust, "Computer-Assisted Instruction in Physical Therapy: A Pilot Program," *Physical Therapy* 951 (October 1971):1113-1120.

McLaren, Alan, "A Computerized Information System," *Hospitals* 46 (August 1972):103-106.

Montgomery County Sanitary Department [Dayton, Ohio], "Ground Water Infiltration and Internal Sealing of Sanitary Sewers, Montgomery County, Ohio," Washington, D.C. (June 1972).

National Governors' Conference, "Innovations in State Government," Washington, D.C. (June 1974).

Nilsson, Ernst K., et al., "Applications of Systems Analysis to the Operation of a Fire Department," U.S. Department of Commerce, National Bureau of Standards, Washington, D.C. (June 1974).

Parsons Brinkerhoff-Tudor-Bechtel, "San Francisco Bay Area Rapid Transit District Demonstration Project," San Francisco (January 1970, NTIS PB 189 333).

Parsons Brinkerhoff-Tudor-Bechtel, "San Francisco Bay Area Rapid Transit District Demonstration Project, Technical Report Number II—Automatic Fare Collection, Supplementary Report," San Francisco (June 1973, NTIS PB 226 131).

Pearlman, Richard L., et al., "An Acute Treatment Unit in a Psychiatric Emergency Service," *Hospital and Community Psychiatry* 25 (July 1973):489-491.

Price, Charlton R., et al., "Fifteen-Oh-One to Sixteen-Thirty Technical and Managerial Lessons from One Experience in Introducing New Technology to Improve Urban Mass Transportation," Social Engineering Technology, Los Angeles (November 1972, NTIS PB 213 448).

Resnik, Henry S., "The Shedd Revolution—A Philadelphia Story," *Urban Review* 3 (January 1969):20-25.

Robinson, Nicholas Wheeler, "Marland's 'Magnificent Gamble'—Pittsburgh's Great High School," *Urban Review* 3 (September 1968).

Roehring, Darryl R., et al., "Studies in Remote Sensing Applications—Barriers to Innovation: The Example of Remote Sensing in Urban and Regional Planning in the Los Angeles Metropolis. Interfacing Remote Sensing and Automated Geographic Information Systems," Department of Geography, University of California, Riverside (September 1972, NTIS AD 752 058).

Roos, David E., et al., "Educational Television in New York State: Program Audit 3.1.73," New York State Legislative Commission on Expenditure Review, Albany (July 1973, ERIC ED 084 832).

Roos, David E., et al., "Dial-A-Ride: Urban Mass Transportation Demonstration Project," Urban Systems Laboratory, Massachusetts Institute of Technology, Cambridge (August 1971, NTIS PB 206 367).

Russell, John R., "Analysis of an Estuary," in *Cases in Management* (Cambridge, Massachusetts: The MIT Press, 1974), pp. 35-76.

"Scottsdale Innovations—New and Better Ways," City of Scottsdale, Arizona. (No date.)

Shuman, Larry J., et al., "The Location of a Network of Ambulatory Health Care Centers (PPGP/HMO) Within a Metropolitan Area," Research Department, Blue Cross of Western Pennsylvania (October 1972).

Singleton, Harvey R., "The Tacoma Project/Cost/Benefit Summary," Tacoma, Washington (January 1973).

Slack, Warner V., and Charles W. Slack, "Seminars in Medicine of the Beth Israel Hospital, Boston: Patient-Computer Dialogue," *New England Journal of Medicine* 286 (June 15, 1972):1304-1309.

Thomas, Dean and Hoskins, Inc., *Comprehensive Study of Solid Waste Disposal in Cascade County, Montana* (U.S. Department of Health, Education, and Welfare, Public Health Service, Environmental Health Service, Bureau of Solid Waste Management, Washington, D.C. (1970).

Urban Systems Laboratory, Massachusetts Institute of Technology, "CARS (Computer Aided Routing System)—A Prototype Dial-A-Bus System," Cambridge (September 1969, NTIS PB 187 647).

Van Brunt, Edmund E., "The Kaiser-Permanente Medical Information System," *Computers and Biomedical Research* 3 (1970):477-487.

Alan M. Voorhees and Associates, Inc., "National City Accident Data Retrieval and Analysis System," Los Angeles, AMV-R-61-1110 (July 1970).

Walker, Warren, et al., "Development and Use of a Fixed Charge Programming Model for Regional Solid Waste Planning," The New York City-Rand Institute, P-5307 (October 1974).

Watts, Frederick G., and Charles R. Work, "Developing an Automated Information System for the Prosecutor," *American Criminal Law Quarterly* 9 (Fall 1970):164-169.

Weiner, Myron E., et al., "A Municipal Information System for Connecticut Local Governments," Institute of Public Service, Storrs, Connecticut, and The Travelers Research Corporation, Hartford, Connecticut (1970).

"Wichita Falls Integrated Municipal Information System: Technical Guidelines," City of Wichita Falls, Texas, USAC Project (July 1973, NTIS PB 223 150).

Widoe, Russ, "ITV In-Service to Assist Music Educators Facing Curtailed Schedules," Cooperative Educational Service Agency Number 9, Green Bay, Wisconsin (August 1974).

Winters, Bruce H., and Luis Hernandez, "A Computerized Drug Inventory Control System," *American Journal of Hospital Pharmacy* 29 (September 1972):781-785.

Wittson, Cecil L., "Nebraska Initiates Cross-Country TV-Psychiatry," *Educational Screen and Audiovisual Guide* (November 1965):22-24.

Wittson, Cecil L., et al., "Two-Way Television in Group Therapy," *Mental Hospitals* (November 1961):22-23.

Multisite Cases (not all technological; see Appendix F for summaries)

Baldridge, J. Victor, "Organizational Innovation: Individual, Structural, and Environmental Impacts," in J. Victor Baldridge and Terrence E. Deal, eds., *Managing Change in Educational Organizations* (Berkeley: McCutchan, 1975), pp. 151-175.

Cohen, Elizabeth G., and Eric R. Bredo, "Elementary School Organization and Innovative Instructional Practices," in J. Victor Baldridge and Terrence E. Deal, eds., *Managing Change in Educational Organizations* (Berkeley: McCutchan, 1975), pp. 133-149.

Corwin, Ronald G., "Innovation in Organizations: The Case of Schools," *Sociology of Education* 48 (1975):1-37.

Corwin, Ronald G., "Strategies for Organizational Innovation: An Empirical Comparison," *American Sociological Review* 37 (August 1972):441-454.

Cushen, W. Edward, "Afterthoughts on Four Urban Systems Studies Performed with Small Cities," in Alvin W. Drake et al., eds., *Analysis of Public Systems* (Cambridge, Massachusetts: MIT Press, 1972), pp. 45-63.

Deal, Terrence, E., et al., "Organizational Influences on Educational Innovation," in J. Victor Baldridge and Terrence E. Deal, eds., *Managing Change in Educational Organizations* (Berkeley: McCutchan, 1975), pp. 109-131.

Feller, Irvin, et al., "Diffusion of Technology in State Mission-Oriented Agencies," Institute for Research on Human Resources, Center for the Study of Science Policy, Pennsylvania State University, University Park (October 1974).

Frohman, Alan, et al., "Factors Affecting Innovation in the Fire Services," Pugh-Roberts Associates, Inc., Cambridge, Massachusetts (March 1972).

Hage, Jerald, and Michael Aiken, "Program Change and Organizational Properties," *American Journal of Sociology* 72 (March 1967):503-518.

Heydebrand, Wolf V., and James J. Noell, "Task Structure and Innovation in Professional Organizations," in Wolf V. Heydebrand, ed., *Comparative Organizations* (Englewood Cliffs, New Jersey: Prentice-Hall, 1973), pp. 294-322.

Hodgson, David A., et al., "The Uniform Hospital Discharge Data Demonstration, Summary Report " U.S. Department of Health, Education, and

Welfare, Public Health Service, Health Resources Administration, Washington, D.C. (July 1973).

Kaluzny, Arnold D., et al., "Diffusion of Innovative Health Care Services in the United States: A Study of Hospitals," *Medical Care* VII (November-December 1970):474-487.

Liebert, Roland J., " 'The Electric Company,' In-School Utilization Study. Volume 2: The 1972-73 School and Teacher Surveys and Trends Since Fall 1971," Institute for Social Research, Florida State University, Tallahassee (October 1973).

Mohr, Lawrence B., "Determinants of Innovation in Organizations," *American Political Science Review* 63 (March 1969):111-126.

Mytinger, Robert E., *Innovation in Local Health Services . . .* U.S. Department of Health, Education, and Welfare, Public Health Service, Division of Medical Care Administration, Arlington, Virginia (1968).

Public Technology, Inc., "Integrated Municipal Information Systems: Program and Projects of the United States of American Urban Information Systems Inter-Agency Committee," prepared for the Office of Policy Development and Research, Department of Housing and Urban Development (January 1975).

Rosner, Martin M., "Economic Determinants of Organizational Innovation," *Administrative Science Quarterly* 12 (March 1968):614-625.

Appendix C:
Checklist

Name of Analyst _____

Date _____

Author of Case _____

Number of Case _____

	Percent Distribution	Percent "Sure" Responses[a]

A. Nature of the Case Study

A-1. The study appears as:

		97.9
(1) A journal article	20.7	
(2) A book	10.0	
(3) Neither, but a final report (regardless of the state of the innovative effort)	48.6	
(4) Neither, but an interim report or working draft	10.7	
(8) Other (specify) _____	10.0	

A-2. The date of the study was:

		98.6
(1) 1973-1975	46.4	
(2) 1971-1972	42.9	
(3) 1969-1970	5.7	
(4) 1968 or earlier	5.0	
(9) · Impossible to answer	5.0	

A-3. The main source of funds for the study was:

		74.8
(1) A federal agency	63.6	
(2) A state or local agency	10.7	
(3) A private source (e.g., foundations)	10.7	
(4) A university	5.0	
(5) Self-support	0.7	
(9) Impossible to answer	9.3	

[a]Percent based on substantive responses only; i.e., impossible-to-answer responses were not considered in the numerator or denominator. Since the impossible-to-answer responses were usually also sure responses, their inclusion would have inflated the percentages.

A-4. The first author of the study is employed by: 80.3

   (1) An academic institution only   26.4
   (2) A state, county, or local government agency   28.6
   (3) A professional association   1.4
   (4) A research organization   32.9
   (5) The federal government   8.6
   (8) Other (specify) _____   2.1
   (9) Impossible to answer

A-5. The innovation being described mainly involves: 94.3

   (1) A new machine or other artifact   35.7
   (2) A new material or chemical   2.9
   (3) A new computer package or system   32.9
   (4) An analysis, using symbolic operations   22.1
   (5) An analysis, using quantitative data but no operations   6.4
   (6) None of the above

A-6. In relation to the innovative effort, the author is: 69.3

   (1) Part of a formal evaluation research project only   24.3
   (2) An observer or reporter about the effort   27.9
   (3) An analyst involved in planning or implementing the effort   32.9
   (4) Any other participant involved in the effort   14.3
   (8) Other (specify) _____   0.7
   (9) Impossible to answer

A-7. The study contains an operational description of: 85.0

  (1) The characteristics of the innovation (e.g., an algorithm, engineering specifications, hardware identification)   10.7

  (2) The performance of the innovation (e.g., a test run, survey results, output measures)   15.0

  (3) Both   67.1

  (4) Neither   7.1

A-8. In terms of the conclusions to be drawn from the innovative effort, the study: 87.9

  (1) Has some relevant research methods or design   40.7

  (2) Not (1), but tries to develop a line of argument that accounts for what happened   27.9

  (3) Not (1) or (2), but covers coherently what happened   24.3

  (4) Is a poorly organized report that suits none of the above   7.1

B. *External Factors*

	Percent Distribution	*Percent "Sure" Responses*
B-1. Among the preexisting conditions at the innovative site, the case study mentions the need to:		89.3
(1) Meet service demands (e.g., rising crime rates)	26.4	
(2) Reduce costs of services	7.9	
(3) Both	14.3	
(4) Respond to any condition besides demands or costs	29.3	
(5) No mention of the above	22.1	
(9) Impossible to answer		

B-2. The case study involved an agency in: 96.4

   (1) Criminal justice (excludes traffic police)   10.7
   (2) Health   22.1
   (3) Education   16.4
   (4) Transportation, traffic, or highways   9.3
   (5) Public works or sanitation   9.3
   (6) Fire   7.9
   (7) Planning, executive staff, or coordination   15.0
   (8) Other (specify) _____   9.3
   (9) Impossible to answer

B-3. In relation to the innovative effort or its setting, there was: 84.8

   (1) A professional association   21.4
   (2) A law or regulation requiring any new action   5.7
   (3) Both   2.1
   (4) Neither   69.3
   (9) Impossible to answer   1.4

B-4. The case study mentions other innovations, whether or not related to the one under study, having occurred in:

	Yes	No	Impossible to Answer	
(a) The same agency	30.7	67.9	1.4	87.8
(b) Other agencies in the same jurisdiction	12.9	86.4	0.7	88.5
(c) Other jurisdictions	51.4	47.9	0.7	87.8

B-5. The innovative effort was mainly supported with new funds from:

(1)	No new funds	10.7
(2)	A federal agency	56.4
(3)	A state or county agency	11.4
(4)	A municipal agency	9.3
(5)	Private sources	7.1
(9)	Impossible to answer	5.0

72.2

B-6. The estimated amount of these funds was:

(1)	No new funds	10.0
(2)	Less than $50,000	10.0
(3)	$50,000–$250,000	14.3
(4)	Over $250,000	22.1
(9)	Impossible to answer	43.9

59.5

B-7. The innovative effort involved the following client or citizen participation:

(1)	A hearing, survey, vote, appeal, or other participatory process before testing or implementation	17.1
(2)	Same, but only after testing or implementation	11.4
(3)	No process, but an organized clients' or citizens' group mentioned	4.3
(4)	No process, but some client or citizen mentioned	26.4
(5)	No client or citizen participation	39.3
(9)	Impossible to answer	1.4

90.6

B-8. The case study mentions the following type of public information about the innovation:

		Yes	No	Impossible to Answer
(a)	A story in the mass media	29.3	65.7	5.0
(b)	A pamphlet, public report, or educational campaign	28.6	67.1	4.3
(c)	Other (specify) _____	18.6	78.6	2.8

C. Agency Characteristics (Prior to the Innovative Effort)

C-1. The agency in which the innovation took place:

	Yes	No	Impossible to Answer	Percent "Sure" Responses
(a) Was created in the last five years	5.7	84.3	10.0	71.4
(b) Had or supported a formal R&D or analysis group	33.6	31.4	35.0	46.2
(c) Had other grants or contracts from outside sources	20.0	19.3	60.7	54.5
(d) Served: _____ (locale and state, or write "unnamed")				

C-2. The agency consisted of the following number of employees:

(1) 0-50	4.3			38.8
(2) 51-100	2.9			
(3) 101-500	10.0			
(4) More than 500	17.9			
(9) Impossible to answer	65.0			

C-3. Among the agency's characteristics, the case study mentions:

	Yes	No	Impossible to Answer	Percent "Sure" Responses
(a) Ad hoc working groups, task forces, or committees	22.1	69.3	8.6	85.2
(b) Unions or benevolent associations	12.1	77.1	10.7	91.4
(c) Use of client-type paraprofessionals or a client-liaison unit	10.0	82.1	7.9	87.6
(d) Travel or meetings outside the jurisdiction	11.4	80.0	8.6	89.1

C-4. The case study mentions the following number of fixed *organizational units* in the agency:

(1) None (the study indicates none exist)   5.7
(2) One   10.7
(3) Two   8.6
(4) More than two   37.9
(9) Impossible to answer   37.1

89.8

C-5. The case study mentions the following layers of line (supervisory) relationship, either between units or individuals:

(1) None (the study indicates none exist)   5.0
(2) One (e.g., a supervisor and his/her employee)   17.1
(3) Two (e.g., the supervisor's superior in addition to above)   14.3
(4) More than two   23.6
(9) Impossible to answer   40.0

86.9

C-6. The case study mentions employee morale, job satisfaction, or turnover in:

(1) A positive sense   5.7
(2) A negative sense   14.3
(3) Both   3.6
(4) A neutral sense   12.1
(9) Impossible to answer   64.3

78.0

C-7. The case study mentions the following characteristics of the agency's employees:

	Yes	No	Impossible to Answer	
(a) More than one specialty or profession as routinely belonging to the agency	55.7	30.7	13.6	80.0
(b) Civil service status	5.7	75.7	18.6	81.7
(c) Participation by service providers in any agency decisionmaking process	8.6	70.0	21.4	86.4

	Percent Distribution	Percent "Sure" Responses

D. Nature of Innovation (The Device)

D-1. The innovative device was (a direct quote is preferred, and should be indicated with quotation marks): — 71.9

D-2. The case study makes a reference or citation to some form of the innovation having previously been:

	Percent Distribution	Percent "Sure" Responses
(1) Tested in some artificial environment only	7.1	
(2) Attempted at the present site	9.3	
(3) Attempted at another locale	14.3	
(4) Attempted at more than one locale	29.3	
(5) Not tested or attempted	26.4	
(9) Impossible to answer	13.6	

D-3. The idea for the innovation came to the agency from: — 57.9

	Percent Distribution	Percent "Sure" Responses
(1) Inside the agency	34.3	
(2) A university	7.1	
(3) A research organization or consultant	11.4	
(4) Some other commercial or private source	2.1	
(5) Some other government agency (federal or local)	21.4	
(9) Impossible to answer	23.6	

D-4. Prior to the innovative effort, the innovation's merit had been demonstrated by:

	Yes	No	Impossible to Answer	
(a) Its continued use in some form at another locale	29.3	46.4	24.3	52.8
(b) Comparison to any existing practice, and an advantage over it	41.4	36.4	22.1	55.0
(c) Support or endorsement by some person or group	29.3	40.7	30.0	51.0
(d) Some other means of establishing merit	10.0	58.6	31.4	56.3
(e) Some test or experience showing the innovation had negative or inconclusive results	5.7	66.4	27.9	71.3

D-5. The primary stated goal of the innovation was:

(1) An actual reduction in existing expenditures	4.3	92.8
(2) A reduction in projected rising expenditures	2.1	
(3) Increased information about a problem or its alternative solutions	25.0	
(4) Service improvements or additions (e.g., improved c/b ratio, a new service, increased efficiency, or more coverage)	64.3	
(5) Other (specify) _____	2.9	
(9) Impossible to answer	1.4	

D-6. The innovation's primary intended effect was to create:

(1) Changes in administrative procedures only	42.9	82.0
(2) Changes in client use or awareness of services, but no new practices in relation to service providers	12.9	
(3) New practices between clients and providers	43.6	
(9) Impossible to answer	0.7	

D-7. Any observable changes resulting from the innovation were expected to be or were:

(1) Apparent within a year of its initial use	80.0	77.3
(2) Uncertain for at least a year	11.4	
(9) Impossible to answer	8.6	

D-8. The observable changes could potentially occur:

(1) Once only	6.4	80.3
(2) More than once, whether regularly or not	91.4	
(9) Impossible to answer	2.1	

D-9. The case study mentions that the innovation could be or was treated by using:

(1) A subset of its components	10.7	63.6
(2) A restricted portion of the eventual population to be served	45.0	
(3) Both	26.4	
(4) Could not be implemented gradually or at limited capacity	10.0	
(9) Impossible to answer	7.9	

D-10. The innovation, its effects, or its activities or actions involved:

(1) An unnamed concrete apparatus, material, action (but *not* computer output)	36.4	86.4
(2) A proper name, but no concrete apparatus, material, or action	7.1	
(3) Both	45.7	
(4) Neither	10.7	
(9) Impossible to answer		

D-11. The case study mentions that the initial use or testing of the innovation involved:

	Yes	No	Impossible to Answer	
(a) Changes in job routines of one category of jobs only	21.4	60.7	17.9	75.2
(b) Changes in routines in two or more categories	47.1	38.6	14.2	70.8
(c) The hiring of new, nonprofessional personnel	18.6	65.0	16.4	78.7
(d) The hiring of new professional or managerial personnel	31.4	52.9	15.7	79.7
(e) Termination of any jobs or personnel	7.9	75.7	16.5	83.6

D-12. Initial use or testing of the innovation was stated to involve:

(1) No changes in existing procedures or practices	10.7	74.2
(2) Some adjustments, possibly reversible	53.6	
(3) Substantial irreversible changes (e.g., employee firing, or new facilities)	30.0	
(9) Impossible to answer	5.7	

D-13. Full use of the innovation could potentially affect:

(1) An agency staff office	8.6	71.4
(2) A line unit of the agency or people throughout the agency	55.0	
(3) Some small group of people within the agency	31.4	
(9) Impossible to answer	5.0	

D-14. Federal resources are mentioned, at any site (including the present one) in relation to:

	Yes	No	Impossible to Answer	Percent "Sure" Responses
(a) The early R&D of the innovation	25.7	72.9	1.4	92.8
(b) Testing in some artificial environment	9.3	88.6	2.1	92.7
(c) Conferences, clearinghouses, or other information-disseminating activities	15.0	82.1	2.9	91.9
(d) Implementation at some locale	60.7	38.6	0.7	87.1
(e) Technical assistance or consultation	28.6	69.3	2.1	94.9
(f) Training of local personnel	26.4	71.4	2.1	92.0
(g) Work by a research organization or university	41.4	57.1	1.4	87.0
(h) Evaluation	50.0	48.6	1.4	92.1
(i) Other (specify) _____	5.7	92.9	1.4	99.3

E. Innovator and Implementation Characteristics

E-1. The case study mentions (individually or generically and including the author's role):

	Percent Distribution		Percent "Sure" Responses
	Yes	No	
(a) The chief executive of the jurisdiction	36.4	63.6	97.1
(b) The head of the agency	52.9	47.1	96.4
(c) Any other manager or decisionmaker in the agency	64.3	35.7	93.6
(d) Any person in a staff, not line position in the agency	74.3	25.7	91.4
(e) Any service provider in the agency	78.6	21.4	97.1
(f) A member of a union	15.7	84.3	95.7
(g) A member of the federal government	32.9	67.1	97.1
(h) A member of a university	43.6	56.4	97.1
(i) A member of an industry	47.1	52.9	96.4
(j) A consultant	53.6	46.4	96.4
(k) Any other elected or public official outside the agency	49.3	50.7	93.5
(l) A client or group of clients	82.1	17.9	97.9

Use the above list, together with the following alternatives to answer the following *five* questions (E-2-E-6):

    (99) Impossible to answer
    (98) Two or more of the above categories (within the agency)
    (97) Two or more of the above categories (outside the agency)
    (96) Two or more of the above categories (inside and outside the agency)
    (95) Other (specify) _____
    (94) None of the above

E-2. The party (*The Innovator*) who first proposed the innovation to the agency was:

_____

E-3. The party in the agency (*The Implementer*) who decided to implement or operate the innovation was:

_____

E-4. The party most identified with the advocacy or support of the innovation was:

_____

E-5. The party most identified as skeptical or opposed to the innovation was:

_____

E-6. The party (*The Operator*) responsible for operating[b] the innovation was:

E-7. The *Innovator* (see E-2) had the following *background characteristics*:

	Yes	No	Impossible to Answer	
(a) An educational degree higher than that of service providers	30.0	6.4	63.6	19.6
(b) Professional meetings, membership, or contacts outside the agency	47.1	0.7	52.1	47.8
(c) Experience at more than one position in the agency	6.4	30.7	62.9	65.4
(d) Simultaneous employment inside and outside the agency	11.4	34.3	54.3	65.6
(e) Over five years employment in the same service area	12.9	13.6	73.6	40.5
(f) An acknowledged role as a veteran in the service area	13.6	14.3	72.1	48.7
(g) Previous work experience at another locale	12.9	12.9	74.3	41.7

E-8. The *Innovator* (see E-2) had the following characteristics in relation to the innovation:

	Yes	No	Impossible to Answer	
(a) Direct access to slack resources (e.g., a grant or agency staff time)	46.4	3.6	50.0	68.6
(b) A report or product associated with his/her name	23.6	16.4	60.0	64.3
(c) Was a single individual, not a group	23.6	33.6	42.9	83.8
(d) A decisionmaking role in the agency	27.1	25.0	47.9	82.2
(e) Contact with clients	30.0	10.0	60.0	75.0
(f) Contact with officials outside the agency	47.9		52.1	69.8
(g) An acknowledged role as an opinion leader in support of the innovation	32.1	5.7	62.1	50.9

---

[b]The user of new equipment or material, the consumer of a research analysis or computer routine.

E-9. The definition of the client in this checklist is: 97.8

    (1) A citizen, with no agency affiliation   82.1
    (2) A member of an agency   14.3
    (3) Other (specify) _____   3.6
    (9) Impossible to answer

E-10. The *Operator* (see E-6) was *first* mentioned along with (or noted as   94.1
     participating during):

    (1) Planning of the innovation (before its initial use)   47.1
    (2) Testing or implementation   41.4
    (3) Evaluation of the innovation   2.1
    (4) The final summary or recommendations
    (5) Not mentioned at all   5.7
    (9) Impossible to answer   3.6

E-11. The *Operator* (see E-6) had the following training about the   61.4
     innovation:

    (1) A formal training session or conference   23.6
    (2) A practice or trial period   11.4
    (3) A written set of procedures (pamphlets or manuals)   7.1
    (4) Oral communications only   7.9
    (5) None of the above   9.3
    (9) Impossible to answer   40.7

E-12. The *Implementer* (see E-3) was *last* mentioned along with (or noted as participating during):

                                                    87.1

(1) Planning of the innovation (before its initial use)   12.1
(2) Testing or implementation   12.9
(3) Evaluation of the innovation   13.6
(4) The final summary or recommendations   20.0
(5) Not mentioned at all   30.7
(9) Impossible to answer   10.7

E-13. The case study mentions the following parties as playing

(1) Supportive
(2) Neutral
(3) Negative
(4) Not mentioned at all
(9) Impossible to answer

roles in relation to the innovation:

	(1)	(2)	(3)	(4)	(9)	
(a) The chief executive of the jurisdiction	30.9	4.3	0.7	63.3	0.7	95.7
(b) The budget bureau	14.3	2.9		80.7	2.1	95.6
(c) The local legislative body	14.3	10.7	2.9	71.4	0.7	92.1
(d) A union or benevolent association	3.6	5.7	6.4	83.6	0.7	97.8
(e) The head of the innovating agency	42.9	5.7	2.1	47.9	1.4	90.6
(f) Citizens or clients	35.0	29.3	10.0	18.6	7.1	86.8

E-14. The innovation was introduced into the agency as:

                                                    66.7

(1) Part of a broader external plan or regulation that the agency had
    to follow   7.1
(2) Part of a broader agency plan   27.1
(3) Not part of any broader plan   64.3
(9) Impossible to answer   1.4

E-15. Introduction of the innovation required:

(1) Creation of a new service provider unit or special project	25.0
(2) Integration into an existing service provider-unit	46.4
(3) Both	10.7
(4) No organizational change	12.9
(9) Impossible to answer	5.0

82.7

E-16. The case study indicates that in the innovative effort the innovation had:

(1) Undergone no changes	20.7
(2) Undergone at least one minor modification	57.9
(3) Been rejected and replaced by some other innovation	2.1
(9) Impossible to answer	19.3

73.5

E-17. During the innovative effort, the study mentions:

	Yes	No	Impossible to Answer
(a) Unexpected events resulting in a hastening of procedures	3.6	90.0	6.4
(b) Unexpected delay within the agency	15.7	77.9	6.4
(c) Unexpected external events, creating some delay	27.9	66.4	5.7
(d) New resistance to the innovation within the agency	14.3	77.9	7.8
(e) New resistance outside of the agency	11.4	82.1	6.4

93.2
88.0
87.9
89.4
87.1

	Percent Distribution	Percent "Sure" Responses

F. Outcomes

F-1. By the end of the case study, the innovation had been:

	Percent Distribution	Percent "Sure" Responses
(1) Operational, and appeared fully incorporated	42.9	80.9
(2) Operational, but with some doubt about its extent, form, or permanence (e.g., still identified as a special project or supported with special funds)	37.1	
(3) Discontinued (according to plan), following a period of operation or testing	7.1	
(4) Discontinued (but not according to plan) following a period of operation or testing	10.0	
(5) Not operated or tested	2.9	
(9) Impossible to answer		

F-2. If the innovation did not appear fully incorporated,[c] this was mainly because of:

	Percent Distribution	Percent "Sure" Responses
(1) A lack of funds	7.9	84.1
(2) Resistance to the innovation by some individuals	5.7	
(3) A lack of a significant benefit from the innovation	12.1	
(4) Other (specify) _____	29.3	
(5) Question not applicable	43.6	
(9) Impossible to answer	1.4	

[c]Answer F-2 if F-1 was answered with any alternative (2) through (9).

94.3

F-3. If the innovation was not now operational,[d] the case study reports the following next steps:

(1) Contact with a decisionmaker, but no plan or recommendation to implement   4.3

(2) A plan or recommendation, but no contact   6.4

(3) Both contact and a plan   9.3

(4) No next steps

(5) Question not applicable   80.0

(9) Impossible to answer

F-4. If the innovation had been operational,[e] the case study mainly uses the following type of evidence

(1) Author's report only

(2) Agency or informal records (e.g., logs, service data)

(3) Interview or survey results

(4) Question applicable, but no evidence

(5) Question not applicable

about:[f]

	(1)	(2)	(3)	(4)	(5)
(a) Service changes	43.6	37.9	14.3	2.9	1.4
(b) Provider use or attitudes	62.1	3.6	23.6	5.7	5.0
(c) Client use or attitudes	25.0	3.6	22.9	25.0	23.6
(d) Organizational changes in the agency	63.6	2.9	7.1	13.6	12.9

---

[d]Answer F-3 if F-1 was answered with any alternative (3) through (9).

[e]Answer F-4 if F-1 was answered with any alternative (1) through (4).

[f]Parts (a)-(d) refer to the evidence used in F-5, F-7, F-8, and F-1.

F-5. The use of the innovation resulted in the following service changes:[g]

(1) Some improvement	55.7	84.6
(2) Some decline	5.0	
(3) Both	7.1	
(4) Evidence showing no change	10.7	
(5) Question not applicable	1.4	
(6) Information only	17.1	
(9) Impossible to answer	2.9	

F-6. The main service change is described as (a direct quote is preferred, indicating the commodity and amount of service change):

F-7. The case study provides evidence that personnel in the innovating agency:

	Yes	No	Impossible to Answer	
(a) Used the innovation	85.7	3.6	10.7	93.2
(b) Were pleased with the innovation	60.0	12.1	27.9	80.6
(c) Failed to use the innovation	12.9	53.6	33.6	76.0
(d) Objected to the innovation	25.0	42.1	32.9	78.2

F-8. The case study provides evidence that clients showed:

(1) Increased use of the service	12.9	89.1
(2) Verbal satisfaction with the service	13.6	
(3) Both	15.0	
(4) Neither or a negative change	7.9	
(5) Question not applicable	23.6	
(9) Impossible to answer	27.1	

[g]Any change in service cost, input, output, or effect.

	Yes	No	Impossible to Answer
F-9. The case study provides evidence that the operation or testing of the innovation involved:			
(a) Any structural or personnel reorganization (e.g., a new unit or switches in personnel assignments)	48.6	20.0	31.5
(b) The permanent addition or reduction of personnel	36.4	29.3	34.3
(c) Changes in procedures within individual jobs	65.0	6.4	28.5
F-10. The case study mentions that, following the current experience, other locales:			89.1
(1) Were considering or had begun innovations of the same sort	25.7		
(2) Were considering or had begun modifications of the innovation	2.9		
(3) Had canceled or postponed innovations of the same sort			
(4) Had canceled or postponed modifications			
(5) No mention of any of the above	69.3		
(9) Impossible to answer	2.1		
F-11. In the author's judgment, the innovative effort:			86.8
(1) Had been successful or showed clear gains	74.3		
(2) Had failed to show clear gains	20.7		
(3) Was still in the planning stage	2.1		
(9) Impossible to answer	2.8		
F-12. The author gives the following reasons for success or failure (a direct quote is preferred):			

F-13. In your own opinion, rate the degree of confidence you place in the overall conclusions to be drawn from the study in relation to the nature of the evidence presented (use 1-5 as defined below):

1 = Good support for conclusions drawn and alternative
    explanations ruled out 15.7

2 = Some support 43.6

3 = "Neutral"—Evidence neither supports nor challenges
    conclusions 31.4

4 = Evidence presented for minor points is contrary to
    conclusions drawn 7.9

5 = Evidence presented for major points is strongly contrary
    to conclusions drawn 1.4

G. 1970 Census Information (based on answer to C-1d)

	Percent Distribution

G-1. Type of locale:

(1) State	7.9
(2) County	10.7
(3) SMSA	8.6
(4) City	69.3
(5) Other	1.4
(9) Impossible to answer	2.1

G-2. Population:

(1) Over 1,000,000	34.3
(2) 500,000-999,999	19.3
(3) 100,000-499,999	20.0
(4) Less than 100,000	21.4
(9) Impossible to answer	5.0

G-3. Population change 1960-1970:

    (1) Increase 20 percent or more   23.6
    (2) Increase 0-19.9 percent   47.9
    (3) Negative change   22.1
    (9) Impossible to answer   6.4

G-4. Median years of education:

    (1) 12.5 or more   15.7
    (2) 11.5-12.4   63.6
    (3) Less than 11.4   14.3
    (9) Impossible to answer   5.7

G-5. Median income (in dollars):

    (1) 11,000 or more   15.7
    (2) 10,000-10,999   20.7
    (3) 9,000-9,999   40.7
    (4) Less than 9,000   17.1
    (9) Impossible to answer   5.7

G-6. Local government per capita expenditure (in dollars):

    (1) More than 350   32.9
    (2) 250-349   11.4
    (3) 150-249   23.6
    (4) Less than 150   21.4
    (9) Impossible to answer   10.7

G-7. Region:

		Percent Distribution
(1)	New England and Middle Atlantic	30.7
(2)	North Central	28.6
(3)	South Atlantic and South Central	15.7
(4)	Mountain and Pacific	21.4
(9)	Impossible to answer	3.6

H. Complex Variables (based on combinations of questions as indicated)

H-1. Quality:

(1)	Moderate [if average of F-4, column 2 = 1 to 2.99]	35.7
(2)	Low [if average = 3 to 3.99]	40.7
(3)	Poor [if average = 4 or more]	23.6

H-2. Publicity:

(1)	Yes = [if any of B-8a, b, or c = 1]	40.0
(2)	No = all others on B-8a, b, or c	60.0

H-3. Previous merit:

(1)	Yes = [if any of D-4a, b, c, or d = 1]	62.9
(2)	No = all others on D-4a, b, c, or d	37.1

H-4. Federal support:

(1)	Implementation only = [if D-14d = 1]	60.7
(2)	Any other = [if any of D-14b, c, e, f, g, h, or i = 1]	14.3
(3)	None = all others on D-14b, c, d, e, f, g, h, or i	25.0

H-5. Cosmopolite:

(1) Yes = [if any of E-7a, b, or E-8f = 1]   55.0
(2) No = all others on E-7a, b, or E-8f

H-6. Veteran:

(1) Yes = [if any of E-7c, e, f, g, or E-8b, g = 1]   45.0
(2) No = all others on E-7c, e, f, g, or E-8b, g   55.0

H-7. Power:

(1) Yes = [if any of E-7d or E-8a, d, e = 1]   50.0
(2) No = all others on E-7d or E-8a, d, e   50.0

H-8. Political support:

(1) Yes = [if any of E-13a, b, c, d, e, f = 1]   70.7
(2) Neutral = all others on E-13a, b, c, d, e, f   25.0
(3) Negative = [if any of E-13a, b, c, d, e, f = 3]   4.3

H-9. Implementation delay:

(1) Yes = [if any of E-17b, c, d, e = 1]   47.1
(2) No = all others on E-17b, c, d, e   52.9

H-10. Provider satisfaction:

(1) Yes = all others on F-7a, b, c, d   58.6
(2) No = [if either F-7c or d = 1]   32.1
(3) Neutral = [if F-7a, b, c, and d all = any of 2, 3, or 9]   9.3

H-11. Organizational change:

(1) Major = [if F-9a and b = 1]   32.1
(2) Minor = [if F-9a = 1; and F-9b = 2 or 9]   20.7
(3) Trivial = [if F-9c = 1; and F-9a = 2 or 9]   20.0
(4) All other = all others on F-9a, b, or c   27.1

H-12. Success:

(1) Incorporated and improvement = [if F-1 = 1; *and* F-5 = 1]   27.1
(2) Partially incorporated and improvement = [if F-1 = 2; *and* F-5 = 1]   23.6
(3) Not incorporated but improvement = [if F-1 = 3, 4, 5, or 9; *and* F-5 = 1]   4.3
(4) Incorporated but no improvement = [if F-1 = 1; *and* F-5 = anything except 1]   15.7
(5) Partially incorporated but no improvement = [if F-1 = 2; *and* F-5 = anything except 1] 13.6
(6) Not incorporated and no improvement = [if F-1 = 3, 4, 5, or 9; *and* F-5 = anything except 1] 15.7

H-13. Detail:

(1) 0-2 [if total number of 1's for E-1a through 1 = 0, 1, or 2]   2.9
(2) 3-4 [if total number of 1's for E-1a through 1 = 3 or 4]   21.4
(3) 5-6 [if total number of 1's for E-1a through 1 = 5 or 6]   25.0
(4) 7 or more [if total number of 1's for E-1a through 1 = 7 or more]   50.7

H-14. Extra resources:

(1) Yes = [if C-1b or c = 1]   44.3
(2) No = all others on C-1b or c   55.7

H-15. Research adequacy:

(1) High = [if A-7 = 3; and A-8 = 1]   30.7
(2) Medium = [if A-7 = 1 or 2; and A-8 = 1] or [if A-7 = 1, 2, or 3; and A-8 = 2]   35.0
(3) Low = all others on A-7 and A-8   34.3

H-16.   Agency actors:

(1) Innovator, implementer, and advocate all in agency = [if E-2 = 2, 3, 4, 15, or 17; and E-4 = 2, 3, 4, 15, or 17; and E-3 = 2, 3, 4, 15, or 17]   14.3

(2) Two of three in agency = [any two of three in first bracket]   17.9

(3) One of three = [only one of three in first bracket]   31.4

(4) None = [if none of three in first bracket]   36.4

H-17.   Formal organization:

(1) Yes = [if C-4 = 3 or 4; and C-3a = 2 or 9]   26.4

(2) No = [if C-3a = 1] or [C-3a = 2 or 9; and C-4 = 1 or 2]   65.0

(3) Impossible to answer = [if C-3a = 2 or 9; and C-4 = 9]   8.6

H-18.   New hires:

(1) Yes = [if D-11c or d = 1]   36.4

(2) No = all others on D = 11c or d   63.6

H-19.   In-job changes:

(1) Yes = [if D-11a or b = 1]   68.6

(2) No = all others on D-11a or b   31.4

H-20.   Inside resistance:

(1) Yes = [if E-17d or F-7d = 1]   26.4

(2) No = all others on E-17d and F-7d   73.6

Appendix D:
Supplementary Tables

The data from the tables in this appendix ($N = 140$ for all tables) are referred to in the text on the following pages:

Table	Chapter	Page
D-1	2	31
D-2	2	31
D-3	2	31
D-4	2	31
D-5	2	31
D-6	2	36
D-7	2	36
D-8	2	36
D-9	2	36
D-10	2	37
D-11	2	37
D-12	2	37
D-13	2	37
D-14	2	37
D-15	2	37
D-16	2	38
D-17	2	38
D-18	2	38
D-19	2	38
D-20	5	99
D-21	5	99
D-22	5	99
D-23	5	99
D-24	5	99
D-25	5	99
D-26	5	99
D-27	5	100
D-28	5	106
D-29	5	106
D-30	5	106
D-31	5	106
D-32	5	106

Table D-1

Relationship Between Types of Measures Used and Rating of Overall Adequacy of Evidence in Case Study

| | Rating of Overall Adequacy | | | | |
| | | | | Contradictions | |
Measures	Good	Some Support	Neutral	Minor	Major
Operational description of both innovative device and outcomes	19	47	21	6	1
Operational description of performance only	3	8	8	1	1
Operational description of innovative device only	0	4	10	1	0
None of above	0	2	5	3	0

Note: χ^2 = 22.83, df = 12, $p < 0.05$.

Table D-2

Relationship Between Types of Measures Used and Rating of Adequacy of Evidence for Each Outcome

| | Adequacy of Evidence for Outcome | | |
Measures	High	Medium	Low
Operational description of both innovative device and outcomes	41	39	14
Operational description of performance only	6	7	8
Operational description of innovative device only	3	6	6
None of above	0	5	5

Note: χ^2 = 13.05, df = 6, $p < 0.05$.

Table D-3

Relationship Between Type of Research Design and Rating of Overall Adequacy of Evidence in Case Study

| | Rating of Overall Adequacy | | | | |
| | | | | Contradictions | |
Research Design	Good	Some Support	Neutral	Minor	Major
Some relevant design	17	13	7	2	0
Line of argument, but no design	5	22	9	2	1
Coherent description only	0	6	21	6	1
None of above	0	2	7	1	0

Note: χ^2 = 46.00, df = 12, $p < 0.001$.

Table D-4

Relationship Between Type of Research Design and Rating of Adequacy of Evidence for Each Outcome

Research Design	Adequacy of Evidence for Outcome		
	High	Medium	Low
Some relevant design	29	21	7
Line of argument, but no design	13	22	4
Coherent description only	8	11	15
None of above	0	3	7

Note: χ^2 = 29.83, df = 6, $p < 0.001$.

Table D-5

Relationship Between Rating of Overall Adequacy of Evidence in Case Study and of Adequacy of Evidence for Each Outcome

Overall Adequacy	Adequacy of Evidence for Outcome		
	High	Medium	Low
Good	18	4	0
Some support	23	31	7
Neutral	9	18	17
Minor contradictions	0	3	8
Major contradictions	0	1	1

Note: χ^2 = 40.73, df = 8, $p < 0.001$.

Table D-6

Relationship Between Research Quality and Publication Status of Study

Publication Status	Research Quality		
	High	Medium	Low
Published	12	21	10
Unpublished	38	36	23

Note: χ^2 not significant.

Table D-7

Relationship Between Research Quality and Date of Study

Date of Study	Research Quality		
	High	Medium	Low
1973-1975	25	31	9
Before 1973	25	26	24

Note: χ^2 not significant.

Table D-8
Relationship Between Research Quality and Federal Support for Study

	Research Quality		
Federal Support	*High*	*Medium*	*Low*
Yes	37	33	19
No	9	19	10
Impossible to answer	4	5	4

Note: χ^2 not significant.

Table D-9
Relationship Between Research Quality and Affiliation of Author of Study

	Research Quality		
Affiliation of Author	*High*	*Medium*	*Low*
Academic institution	12	16	9
Research organization	15	23	8
Other	22	18	14
Impossible to answer	1	0	2

Note: χ^2 not significant.

Table D-10
Relationship Between Research Quality and Population of City of Innovative Effort

	Research Quality		
Population	*High*	*Medium*	*Low*
Over 1 million	13	23	12
500,000 to 999,999	10	11	6
100,000 to 499,999	14	9	5
Less than 100,000	11	11	8
Impossible to answer	2	3	2

Note: χ^2 not significant.

Table D-11

Relationship Between Research Quality and Region of Innovative Effort

	Research Quality		
Region	High	Medium	Low
New England and Mid-Atlantic	12	24	7
North Central	20	9	11
South Atlantic and South Central	6	8	8
Mountain Pacific	12	12	6
Impossible to answer	0	4	1

Note: χ^2 not significant.

Table D-12

Relationship Between Research Quality and Type of Innovative Agency

	Research Quality		
Type of Agency	High	Medium	Low
Criminal justice and fire	8	16	2
Public works and transportation	15	10	1
Health	11	12	8
Education	9	7	7
Planning and coordination	7	12	15

Note: $\chi^2 = 22.31$, df = 8, $p < 0.01$.

Table D-13

Relationship Between Research Quality and Federal Support for Innovative Effort

	Research Quality		
Federal Support	High	Medium	Low
Yes	35	25	19
No	13	29	12
Impossible to answer	2	3	2

Note: $\chi^2 = 7.54$, df = 2, $p < 0.05$ (excludes impossible-to-answer cases).

Table D-14

Relationship Between Research Quality and Level of Funding Support

	Research Quality		
Level of Funding	High	Medium	Low
Less than $50,000	5	13	10
$50,000 to $250,000	13	6	1
More than $250,000	13	16	2
Impossible to answer	19	22	20

Note: $\chi^2 = 17.80$, df $= 4$, $p < 0.01$ (excludes impossible-to-answer cases).

Table D-15

Relationship Between Research Quality and Client Participation

	Research Quality		
Client Participation	High	Medium	Low
Some participation	20	17	3
No participation, but client mentioned	13	22	8
No participation	16	18	21
Impossible to answer	1	0	1

Note: $\chi^2 = 15.33$, df $= 4$, $p < 0.01$ (excludes impossible-to-answer cases).

Table D-16

Relationship Between Research Quality and Incorporation of Innovation

	Research Quality		
Incorporation	High	Medium	Low
Full	19	28	13
Partial (some doubt)	23	18	11
Discontinued or not operated	8	11	9

Note: χ^2 not significant.

Table D-17

Relationship Between Research Quality and Service Improvement

	Research Quality		
Service Improvement	High	Medium	Low
Yes	33	35	10
No	9	13	10
Useful information produced	7	8	9
Impossible to answer	1	1	2

Note: χ^2 not significant.

Table D-18

Relationship Between Research Quality and Outcome of Innovative Effort

	Research Quality		
Outcome of Innovative Effort	High	Medium	Low
Success$_1$	30	32	9
Success$_2$	5	9	8
Failure	15	16	16

Note: χ^2 = 10.21, df = 4, $p < 0.05$.

Table D-19

Relationship Between Research Quality and Author Judgment of Success of Innovative Effort

	Research Quality		
Author Judgment	High	Medium	Low
Success	38	47	19
All other	12	10	14

Note: χ^2 = 6.89, df = 2, $p < 0.05$.

Table D-20

Relationship Between Transitivity and Service Improvement

	Service Improvement			
Transitivity	Yes	No	Information Only	Impossible to Answer
Changes in administrative procedures only	22	17	17	4
Changes in services	8	7	3	0
New practices between clients and providers	48	10	3	0
Impossible to answer	0	0	1	0

Note: χ^2 = 23.38, df = 4, $p < 0.001$ (excludes impossible-to-answer cases). Examination of higher quality cases alone significantly supports this relationship.

Table D-21
Relationship Between Divisibility and Service Improvement

	Service Improvement			
Divisibility	Yes	No	Information Only	Impossible to Answer
Yes	45	13	3	2
No	31	18	15	2
Impossible to answer	2	3	6	0

Note: $\chi^2 = 11.32$, df = 2, $p < 0.01$ (excludes impossible-to-answer cases). Examination of higher quality cases alone fails to show any relationship.

Table D-22
Relationship Between Practitioner Training and Service Improvement

	Service Improvement			
Practitioner Training	Yes	No	Information Only	Impossible to Answer
Yes	47	14	5	4
No	31	18	19	2

Note: $\chi^2 = 11.93$, df = 2, $p < 0.01$ (excludes impossible-to-answer cases). Examination of higher quality cases alone significantly supports this relationship.

Table D-23
Relationship Between Implementation Delay and Service Improvement

	Service Improvement			
Implementation Delay	Yes	No	Information Only	Impossible to Answer
Yes	38	22	4	2
No	40	10	20	4

Note: $\chi^2 = 14.99$, df = 2, $p < 0.001$ (excludes impossible-to-answer cases). Examination of higher quality cases alone significantly supports this relationship.

Table D-24
Relationship Between New Hiring and Incorporation

	Incorporation		
New Hiring	Full	Partial (some doubt)	Discontinued or Not Operated
Yes	13	28	10
No	47	24	18

Note: $\chi^2 = 12.46$, df = 2, $p < 0.01$. Examination of higher quality cases alone significantly supports this relationship.

Table D-25

Relationship Between Support of the Chief Executive and Incorporation

	Incorporation		
Support of Chief Executive	Full	Partial (some doubt)	Discontinued or Not Operated
Yes	25	8	10
Neutral	1	3	2
No	33	41	15
Impossible to answer	1	0	0

Note: $\chi^2 = 11.09$, df = 4, $p < 0.05$ (excludes impossible-to-answer case). Examination of higher quality cases alone significantly supports this relationship.

Table D-26

Relationship Between Agency Affiliation of Main Actors and Incorporation

	Incorporation		
Agency Affiliation	Full	Partial (some doubt)	Discontinued or Not Operated
Innovator, implementer, and advocate in agency	14	6	0
Two of above in agency	13	8	4
One of above in agency	12	16	16
None in agency	21	22	8

Note: $\chi^2 = 17.98$, df = 6, $p < 0.01$. Examination of higher quality cases alone significantly supports this relationship.

Table D-27

Relationship Between Implementation Delay and Incorporation

	Incorporation		
Implementation Delay	Full	Partial (some doubt)	Discontinued or Not Operated
Yes	20	30	16
No	40	22	12

Note: $\chi^2 = 8.03$, df = 2, $p < 0.05$. Examination of higher quality cases alone significantly supports this relationship.

Table D-28

Relationship Between Divisibility and Type of Innovation

	Type of Innovation		
Divisibility	Hardware	Computers	Data Analysis
Yes	40	15	8
No	13	28	25
Impossible to answer	1	3	7

Note: $\chi^2 = 26.40$, df = 2, $p < 0.001$ (excludes impossible-to-answer cases). Examination of higher quality cases alone significantly supports this relationship.

Table D-29
Relationship Between Visibility and Type of Innovation

	Type of Innovation		
Visibility	Hardware	Computers	Data Analysis
Concrete artifact or action	27	7	17
Proper name only	0	3	7
Both	26	33	5
Neither	1	3	11

Note: x^2 = 50.46, df = 6, $p < 0.001$. Examination of higher quality cases alone significantly supports this relationship.

Table D-30
Relationship Between Reversibility and Type of Innovation

	Type of Innovation		
Reversibility	Hardware	Computers	Data Analysis
Yes	30	35	33
No	24	11	7

Note: x^2 = 9.15, df = 2, $p < 0.05$. Examination of higher quality cases alone fails to show any relationship.

Table D-31
Relationship Between Existence of a Prior Need and Type of Innovation

	Type of Innovation		
Prior Need	Hardware	Computers	Data Analysis
Yes	26	16	26
No	28	30	14

Note: x^2 = 7.82, df = 2, $p < 0.05$. Examination of higher quality cases alone fails to show any relationship.

Table D-32
Relationship Between New Hiring and Type of Innovation

	Type of Innovation		
New Hiring	Hardware	Computers	Data Analysis
Yes	22	19	10
No	32	27	30

Note: x^2 not significant. Examination of higher quality cases alone shows a significant positive relationship between new hiring and computers.

Appendix E:
Examples of Checklist Coding
of Case Study Evidence

Factors in the Innovative Process	Attribute	Checklist Question
Outcomes		
CVIS has become part of the regular operating programs of the three high schools in District 88.	Full incorporation	F-1
El Camino Hospital . . . was selected for the HEW-supported demonstration and evaluation project of a total hospital information system. . . . the demonstration and evaluation effort is not completed.	Partial incorporation	F-1
. . the project never proceeded beyond initial data gathering.	Discontinued	F-1
The implementation of MIS is effecting a general decrease in the turnaround time associated with tests and procedures.	Service improvement	F-5
Respondents clearly felt that ITV is a very effective device for aiding in the improvement of teaching performance.	Service improvement	F-5
Although not all installation showed every potential attribute of the ECE, a composite picture demonstrated that steam buses can equal the road performance of diesel buses, and with greatly reduced exhaust emissions.	Service improvement	F-5
. . 23,541 passenger trips were provided [by the dial-a-ride system].	Service improvement	F-5
Whereas 70 percent of the dictated exams were not available until the next day, 75 percent of our [computerized] reports now go out the same day and 93 percent by the end of the second day.	Service improvement	F-5
. . . MIS has not significantly altered the speed with which a patient progresses through his episode of hospitalization	No service change	F-5
EMPIRIC has had virtually no effect on local policies or policymaking as yet.	No service change	F-5
The results of the data transmittal pilot test revealed the Telecomputer Grid to be a currently unacceptable technical device incapable of reliably supporting sustained instruction.	No service change	F-5

Device Factors

... [he] became program director in November 1971, and reoriented the ITV program around the microteaching concept.	Adaptability	E-16
Changes in the original EMPIRIC model estimated for Boston had been specified and carried out	Adaptability Visibility	E-16 D-10
CVIS is not designed to replace counselors. It is a powerful technological tool that assists students and counselors in collecting and sorting information before the career decisionmaking stage.	Transitivity	D-6
A study of the methods used by the Oklahoma Highway Department and the Tulsa Police Department revealed that the proposed method offered better potential use than the variations used elsewhere.	Relative advantage	D-4b

Background Factors

All of the nineteen specialties recognized by the AMA, plus many subspecialties, are represented on the medical staff.	Diversity	C-7a
Two other hospital information system programs were not being particularly successful at that time ... there were several other full-scale information systems that had reached a demonstrable stage in a hospital.	Rich environment	B-4c
[Patrol Bureau, Safety-Emergency Division, Planning and Operations Division ....]	Formalization	H-17
[Aside from the analytic work], the department was planning to install a new communication system that would computerize and record the dispatching process.	Agency history of innovation	B-4a
[Chief inspector, assistant chief inspector, deputy chief inspector, inspector, captain, lieutenant, sergeant ....]	Centralization	C-5
... a study team ... from the department's [NYPD] planning bureau was assigned to perform a management survey and analysis of the CCR.	R&D analysis group	C-1b

Factors in the Innovative Process	Attribute	Checklist Question
. . . Director of Guidance . . . was joined by two counselors . . . , and a school psychologist . . . the Chairman of the Mathematics Department in the school joined the project	Diversity Formalization	C-7a H-17
BART's Office of Research conducted a public survey of attitudes and awareness about BART in 1971.	R&D analysis group	C-1b
Implementation Factors		
East Lansing was faced with the prospect of building two additional fire stations because of its continuing growth and the replacement of its central fire station.	Prior need	B-1
City officials decided that the systems project should focus on the need for increasing the quality of life of residents of the Fallkill area.	Service goal	D-5
Approximately 120 teachers . . . have been exposed to and basically trained in microteaching.	Practitioner training	E-11
Everything went smoothly and the city was cleaned up within a few hours, with credit properly going to the mayor, the Department of Sanitation, and the new plan.	Chief executive support	E-13a
There was some early opposition to model development among some of the local public officials.	Implementation delay	H-9
During the seven-month evaluation period . . . poor weather conditions often canceled flight operations to further contribute to the decrease in flying hours.	Implementation delay	H-9
An additional feature of the CVIS program was the use of community support in developing the program. Local businesses and industries continue to play an important role in updating CVIS data files and programs.	Client participation	B-7
Formation of local citizen groups to influence BART took place mainly at the individual city level. Generally, these were informal, short-lived groups that campaigned for a particular objective.	Client participation	B-7

Federal Factors

Its funds were limited to normal city operating expenditures, augmented by HUD support of the NBS technical advisors.	Federal technical assistance Local funds	D-14e B-5
Through three grants totalling $343,243, the Law Enforcement Assistance Administration has underwritten a sizeable portion of the costs to date for helicopter operations.	Federal funds	B-5

Appendix F:
Multisite Case Study
Summaries

This appendix contains reviews of the following studies:[a]

Baldridge, J. Victor, "Organizational Innovation: Individual, Structural, and Environmental Impacts" (1975).

Cohen, Elizabeth G., and Eric R. Bredo, "Elementary School Organization and Innovative Instructional Practices" (1975).

Corwin, Ronald G., "Strategies for Organizational Innovation: An Empirical Comparison" (1972).

Corwin, Ronald G., "Innovation in Organizations: The Case of Schools" (1975).

Cushen, W. Edward, "Afterthoughts on Four Urban Systems Studies Performed with Small Cities" (1972).

Deal, Terrence E., et al., "Organizational Influences on Educational Innovation" (1975).

Feller, Irwin, et al., "Diffusion of Technology in State Mission-Oriented Agencies" (1974).

Frohman, Alan, et al., "Factors Affecting Innovation in the Fire Services" (1972).

Hage, Jerald, and Michael Aiken, "Program Change and Organizational Properties" (1967).

Heydebrand, Wolf V., and James J. Noell, "Task Structure and Innovation in Professional Organizations" (1973).

Hodgson, David A., et al., "The Uniform Hospital Discharge Data Demonstration, Summary Report" (1973).

Kaluzny, Arnold D., et al., "Diffusion of Innovative Health Care Services in the United States: A Study of Hospitals" (1970).

Liebert, Roland J., " 'The Electric Company,' In-School Utilization Study. Volume 2: The 1972-73 School and Teacher Surveys and Trends Since Fall 1971" (1973).

Mohr, Lawrence B., "Determinants of Innovation in Organizations" (1969).

Mytinger, Robert E., *Innovation in Local Health Services* . . . (1968).

Public Technology, Inc., "Integrated Municipal Information Systems: Program and Projects of the United States of America Urban Information Systems Inter-Agency Committee" (1975).

Rosner, Martin M., "Economic Determinants of Organizational Innovation" (1968).

---

[a]The full citations are given at the beginning of each review.

Study: J. Victor Baldridge, "Organizational Innovation: Individual, Structural, and Environmental Impacts," in J. Victor Baldridge and Terrence E. Deal, eds., *Managing Change in Educational Organizations* (Berkeley: McCutchan, 1975), pp. 151-175.

This article reports on two studies designed to test the following three hypotheses about the determinants of nontechnological innovations in school districts:

Certain individuals are more prone than others to innovate; hence, organizations with a high percentage of such individuals are more prone to innovate;

Organizational complexity size promote innovation; and

Heterogeneous or changing environments cause performance gaps that in turn lead to innovation.

Definitions and Measures

The following definitions and measures were used:

Individual, organizational, and environmental characteristics. Individuals were denominated by administrators as "opinion leaders" or "change participants." Through interviews, data were collected on variables associated with innovators—e.g., social status, education, cosmopolitism. For organizational considerations, the size of each school district was determined by its number of students. Complexity was defined by the number of programs and positions formally organized in each district, the number of full-time administrators assigned to the programs, and the policy statements, job descriptions, and organizational charts. As for the environment, heterogeneity was defined by: population density, percentage of urbanization, percentage of nonwhite residents, number of agencies competing with the school district for tax revenue, home ownership, and proportion of government expenses used for noneducational uses.

Innovations. Innovations were defined as changes in curriculum or organization that covered a large number of people or processes in the organization, that were considered "important" by knowledgeable observers, and that were well established in the organization.

Method

The first study included in this overview examined twenty randomly selected schools in seven districts in the San Francisco Bay area. Information about the districts and the schools was collected through interviews with the superintendents and principals and from district records. Three categories of teachers were also interviewed: opinion leaders ($N = 53$), change participants ($N = 309$), and a 50 percent random sample of all faculty ($N = 775$).

The second study randomly selected 264 schools from elementary and secondary districts in Illinois. The sample consisted only of large school districts. Data came from four sources: questionnaires mailed to district superintendents, punched-card records of enrollments, district records, and *The County and City Data Book* and the *Census of Government, 1962.* The usable sample was 184 schools, representing a 70 percent response rate.

Findings

The results of the bay area study showed no significant differences among opinion leaders, participants, and randomly selected faculty on measures of individual characteristics presumed common to innovators. This result contradicts much previous research on innovation. However, *positional* characteristics were important in understanding how individuals influence change. Administrative leaders and department chairmen were found to be initiators out of proportion to their number, to have strong control over the incentives and sanctions in the organization, and to serve as communication links between those carrying out changes and those supporting them.

Both the bay area and Illinois data showed size and complexity to be directly related to innovation. In California, more than three times as many major innovations were listed for the ten largest as for the ten smallest schools. In Illinois, high adopters had 50 percent more administrative positions and twice as many full-time administrators as low adopters. The six indicators of heterogeneity all correlated positively with innovation.

Conclusions

This report stresses that organizational factors have been ignored in diffusion studies. There is a fundamental difference between the adoption of a tested, easily evaluated, quickly effective technology by an individual adopter and the adoption of a hard to evaluate, uncertain social innovation by an organizational adopter.

The author also concludes that the impact of environmental variability on innovation suggests that social organizations seeking to innovate should open channels of communication with their environments through such mechanisms as advisory boards.

Comment

The study challenges the individualistic approach to the diffusion of innovation. The methods are clearly explained, although no justification is given for the restriction of sampling to large districts—which is especially curious since size, the author argues, is a major factor in innovation. The impact of the strong relationship between size, complexity, and innovation is somewhat weakened by the lack of data on small school districts. The sampling limitation also makes the author's recommendations to consolidate districts, increase administration, and hire experts much less persuasive.

These conclusions also go far beyond what the data, gathered at one point in time, can support. The conclusions would only be justified if extensive longitudinal data permitted the construction of a model of the innovation process in which the direction of causality could be known with a high level of certainty.

Another weakness of this report is a lack of both data on what projects were selected as "innovations" and a discussion of the rationale for aggregating the (assumed) diversity. In the absence of this information, it is hard to know if the relationships found are more than a function of arbitrary definition.

Study: Elizabeth G. Cohen and Eric R. Bredo, "Elementary School Organization and Innovative Instructional Practices," in J. Victor Baldridge and Terrence E. Deal, eds., *Managing Change in Educational Organizations* (Berkeley: McCutchan, 1975), pp. 133-149.

This report analyzes the adoption of nontechnological instructional and organizational practices in elementary education. The first research issue is whether it is possible to generalize about the type of instructional practice of a given teacher across subjects; the second issue is the association between structure and innovation variables. The report hypothesizes that team teaching, representing a more complex organizational structure than isolated teaching, will be positively associated with complex instructional practice, such as multiple-classroom groups; that teams with a rigid division of labor and low interdependence will be positively associated with preprogrammed instruction; and that teams with a flexible division of labor and high interdependence will be positively associated with nonprogrammed instruction.

The following definitions and measures were used:

Teaming is defined as collaboration in one or more of the following practices: planning, student evaluation, joint instruction, and coordination of discipline. Cross-grouping on the basis of pupil ability or teacher specialization was taken as an indicator of a rigid division of labor, while joint teaching was taken as an indicator of a flexible division of labor and high interdependence.

Innovation is broadly defined to refer to the educational means used to achieve outcomes. It is conceived as varying in complexity on two dimensions:

Differentiation: the degree to which a classroom is organized so that teachers treat students differently; and

Nonprogrammed instruction: the mode of teacher decisionmaking (preprogramming makes decisions routine; nonprogramming is based on a continuous assessment of students' needs in the course of teaching).

Method

Sixteen elementary schools in the San Francisco Bay area were selected from a larger stratified random sample on the basis of the principals' questionnaire response. The objective was to maximize the variation of the aspects of structure and innovations described above. Questionnaires were sent to all teachers, and a 95 percent response rate was obtained. The questionnaire contained items designed to permit the construction of indices for the measurement of structural and technological variables. Teachers were asked to report on their teaching practice in the areas of reading, mathematics, and social studies.

Findings

There was a positive association between indices of complexity across subject matter areas, despite differences within subject matter areas. Second, differentiated and nonprogrammed instruction were positively associated. Third, teams reported more differentiated instructional practices and fewer programmed instructional practices. Fourth, flexibility in team organization was related to nonprogrammed instruction.

Conclusions

The first research question can be answered affirmatively. There is a positive association among indicators of complexity of practice across subject matters for a given classroom.

Team teaching, a more complex structure, was associated with more differentiated, less routinized instructional innovations. Therefore, the argument can be advanced that some types of innovations may not be feasible without supportive structural modes. Practices such as flexible group instruction are impossible without role flexibility and interdependence. If schools wish to implement such innovations, the way the team works together deserves attention.

Comment

The definition and role of innovation is not clearly spelled out, although the thrust of the study is obviously to conceptualize conditions that favor implementation. There is no comparative analysis of innovations from the point of view of length of existence, adoption difficulties or circumstances, or service changes. There are no data on teacher attitudes or on the number of schools where teaming was itself an innovation or where innovations that needed the structural support of teaming were implemented without it. The latter would complement this study and strengthen the argument that a congenial structure is a necessary (but not sufficient) condition for some innovations.

Study: Ronald G. Corwin, "Strategies for Organizational Innovation: An Empirical Comparison," *American Sociological Review* 37 (August 1972):441-454.

This study reports on nontechnological innovations in low income schools, using data from a larger, longitudinal study of the Teacher Corps. *Innovation* is defined as a deliberate change in structural relationships and procedures in a particular organization in order to change outputs. For most of the innovations, faculty from local colleges and universities assisted in the implementation process. The main research objective was to identify the mix of variables pertaining to the characteristics of the key innovating personnel as well as the organizational context that account for the amount of organizational innovation.

Thirty-seven indicators were used to guide the collection of data. The author acknowledges that these indicators are proxies for more complex social facts. The indicators covered the following areas:

Characteristics of new members (e.g., political liberalism, measured by a nine-item Likert scale assessing political attitudes towards public policies);

Characteristics of boundary personnel—i.e., those school staff that had to relate to the colleges and universities (e.g., the competence of the principal, measured by the ratings given him on a six-item Likert scale by interns and other teachers);

Characterization of socialization agents (e.g., quality of the university, measured by a combined index of college resources and selectivity of student body);

Organizational structure (e.g., centralization, measured by the combined estimate of teachers and principals about where final decisions are made);

Resources available (e.g., amount of federal funds per intern);

Status security (e.g., proportion of teachers, by self-report, who are members of a union); and

Interorganizational content (e.g., cooperation between the public school and the college, measured by content analysis of interviews).

The dependent variable was the adoption of innovations in schools. Each school was given a score based on all reported or observed changes and weighted for the innovativeness of each change (rated by two judges). Each change was scored on a three-point scale on five dimensions: new classroom methods, new materials, changed relationship with clientele, the addition of implementing personnel, and extracurricular activities. The weighting was based on the assumption that changes requiring altered relationships and affecting basic curriculum are more important than additive changes or peripheral activities. Thus team teaching, for example, received a higher weight than a new photography club.

Method

Ten universities with Teachers Corps programs and forty-two cooperating schools were visited for one week each by teams of interviewers. Two hundred sixty-six interns, 872 classroom teachers, fifty-three team leaders, sixty principals, one-hundred graduate students not in Teacher Corps, and forty-five university faculty members constituted the sample for a written questionnaire. Nine hundred thirty-two persons were interviewed. The average rate of questionnaire return was 73 percent. The ten programs were selected to represent the range and quality of the thirty-five programs that constitute the Teacher Corps programs.

Analysis of the data was organized into three steps: the degree of association between independent and dependent variables was computed; the thirty-seven independent variables were factor analyzed to identify inductively the common factors underlying these indicators; and the amount of variance in the dependent variable explainable by the emergent factors was examined by regression analysis.

Findings

The factor analysis yielded seven dimensions:

Quality and modernization of context;

Professionalism and liberalism of staff;

Organizational control by schools;

Competence of administration;

Quality and interdependence of boundary personnel;

Status of teaching staff; and

Uniqueness of outsiders.

The seven factors accounted for 51 percent of the variance when regressed against the dependent variable. Three factors accounted for 48 percent of the explained variance: quality and interdependence of boundary personnel, organizational control exercised by the school, and uniqueness of the outside change agent.

Thus the most salient factor in innovation was the quality and interdependence of boundary personnel. This includes faculty competence as perceived by interns, faculty political liberalism, extent of cooperation between university and school, and competence of team leaders. The importance of this factor supports others' findings that organizations change in response to an outside stimulus.

The second most important factor—organizational control—reflects the capacity of the host organization to filter the effects of the outside organization. This includes centralization, stress on procedures and rules, emphasis on discipline, and proportion of program funds controlled by the school. Centralization was the only variable of this cluster positively associated with innovation to a significant degree ($r = 0.33$), which is at variance with the assumption that decentralized systems are more adaptable. Centralization may give the capacity to enforce rather than resist innovation.

The third factor reflects the amount of dissonance between change agents and members of the host organization. Contrary to theory, the correlation is negative ($r = -0.32$) for politically liberal interns. The author concludes that conflict per se does not necessarily produce change. Finally, despite the theoretical importance one might attribute to them, the variables related to the professionalism and competence of teachers and school administrators were less important.

Conclusions

These findings have implications for school decentralization. The data support the contentions that professionalization may not speed innovation and that decentralization may cripple an administrator's ability to mandate change.

In conclusion, the author offers the following general proposition, with an injunction to be cautious because of the crude measurements: the way an innovation is conceived and implemented is a product of forces inside and outside the organization. The necessary ingredients include: a dominant outside organization staffed by competent liberals; competent, receptive boundary personnel in the host; and a functional interdependence between the two.

Comment

This is a well-organized, coherent study that explores the empirical usefulness of several conceptual approaches to innovation. The problems of the validity of the indicators are confronted openly and counteracted to some extent by the factor analysis of the data. The extensive interviews and site observations further strengthen the conclusions drawn in this report. All the data relate coherently to the conclusions, and no conclusions go beyond what the data will support, except the final general propositions, which are clearly identified as tentative.

Study: Ronald C. Corwin, "Innovation in Organizations: The Case of Schools," *Sociology of Education* 48 (Winter 1975):1-37.

This is a densely organized report that compares the importance of six classes of variables to the adoption of an innovation. Innovation is defined nontechnologically as a deliberate change in the structural relationships in a particular organization. The innovating organization is a public school, and the six types of variables include: (1) the role of the administration; (2) the role of subordinates; (3) the personal characteristics of the administrator's subordinates; (4) the moral and financial support for change from outside the organization; (5) the community context; and (6) the structural characteristics of the organizations themselves. The existing literature on these types of variables is reviewed, and the alternative explanations for innovation that have been suggested are summarized. Thirty-three independent variables emerge, and Corwin uses them in his study.

The following definitions and measures were used:

Sample. Data were collected as part of a larger, longitudinal study of graduates of the Teacher Corps after they had entered teaching. Measurements were based on questionnaires returned by principals and interns in 131 schools. Two-thirds of these schools were strictly elementary schools, and 85 percent were either elementary or combined elementary and junior high schools. The sample is called a comparative multicase study, which, while it is not random, provides a range of variation on variables thought to be relevant, and is large enough to accommodate a statistically controlled analysis.

Dependent Variable. Innovativeness is defined as the number of innovations undertaken during a two-year period, weighted by a panel of three judges on the basis of centrality to teaching practice (e.g., new classroom methods versus extracurricular activity) and extensiveness of adoption (e.g., ranging from rejection to adoption by the whole school).

Independent Variables. The major independent variables were made operational in the following manner:

Levels of education of principals and teachers: type of college degree held; percentage of teachers with M.A. or better

Experience of the principal: age, tenure in school, tenure in system

Experience of the teachers: percentage of new teachers in the year of research, percentage teaching over ten years

Sex: principal's sex; percentage of male teachers

Racial and ethnic composition: race of the principal (white/nonwhite); percentage of pupils as reported by the principal

Teacher characteristics: a three-item factor score based on sex, education, and experience

Liberalism: principal's self-identification on a five-point scale from conservative to radical

Professionalism: percentage of teachers in the National Education Association; percentage of teachers in the American Federation of Teachers; professional activities of the principal

Principal's competence: mean of six items describing the former intern's evaluation of the principal's competence

Formalization: flexibility as rated by former interns on four items related to freedom in role performance

Standardization: interns' agreement with eight statements about school procedures related to rules

Specialization: ratio of full-time people in specialized jobs to total enrollment

Centralization of system: principal's judgment of the school's autonomy on seven issues

Size: faculty size (full time)

Outside financial support: number of federally funded programs in the school, reported by the principal

Community support for change: principal's rating of community support

National Education Association support for change: principal's rating of NEA support

American Federation of Teachers support for change: principal's rating of AFT support

School community cooperation: index based on activities identified by the principal

Size of city: population

Modernization of region: summed weights of five indicators: percentage of males in nonagricultural labor; percentage of population in urban areas; per capita income; per capita physicians; number of telephones per housing unit

Students' characteristics: four-item factor score including the average daily absence rate; the percentage at least a year behind in reading level; the percentage with a discipline problem; the percentage from homes with incomes less than $4000 a year

Findings

Three types of analysis were undertaken: linear correlations, chi-square tests, and regression analysis.

The correlational analysis revealed the following variables with a significant relationship to innovativeness:

Principal's and teacher's education

Proportion of male teachers

Teacher professionalization

Community support

Size of community and school

Number of federal programs in the school

However, several variables usually thought to be related to innovativeness were found not to be correlated. These included:

Principal's length of tenure and competence

Specialization

Centralization

Regional location

Student characteristics

Chi-square analysis divided the schools into three approximately equal groups on the basis of innovativeness scores. These three groups were then cross-tabulated against other variables, dichotomized or trichotomized. This analysis yielded two significant findings:

Principals with fewer than three years' tenure who had been assigned from within were more innovative than those who came from "outside"; and

White principals were located in more innovative schools; when race was dichotomized and treated as a variable, it was found that nonwhite principals were in smaller schools with less educated and professional teachers.

The regression analysis attempted to assess the relative contribution of five classes of independent variables to innovativeness:

In the case of the personal characteristics of the administrators, the ten relevant variables accounted for only 6 percent of the variance; activity in professional associations was negatively associated with innovation;

Seven variables representing teacher characteristics accounted for 20 percent of the variance; however, the importance of teachers' education and experience diminished when other factors were controlled, while the significance of professional activities increased, accounting for 17 percent of the variance;

Eight contextual variables accounted for 17 percent of the variance; the number of federal programs, the community support, and the size of the city were statistically significant factors;

Six of the eleven variables pertaining to structural characteristics accounted for 11 percent of the variance; only school size and standardization were statistically significant; and

Finally, student characteristics accounted for a negligible (2 percent) amount of the variance.

Next, all of the variables were entered into a stepwise regression analysis. Teacher characteristics emerged as the single most important set of variables, but only explained 12 percent of the variance. The number of federal programs, the size of the city, the community support, the percentage of teachers in professional organizations, and the size of the faculty raised the amount of variance accounted for up to 29 percent. The remainder of the 33 variables together accounted for 32 percent of the remaining variance. Thus six variables were considered the most important to emerge from this analysis: Innovation is more likely to occur in the large schools of big cities where teachers are organized, where federal funds are available, and where the community supports the school's efforts.

Conclusions

The study concludes that a combination of variables is needed to account for innovation, with the following factors appearing to be most important:

1. A well-educated male faculty active in professional organizations;
2. Moral support in the community and a school-community partnership;
3. Resources for change from outside the school;
4. A school that is large enough to provide the necessary manpower for change; and
5. A community that is large enough to offer a variety of sources of pressure and support for change.

The priority of these variables differs between classes of communities, with the principal's characteristics having more weight in the middle-class schools.

Comment

This is an interesting and imaginative piece of research that addresses questions about the relationship of many variables to innovation. However, there is more than one threat to the validity of the data as presented in this report. For instance, the author does not comment upon the range of variability in the dependent variable with respect to the kinds of innovations represented, leaving doubt as to the true comparability among organizations that have the same innovativeness score. Conceivably an organization with many marginal innovations could get the same score as one with only one or two very central new programs, and it is hard to equate these as "equally innovative." Second, there is no description of salient characteristics of the sample (e.g., urban/rural) that might give the reader a sense of the direction of bias that operated as a function of sample selection. Third, some of the measures for independent variables have weak face validity, especially those for principal competence. The measures of centralization and standardization are open to the same criticism, and this may be why they are not more strongly related to innovativeness in a systematic way.

With respect to the analysis, the strength of the data does not seem adequate to meet the assumptions for regression analysis. Even though a cautious interpretation is encouraged where ordinal data are involved, there is no evidence that the rank-ordered data are comparable among subjects, as no questionnaire items are included to demonstrate shared anchors for ratings. It may be this methodological problem that accounts for the fact that less than one-third of the variance in the dependent variable is explained by variables that seemingly should be more systematically related to innovation.

Study: W. Edward Cushen, "Afterthoughts on Four Urban Systems Studies Performed with Small Cities," in Alvin W. Drake et al., eds., *Analysis of Public Systems* (Cambridge, Massachusetts: MIT Press, 1972), pp. 45-63.

This report is aptly titled an "afterthought." It is an admittedly incomplete narrative description of four cases in which cities participated in a one-year, HUD-sponsored experiment to introduce a technological systems-analysis approach to city problems. City governments were the innovating organizations and were chosen in the following manner: The International City Management Association (ICMA) and the American Society of Planning Officials (ASPO) initially selected thirty-two attendees for a one-week training course in systems analysis designed by Fels Institute and the Technical Analysis Division (TAD) of the National Bureau of Standards. Within a month, four cities indicated to ICMA that they were seriously interested in being experimental locales. The plan called for a conference to decide what to study and how to design a plan of action.

The city manager and/or planner was taken to be the prime client and was expected to spend a lot of time on the study. TAD was to provide city staff with technical assistance, and a university and a commercial organization were to participate in an unspecified fashion. At the completion of the study, an evaluation report was to be submitted to HUD, and the city was expected to be able to implement system studies without continuing advice. The four cities were East Lansing, Michigan; Dayton, Ohio; Charlotte, North Carolina; and Poughkeepsie, New York. All four cities had staff that were well prepared for start-up. They had identified the problems they wished to study, and the scope was reasonable for a nine-month project.

East Lansing wanted to determine how many fire stations it needed and where they should be located. Extensive data on fire alarms existed, and University of Michigan staff were involved in the computer analysis of the data and in the model construction. The city planner, the city manager, and the fire commissioner assisted in the design of the project, the acquisition of the data, and the process of applying the logic of the analysis to the data by means of a computer.

In Dayton, resource-allocation strategies were explored to maximize the benefits from the various federal programs in which Dayton participated. According to HUD, this fell outside of the legally permissible ways to use the appropriation from which the study was funded. Dayton meanwhile solved the problem in what is referred to as "a more routine way."

Charlotte's study was described more elaborately in the report, reflecting the bias inherent in the author's acknowledged "missionary" commitment to that venture. The problem to be analyzed was the location of public facilities within a model neighborhood. Neighborhood residents participated in the project planning, which did not occur in other projects. Questionnaire design slowed up implementation, and pressures for immediate action in many other Model Cities programs competed for the attention of city staff. As one result, the analytic plan was modified repeatedly in implementation.

In Poughkeepsie, the project was a benefit/cost comparison of strategies the city might take to bring about building code compliance in the Model Cities neighborhood. The social welfare agencies, the city building inspectors, and the planning agency were involved. The analysis went through the design stage six times because city personnel were constantly turning over, and each new team revised the data collection sheets and the format for the analysis.

Findings

East Lansing was the most successful project undertaken (in the sense that the city now has an analytic capability). No reasons are advanced for this outcome, but the judgment is explicitly made, along with reference to other jurisdictions that are building directly on the work done in East Lansing on fire research.

The main accomplishments in Charlotte were to bring together a number of constituencies in a problem formulation process and to help the city's staff to acquire a better socioeconomic data base. The study also identified a need for six facilities, rather than the one facility that would have been constructed without the study. Several of these have been constructed.

The Poughkeepsie effort is characterized as "informative, but not particularly productive." The costs of high turnover were unanticipated and severely debilitated the project. There is no evidence of implementation.

Conclusions

This report does not systematically compare the situations related to differential outcomes, but rather discusses "lessons learned":

A "nuts and bolts" situation is easy to understand, solve, and communicate;

User organizations must be involved;

City staff have less time to do analytic work than one expects;

Problems related to improving the quality of life have a degree of urgency that precludes the lengthy research investment that systems analysis requires; and

Analysis teams need a designated leader responsible for delivering a result and shielding the team from the many experts who give conflicting advice.

Comment

This piece is an example of straight journalistic reporting. There is no systematic research design, and the conclusions, although quite plausible, are nevertheless based solely on the author's report. The quality of information would have been improved if the "lessons" had been linked to specific city examples, but the piece was intended to be an "afterthought" rather than a rigorous analytic account.

Study: Terrence E. Deal et al., "Organizational Influences on Educational Innovation," in J. Victor Baldridge and Terrence E. Deal, eds., *Managing Change in Educational Organizations* (Berkeley: McCutchan, 1975), pp. 109-131.

This preliminary report of an ongoing longitudinal study focuses on organizational features that support and maintain complex innovations. The report is limited to the analysis of data from the first wave of the study. It presents an analysis of the organizational characteristics of both the school district and the individual school that are related to two types of nontechnological innovation: differentiation of reading instruction, and organization of teachers into small groups to teach reading.

Definitions and Measures

The report measured the following independent variables:

Per student expenditure of district funds

External funding: state and federal money spent on reading programs in grades 1-3

Proportion of special administrators to total administrative staff

Size: the total number of schools in the district

At the individual school level, characteristics associated with innovation were:

Principal's leadership: measured by an index based on the principal's report of his own influence relative to the influence of teachers and of the time he spent on change

Evaluation structure: measured by an index based on the principal's report of evaluation activities

Open space: measured by the number of instructional spaces used by two or more teachers at the same time

Size: the number of students enrolled

Community climate: the principal's estimates of the community's attitude toward change as innovative, traditional, or mixed

The dependent variables were innovation in instruction and work arrangement. In this report, *innovation* was equated with complexity. *Complexity in instruction* was measured by an index based on the number of distinct sets of reading materials used in grades 1-3, student pacing, the degree of teachers' choice in selecting materials, and scoring of curriculum materials by experts. *Complexity in organization* was measured by an index of teacher collaboration— i.e., the percentage of teachers in grades 1-3 that grouped into teams for teaching reading.

Method

Data were taken from a stratified random sample of 188 schools located in thirty-four districts in the San Francisco Bay area. The sample included urban, suburban, and rural districts. Within districts, the number of schools varied with the size of the district. Ninety percent of the principals completed the research questionnaire and a field interview. At the district level, all superintendents and their associates completed the questionnaire and interview.

An initial analysis attempted to organize the data according to two alternative models (staff-line centralization or professionalized decentralization). The hypothesis was that innovative districts and schools would follow one of these alternatives. However, neither model accounted for the findings, and a subsequent analysis served as a filter for an original, more comprehensive set of independent variables that yielded the previously described set of independent variables. There was no information on the variables and indicators screened out of subsequent multiple-regression analysis.

Findings

The size of both the individual school and the school district is negatively related to innovation. Wealth and external funding (correlated with districts in urban areas) are correlated to innovation. A strong principal and a vigorous evaluation program are positively related to instructional differentiation. Open space schools (correlated with suburban areas) are also positively related in instructional differentiation.

Open space schools with strong principals and in innovative communities are likely to have teachers organized in teams for teaching reading. Wealth and special administrators are also correlated with reading teams, with each of these variables having statistically significant regression coefficients.

Conclusions

The report points out that although the results of the analysis are clear, they are inconsistent. It is impossible to construct a causal model that accounts for all the significant relationships. There is some cautious optimism that the continuing accumulation of longitudinal data will clarify the linkages. The authors conclude that there is a disconnected pattern of district and school influences on innovation at the classroom level. The educational system is viewed as a series of loosely connected units where higher organizational levels do not appear to control or coodinate the responses of lower ones. This pattern may promote the adoption of innovation, but not the structural support for the maintenance of innovation.

Comment

The definition of innovation as complexity, with little reference to organization-al novelty, has little face validity. There is no theoretical rationale for this departure, and this definition (and the subsequent indices that follow from it) may account for the finding of a negative relationship between size and innovation—a finding which contradicts much of previous research.

Another limitation on the validity of the data is the limited sampling of roles. Principals and superintendents were the only level of the hierarchy to be queried on many points that contributed most heavily to the construction of the indices. This may have introduced a serious bias that accounts for the inconsistent results.

Finally, the conclusions about organizational segmentation seem to be independent of the data presented. No coherent argument links the findings of the regression analysis to a conclusion of fragmentation, and confusion is compounded by the interchangeable use of the terms *innovation, complexity,* and *change.*

Study: Irwin Feller et al., "Diffusion of Technology in State Mission-Oriented Agencies," Institute for Research on Human Resources, Center for the Study of Science Policy, Pennsylvania State University, University Park (October 1974).

The study reported the results of an exploratory effort concerning the diffusion of technological innovations in the public sector. The study attempted to answer the following questions:

1. Is there a systematic tendency for some states to be early adopters and others laggards?
2. What factors influence patterns of adoption?
3. Do diffusion networks (leader-follower relationships) exist among agencies in the different states?
4. What are the characteristics of the diffusion process in the public sector?

The conceptual framework was derived from the literature on organizational innovation. The research focused on: inputs (variables that predispose an organization to innovate); outputs (the number and kind of innovations adopted); and process (the sequence of events from input to output). The report contains two types of data presentation: quantitative presentations of interstate variations in diffusion, and qualitative assessments of the factors that shape the diffusion pattern.

The following definitions and measures were used:

Technological innovation was defined as the adoption of either a process or a product by state agencies. Specifically, the study covered the adoption of impact attenuators (a product) and transportation modeling (a process) by state highway agencies, and the adoption of automatic telemetry systems (a product) and air pollution modeling (a process) by state air pollution control agencies. *Impact attenuator adoption* was defined as the use of any one or combination of marketed devices designed to prevent serious injury or death should the fixed obstacle be struck by a vehicle. *Transportation modeling adoption* was operationally defined as the first use of a packaged program for modeling the journey to work and other travel behavior. *Air telemetry adoption* was operationally defined as the installation of hardware and software to ensure the technical capability for continuous monitoring of air quality and the transmission of this information to a distant point. Finally, *air pollution modeling adoption* was defined as an agency's first use of multiple-point source modeling, such as the Air Quality Display model developed by National Air Pollution Control Commission.

Method

The study stresses that a line of inquiry that focused on "the decision to adopt" was followed but with great flexibility, thereby allowing investigators to pursue interesting leads. An interview schedule was developed to cover the following topics: date and extent of adoption; reasons for adoption or nonadoption; composition of the decision unit; size and resources of the organization; environment in which the decision was made; and personal and professional backgrounds of the individuals involved. In addition, a Likert scale was administered at the end of the interview. The scale had thirty-one items and covered organizational and leadership dimensions and personal efficacy in the decision process.

Field interviews were conducted in ten states (Michigan, North Carolina, California, Kansas, Maryland, Minnesota, West Virginia, Illinois, New Jersey, and New York). The interviewees were not systematically selected; instead, the researchers chose to concentrate on people reputed to be involved in relevant decisionmaking. An average of four or five persons per agency was interviewed. Interviews with Federal Highway Administration engineers and staff in six states were also held.

These interviews suggested the subsequent extension of interviewing to cover commercial and noncommercial entrepreneurs. Thus interviews were also conducted with an unspecified number of people in a half dozen profit and nonprofit organizations.

The ten states were chosen on the basis of their adoptive behavior and their reputations as national or regional leaders. With respect to adoptive behavior, the telemetry and impact attenuation technologies were given priority to determine a mix of early and late adopters. With respect to reputation, telephone surveys of fifty pollution-control agencies, Department of Transportation data, and Walker's study of diffusion of innovation among states provided a categorization of states as leaders or followers.

Findings

This study presents two types of findings. The first involves the adoption trends for the technologies and gives diffusion curves based on the date of first adoption. The results support a systematic adoption trend in the air pollution field but not in the highway field. Further, there was not a consistent pattern of adoption of new technologies within particular states. A state that adopted new highway technology did not necessarily adopt new pollution control technology. The second type of finding was the isolation, cataloguing, and assessment of the key variables that facilitate or inhibit adoption. The analysis is both qualitative and quantitative, and at points is almost haphazardly impressionistic. It includes (besides the anticipated topics of adoption decisions, decision unit characteristics, and tests of relationships from the literature) the unanticipated topics that evolved in the course of the research, such as the role of the outside entrepreneur, the role of federal influence, and the role of professional intermediaries.

Air Pollution Agencies. With respect to air pollution telemetry, adoption was positively related to statewide problems of long duration in states which were responsible for pollution management. Obstacles to adoption were insufficient resources, lack of confidence in technology, disbelief in federal approval for innovation, and bureaucratic aversion to taking risks. As for modeling, the factors influencing adoption included federal legislation, the presence of personnel qualified to model, and a perceived need to do so. Consideration of the decision unit revealed that decisions on "hardware" technologies such as telemetry were more likely to involve high ranking officials and outsiders than were decisions on "software" technologies such as modeling.

Highway Agencies. Impact attenuator adoption was widespread (forty-eight states in 1973), apparently as a result of public awareness, the publication by the American Association of State Highway and Transportation Officials of a pamphlet titled *Safety Practices*, and the publicity given to the 1967 Congressional hearings. In addition, both the large body of research that attests to the efficacy of the technology and the resources provided by the Federal Highway Administration promoted rapid diffusion. The need for the diffusion of computer modeling seemed to be largely the result of people moving from one state to another in the 1950s and the passage of the Federal Highway Act (1962) requiring states to develop plans for the orderly expansion of highways and related modes of transport. These were the only factors cited in the report.

The composition of decision units resembled that found in the air pollution agencies, and decisions on "harder" technology involved more persons of higher status and more outsiders than decisions on "soft" technology.

Adoption Characteristics. The report started with seven hypotheses relative to the major attributes of decisionmakers, decision units, and the environment in which decisions are made. Variables included the size, prestige, and professionalism of the staff, the staff's interaction with leaders (both personal and professional), agency resources and autonomy, and organizational professionalism. Only one of these systematically related to adoption: nonadopting air pollution agencies had fewer resources than adopting ones. Further, no rank-order relationship was found between date of adoption and current resources in either field.

External Change Agents. The study's research also diverged from its original plan and examined the role of external influences in the diffusion process. First, the study identified three areas of federal influence: legislation, funding, and technical assistance. The relevant findings were that federal money was critical to adoption for one-third of the respondents; that 60 percent of the respondents reported attending federally sponsored technical seminars; and that over half felt that the seminars were very effective. Fifty-eight percent of the respondents felt that federal demonstrations were helpful, but the contrast among agencies was marked: 72 percent of the highway personnel reacted favorably, whereas 64 percent of the air pollution officials reacted negatively. The report suggests that different federal and state relations exist in highway and air pollution agencies: state and federal highway agencies cooperate, thereby promoting diffusion; state environmental agencies submit to the dominance of the federal agencies, thus retarding diffusion and risk bearing.

Second, the study identified at least six other types of external change agents that appear to facilitate adoption: manufacturers, consultants, contractors, universities, research institutes, and professional associations. The findings are impressionistic, but plausible. For instance, manufacturers will not aggressively market in the public sector if there is another market, perhaps because of the costs of dealing with federal regulatory agencies. This varies with the type of technology, however; the links between the federal agencies and the commercial corporations are much better developed in transportation than in air pollution control. As a second example, the Highway Research Board and the American Association of State Highway and Transportation Officials were cited as having critical roles in the diffusion process. In general, these associations legitimate innovations, disseminate information, and serve as liaison between states and the Congress. Both associations rely on state agencies for financial support. The Air Pollution Control Association and the State and Territorial Air Pollution

Prevention Agencies occupy analogous niches in pollution control, but do not serve as adequate links between states and the Congress because of limited membership and a lack of effective information services.

Conclusion

The main conclusion of this report is that external change agents (federal agencies, commercial entrepreneurs, and intermediary associations) are more important than other factors in producing differential patterns of adoption. The patterns of innovation, induced by changing intergovernmental relations and interstate communication, are changing rapidly among public agencies. Thus the innovation process is a mutual accommodation of a multitude of factors, including individual motives, organizational perspectives, and institutionalized ways of disseminating information.

Comments

This study presents a nice balance between rigid research design and serendipitous findings. The uncovering of the role of external actors should enrich the diffusion model and stimulate research. The study's major weakness is its refutation of the relationships (posited in the literature) of agency, size, professionalism, etc., as correlates to innovativeness without at least mentioning the noncomparability of definitions between the study and the previous ones that asserted relationships. It is also unfortunate (although an acknowledged admission and one of the risks of an exploratory research) that the study's most important findings rest on the most limited data base: an unspecified number of interviews unsystematically selected and thus not protected from bias.[a]

With regard to the larger data base, it is clear that the report incorporated only a fraction of the data. The questionnaire alone covers almost 1000 items. Although it is clear from the text that the investigators became disenchanted with their original set of questions, some explanation of the analysis of the questionnaire and the construction of the variable would have been appropriate.

Study: Alan Frohman et al., "Factors Affecting Innovation in the Fire Services," Pugh-Roberts Associates, Inc., Cambridge, Massachusetts (March 1972).

[a]An inspection of those interviewed shows that four out of six "external agents" are concerned only with the impact attenuation innovation; thus, some qualifying comments were in order.

This study concerns a technological innovation called the *jet-axe*, an adaptation of an explosive system developed for military purposes. The study is but one part of the full report, which deals with factors affecting innovation in the fire services. Although it was a multisite study, there is no systematic comparison of the sites. The innovating organization was a fire department, and the jet-axe innovation is described as a tool designed to cut rapidly through surfaces that are too thick or hard for an axe or chain saw.

The study is not an empirical investigation, but takes the form of a case report on the development of the jet-axe. Product development was undertaken in 1967 by an aerospace firm, Explosive Technologies, Inc., with the encouragement of the Fire Chief of New York City. Prototypes were demonstrated at the Washington State Command School in Seattle in the presence of 400 fire service officers from seven states and two Canadian provinces. Demonstration projects were implemented in Seattle, San Francisco, and Los Angeles, at training schools in New York, and at a meeting in Louisville in 1968. Explosive Technologies, Inc. also worked with the Department of Commerce's Bureau of Explosives and with several insurance companies interested in evaluating the jet-axe. The product was ready to market within a year and a half, and preliminary market surveys related enough sales potential to warrant production. However, although a conservative prediction of sales was 2500 jet-axes, the 1970-1973 sales were only 400 jet-axes.

The report summarizes interviews that were held with service personnel to learn what factors retarded adoption. The interviews related that even among cities that purchased the jet-axe and even where the fire chief was in favor of the innovation, its use was very limited. This appeared to be because the men who had to use the innovation were uncomfortable with it and preferred to use conventional axes and chain saws.

Conclusions

The study presents the following key characteristics about this experience with innovation:

The developer had produced the technology for a different market, which had shrunk, creating the necessity of marketing it elsewhere;

Influential fire chiefs worked with and encouraged the private firm;

The top-level management in the firm was committed to development of a new market;

Distribution channels were readily available; but

Diffusion was nevertheless very slow due to the reluctance of firemen to use it.

Comment

The study gives no systematic description of its research methods. It refers to an "in-depth look" but does not specify the scope, selection process, or data-gathering tools. The problem addressed, however, is important and interesting: how do private sector firms successfully penetrate public markets as agents of technological change? Although this study does not methodically develop an argument from specific data, it is suggestive in pointing out areas that may be crucial for such penetration.

Study: Jerald Hage and Michael Aiken, "Program Change and Organizational Properties," *American Journal of Sociology* 72 (March 1967):503-518.

This well-organized study concentrates on the relationship between structural, performance, psychological, and contextual variables and the rate of program change in organizations. The authors investigated sixteen social welfare organizations that were staffed largely with professional personnel and that provided service to the physically handicapped and emotionally disturbed in a midwestern city. The number of new programs adopted (not necessarily technological innovations) over a five-year period was the measure of change. The crucial research question was whether organizational characteristics (complexity, centralization, formalization, and job satisfaction) were correlated with the measures of change. The authors hypothesize: (1) positive relationships between complexity and both job satisfaction and the rate of change, and (2) negative relationships between both centralization and formalization and the rate of change.

Three empirical indicators were used for measuring complexity: occupational specialties included in an organization, the length of training required by each occupation, and the degree of professional activity associated with each occupation. Centralization was scored by the average degree of staff participation in the hiring decisions, the promotion of personnel, the adoption of new organizational policies, and the adoption of new programs or services. Formalization consisted of two factors: job codification and rule observation. *Job codification* referred to the number of rules specifying who is to do what, where, when, and how, whereas *rule observation* referred to the diligence used in enforcing the codification. Two indices of formalization were developed from a factor analysis of scales employed in a previous investigation. Admittedly, these indices provided only rough indicators of formalization. Job satisfaction was measured by two indices, developed for this study, reflecting both satisfaction with the job as a task and satisfaction with opportunities for expressing their views about their work.

The study attempted to examine the effects of these organizational characteristics independently of personality and contextual characteristics. To make the personality characteristics operational, the Neal battery of measures (devised to quantify individual attitudes and orientations to change) was administered to organizational members.

The main contextual characteristics were the auspice, age of organization, and major organizational function. *Auspice* refers to whether the agency was public or private. *Function* refers to the division of the agencies into two groups—those that dealt with their clients in a relatively short period of time (e.g., social casework agencies), and those that dealt with their clients for a relatively long period of time (e.g., the sheltered workshop).

Method

Sixteen social welfare agencies (ten private and six public) located in a large midwestern metropolis in 1964 served as the subjects of study. The agencies varied in size from twelve to several hundred employees. Interviews were conducted with 314 staff members, selected by the following criteria:

All executive directors and department heads were selected;

In departments of fewer than ten members, one-half the staff was selected randomly; and

In departments of more than ten members, one-third of the staff was selected randomly.

Nonsupervisory administrators and maintenance staff were not interviewed.

The number of interviews varied from seven in the smallest agency to forty-one in one of the largest agencies. Because the units of analysis were organizations, not individuals within organizations, the information obtained from respondents was pooled to reflect properties of the organizations. The authors admit that this procedure presents some methodological problems (e.g., too much weight given to respondents lower in the hierarchy because of their sheer number) and attempt to compensate by calculating organization scores from the mean score of the different strata of the organization.

Findings

The simple relationship between each independent variable and program change are shown in Table F-1. Generally, the relation between organizational properties and the rate of program change remained when contextual variables were

Table F-1
Relationships to Program Change

Variable	Values of Pearson r
Complexity	
Number of occupational specialties	0.48
Amount of professional training	0.14
Extra organizational activity	0.39
Decentralization	
Participation in agency-wide decisions	0.49
Hierarchy of authority	0.09
Formalization	
Job codification	−0.47
Job satisfaction	0.38
Personality variables	0
Contextual	
Age of organization	−0.03
Public versus private auspice	−0.06
Size of organization	0.61
Social service function (long-term versus short-term)	0.58

held constant by means of partial correlation analysis. Only complexity (measured by number of specialties) and centralization (measured by hierarchy of authority) were affected. When function, size, and auspices were held constant, the relationship between complexity and change disappeared, but the relationship between centralization (hierarchy) and change was strengthened.

Conclusions

The authors offer two plausible lines of reasoning to account for their results. The first points a high rate of program change as a prior condition to the structural and performance situations correlated with the rate of program change. The second places the structural and performance conditions as necessary conditions for a high rate of program change. Without longitudinal data, no final argument can be made about the direction of the causality. The strongest statement the authors make is that the rate of program change is associated with configurations of other organizational properties.

Comment

This report makes an attempt to view an organization as a social entity—i.e., a collection of social positions—rather than as a theoretical construct ultimately reducible to individual behavior. However, the ability to generalize the results based on research in service organizations is questionable, and the comparability claimed with work in industrial settings is not persuasive.

The weakest points in the research design that was employed are the unspecified transformation of interviews into organizational scores and the assumption that all program changes are the same. Some examples of what were judged to be comparable changes would have been reassuring. The lack of detail about how the interview results became scores raises questions about the suitability of the parametric statistic used to measure the strength of the relationships (Pearson product-moment). The authors make the point that their data are not ordinal, but that does not therefore ensure that they comprise an interval.

If one is willing to grant the authors the network of assumptions that underlies their attempt at quantification, their data are consistent with their conclusion that rate of program change seems systematically related to organizational variables. This conclusion, in turn, supports their main methodological assumption that an organization is best viewed as a system of social, not personal, variables. The authors are justifiably reserved about the direction of the causal sequence, since they lack longitudinal data that would allow a more definitive choice among competing explanations.

Study: Wolf V. Heydebrand and James J. Noell, "Task Structure and Innovation in Professional Organizations," in Wolf V. Heydebrand, ed., *Comparative Organizations* (Englewood Cliffs, New Jersey: Prentice-Hall, 1973), pp. 294-322.

This article focuses primarily on the relationships of professionalization, bureaucratization, rationalization of specialized knowledge, control of organizational resources and goals, and innovativeness. Only two aspects were investigated empirically: the interrelationship of professionalization, bureaucratization and the complexity of task structures, and the effect of this set of relationships on innovativeness, defined (nontechnologically) as the extension and application of specialized, professional knowledge in new areas.

The following definitions and measures were used:

Professionalization is defined as the degree to which the organized labor force, excluding the managerial staff, consists of holders of the M.S.W. professional degree

Complexity of task structure s defined according to three dimensions:

(1) geographic dispersion—the number of branch offices the organization has

(2) number of programs, indicating the diversity of services

(3) size

Bureaucratization is defined in two ways:

(1) number of levels—determined by counting vertically the job titles within the central division of the agency

(2) administrative/clerical staff—determined by the proportion of managerial and clerical workers to the total personnel

Innovativeness, the dependent variable, is defined as the number of research and demonstration projects executed by an agency in the four-year period 1961-1964; it is acknowledged that the range of the projects was wide in terms of topic area and scope

Method

The organizations included in this study are private welfare agencies, specifically, neighborhood centers affiliated with the National Federation of Settlements and Neighborhood Centers. In 1964, a detailed questionnaire was sent out by the National Federation to all 270 member agencies; 122 (about 45 percent) returned the questionnaire. The questionnaire data and information from a separate listing of R&D projects compiled by the same agency in 1964 were transformed into quantitative variables and analyzed with correlation and regression statistics.

The findings of this study included:

There is a moderate positive correlation ($r = 0.17$) between professionalization and bureaucratization, which disappears when size and task complexity are controlled;

Professionalization is moderately related to complexity ($r = 0.24$) and size ($r = 0.28$);

Bureaucratization is more strongly related to complexity ($r = 0.51$) and size ($r = 0.58$);

Complexity is positively related to the degree of innovation (0.48 for the zero-order correlation, 0.37 for the partial correlation);

Size is virtually eliminated as a factor in innovation when complexity is controlled;

Professionalization is positively, but not strongly, related to innovativeness (0.25 for zero-order correlation, 0.16 for the partial correlation);

Bureaucratization is negatively related to innovation when other variables are controlled (−0.11 partial correlation); and

The joint effect of the independent variables on innovativeness is not sufficiently strong to permit talking of an "explanation" ($r^2 = 0.282$); however, the multivariate analysis shows that professionalization and complexity (as defined by the number of branches) are the most important determinants of innovation ($r^2 = 0.257$) and that bureaucratization is not a major determinant.

Conclusions

The results of the empirical analysis support the theoretical expectation that in private welfare agencies having professionals in resource-control positions, professionalization and bureaucratization coexist. Innovation, however, is positively associated with professionalization and negatively related to the organizational distance (in terms of number of levels) between the executive and the "point of production."

Comment

In spite of the above summary, this report is largely theoretical. It devotes greater attention to conceptual rather than empirical analysis. It is aimed at challenging Parson's assertion about the normative conflict between bureaucratization and professionalization, and its choice of sample reflects the bias of intent. The challenge would have been more telling if the sample had included organizations where professionals were *not* in positions of administrative control. It is also not clear that a hierarhical organization is ipso facto a bureaucratic one. In an organization where all employees have equivalent professional degrees, one might expect collegial relationships to prevail, despite the existence of an organizational chart. If this is the case, the conditions of a Weberian bureaucracy may not hold, and the data do not challenge the possible normative duality.

With respect to method, the authors acknowledge the crudeness of the operationalization and quantification of variables. However, the study provides no detail about how the questionnaire data were actually converted into variables in the regression analysis. Similarly, there is no detailed treatment of the dependent variable with respect to differences among "innovations" in substantive area, scope, effectiveness, or survival.

Study: David A. Hodgson et al., "The Uniform Hospital Discharge Data Demonstration, Summary Report," U.S. Department of Health, Education, and Welfare, Public Health Service, Health Resources Administration, Washington, D.C. (July 1973).

This is not an analytical research report, but rather a final report of a demonstration project implemented at a number of sites. There are no numerical measures of inputs, processes, or outputs, nor is there any conceptual scheme employed to develop a systematic understanding of the innovation process. There is no mention of any research instruments or strategies, so we assume that the report's conclusions are based on staff visits to demonstration sites.

The innovation qualifies as a technological one: a new method of abstracting data and deriving from them medical, demographic, and administrative information on hospital inpatients in the United States. The usefulness of such a data set was suggested at a conference, following which the Health Services Foundation (HSF) was awarded a contract to organize a demonstration project. The innovating agencies were of two kinds: abstracting agencies, nonprofit organizations supported by client hospitals and designed to serve hospitals by collecting and processing discharge data and disseminating information to other health care organizations, and the hospital itself—particularly the administration and medical records departments.

At the initial stages of the project, a steering committee was formed; and from it, a technical subcommittee, which developed the basic data set for the demonstration, provided technical assistance for project implementation and designed a suitable recording form. Also, state and local agencies, both public and private (e.g., health departments, Blue Cross) were polled by letter in an attempt to compile an inventory of agencies involved in the collection and processing of discharge data. Three hundred twenty-two or 89 percent of 361 agencies replied. Subsequently, a detailed questionnaire was sent to 232 agencies identified as being involved in data collection and processing and as having a system in an advanced developmental stage. One hundred seventy agencies replied, ninety-four of which were judged to be operating in the desired manner (i.e., collecting data on individuals and operations beyond the experimental stage).

The steering committee developed criteria for potential test sites. These criteria focused primarily on the potential utility of the innovation to a coalition in the site community. The coalition included hospitals, abstracting agencies, third-party payers, and planning councils. Visits were made to the sites, and four sites were selected for contracts: the Maine Hospital Association; the Hospital Utilization Project, Pittsburgh; Health Service Data, Wisconsin; and the Hospital Council of Southern California. Each of the contractors had six areas of task activity: data-base development, implementation, reabstracting analysis, billing, data use, and interregional comparison among regions.

Findings

Hospital Selection. The test hospitals varied unsystematically in bed size, control, and occupancy rate. Hospitals were self-selected, and generally considered by themselves to have the best data systems. There was evidence of strained relationships by the time the test was completed, and there was little sign of wide acceptance of the new approach to abstracting. This was attributed to insufficient attention to briefing all personnel involved.

Electronic Data Processing Modification. Two test sites (Pittsburgh and Southern California) required extensive modification. However, the report does not attempt to link this fact with process or outcome.

Training. The following categories of personnel were trained about the innovation by on-site visits by HSF staff:

Admitting Office staff

Billing Office staff

Medical Records staff

Physicians

The report states that training was a much greater task than anticipated and that involving physicians was found both to be crucial and to require a major effort.

Implementation. All sites completed implementation within six months. The report identifies insufficient familiarity with project objectives and difficulty in obtaining certain data items as the main sources of difficulty encountered. Sources of the latter difficulty are hospital and informant refusals to supply information, clerical carelessness, lack of physician involvement, abstractors' disagreements about definitions, and lack of perceived utility.

Utility of BDS (Basic Data Set). HSF developed forty reporting formats, none of which was adopted by the test sites. Non-hospital users did not perceive the discharge data as a major information source. Generally, there was an inconsistency between what hospital personnel and non-hospital users saw as useful information.

Interregional Comparison. Comparison in this report refers to the inspection of data collected from different test sites to determine if data items were in fact comparable among sites or if each site was generating data by "local rules." It was found that data items were comparable, and some comparative tabular reports were generated. No analyses were attempted.

Conclusions

The report concludes with some recommendations for what should be included in a basic data set. These recommendations are based on project experience, but are not systematically related to any data collected in the field. There is no report on the fate of the innovation at any test site, but the report presents the following factors that retard implementation:

Sources of resistance among groups interested in a data base vary;

Protection of confidentiality requires development of satisfactory safeguards;

Training must be thorough, ongoing, and motivating, even though it consumes time; and

Hospitals may not clearly see how such data systems reduce costs.

The final section of the report comments on the need for education in the health care community about the uses and sources of health-related data.

Comment

This report provides sketchy documentation of an innovation attempt that failed. There is no perspective taken on the problem of innovation per se, and there is no reference to the literature on public technology or organizational change. No attempt was made to define variables or to develop systematic functional relationships among sets of circumstances, except in the most cursory way.

Study: Arnold D. Kaluzny et al., "Diffusion of Innovative Health Care Services In the United States: A Study of Hospitals," *Medical Care* 7 (November-December 1970):474-487.

This report describes one portion of a large study of the diffusion and implementation of selected health care (nontechnological) programs in hospitals and health departments. The general objective of the study was to identify three community, organizational, and personal variables that affect implementation. The report focuses on (1) the amount and rate of implementation of innovative health care services in a representative sample of hospitals in the United States, and (2) on the relationship of the amount and rate of implementation to the geographic location of the hospital (by region), the rural or urban nature of the community, the percentage of the population below the poverty level, the type of hospital control (governmental, voluntary, proprietary) and the hospital size (defined by the number of beds).

The following definitions and measures were used:

Implementation is defined as the presence of selected services and activities in the organization. The *rate of implementation* is defined as the speed with which hospitals adopt programs. This is measured by the cumulative percentage of hospitals implementing services within specified time periods. The programs covered are home health, family planning, medical social work, rehabilitation, and mental health services. A hospital's implementation status within a program is determined by the average number of years that it has made the innovative services available to its patients. This average time, expressed in years, is subtracted from 1969, permitting the classification of a hospital into a designated time period for each program.

Method

Data were collected from a 10 percent stratified random sample of the 6,520 short-term acute hospitals listed in the Master Facility Inventory of the National Center for Health Statistics ($N = 652$). The final selection procedure was based on the number of beds per hospital to ensure that the sampling units approximated population coverage. Questionnaires, and two follow-up mailings, were sent to administrators, yielding 480 respondents. The questions tapped five major areas: the presence or absence of the innovative services; whether these services were provided by others in the community; the administrator's attitudes toward such services; the hospital's place in the community resource network; and the sociodemographic characteristics of the administrators. Information regarding geographic region, type of community (rural/urban), and percentages of poverty within the community was obtained from the *County-City Data Book* published by the Bureau of the Census.

The relationship between the independent variables and implementation status was analyzed by a chi-square test, with a 0.05 level of significance used for all findings. Only simple relationships are presented (i.e., there is no control for interaction effects).

Among the findings in this study were the following:

Findings

Total implementation by programs: In all programs, hospitals with more than 500 beds provide proportionately more services and activities than smaller hospitals; in hospitals in both size categories, proportionately fewer home health services than rehabilitative services are provided—family planning is present less frequently than mental health or rehabilitative services;

The provision of services by other agencies varies by program; generally, hospitals that provide a service tend to have links to other agencies that provide similar services;

Implementation by selected variables: In the case of larger hospitals (500 or more beds), there was little variation in the implementation of programs; hence, there were fewer significant relationships between independent variables and the dependent variable;

Geographic region: The number of hospitals implementing service programs, except those in mental health, was greatest in the Northeast; the north-central region hospitals were next, adopting all but the family planning program; the mountain-pacific west and the south-central region hospitals implemented the lowest number of programs; implementation also took place earlier in the Northeast;

Community type: Communities with a population of one million or more have the largest proportion of hospitals implementing the innovative programs, except for mental health services where the reverse is true;

Poverty level: The proportion of hospitals that have implemented services in all areas is smallest in areas having 24 percent or more families with incomes less than $3000; however, except for rehabilitation and social work, the hospitals in the middle poverty group (12.1 to 24 percent) have the greatest proportion of implemented programs; a similar pattern exists for larger hospitals, except in the cases of home health and family planning where the pattern is reversed;

Type of administrative control: Within voluntary and governmental programs, smaller hospitals were significantly associated with implementation in all categories except family planning, which has been implemented more in large government hospitals; proprietary hospitals have been notably slow in the implementation of all programs;

Size: Among smaller hospitals (less than 500 beds), implementation varies directly with the number of beds, except for home health and family planning; the pattern of late implementation of rehabilitation programs by small (fewer than fifty beds) hospitals is in direct contrast to early implementation by larger hospitals (251 to 500 beds); this pattern appeared to a lesser extent in other programs; and

Rate of implementation by program: Within the two categories of size, three patterns were identified—among smaller hospitals, rehabilitation services increased rapidly and smoothly from a 5 percent acceptance rate in 1950 to a 52 percent rate in 1969; mental health and medical social work programs started at a lower acceptance rate and progressed less rapidly, with 29 percent of the programs being accepted in 1969; family planning and home health programs were accepted at only a 2 percent rate in 1954, hit a 5 percent rate in 1965, and then took off abruptly, reaching about a 15 percent rate of acceptance by 1969.

Among larger hospitals, mental health, medical social work, and rehabilitation programs exhibited one pattern of steady increase in implementation from about 20 percent in 1950 to about 70 percent in 1969. A second pattern was exhibited by family planning services. Only 1 percent of the hospitals provided these services in 1950, and there was only slow growth until a takeoff in 1960 that resulted in 65 percent of the hospitals implementing them in 1969. The home health program showed a third pattern. Four percent of the hospitals had implemented this program by 1954. There was a slow, steady growth to a 25 percent acceptance rate in 1969.

Conclusions

This report does not draw conclusions from its findings, except that implementation appears to be usefully conceived of as a diffusion phenomenon. The value of the data in providing a baseline for comparing organizations and innovative programs and for pointing to gross factors associated with implementation is presented as a justification for this preliminary analysis. A sketch is provided for the subsequent analytic program aimed at teasing out interactions and identifying relevant environmental and organizational factors that bear on the trends presented. A tentative explanation of the trends in terms of the relation of the programs to traditional areas of hospital responsibilities is offered, but the data are neutral with respect to this explanation.

Comments

The research method is clear, appropriate, and presented in detail. It is not clear, however, how the questionnaire yielded information on the dependent variable or if any distinctions were made between programs that were implemented but discontinued and programs that were implemented and then incorporated. This distinction seems appropriate even at the preliminary level of analysis. Although it is acknowledged that no distinction was made about the quality or scope of the service being provided, there was no attempt to identify the constraints that this omission might have set on findings.

Study: Roland J. Liebert, " 'The Electric Company,' In-School Utilization Study. Volume 2: The 1972-73 School and Teacher Surveys and Trends Since Fall 1971 " Institute for Social Research, Florida State University, Tallahassee (October 1973).

This report contains both a study of the diffusion of a technological innovation and a methodological "study of the study" that sought to buttress the validity of the findings. The research was styled after market survey research, and therefore the study design was not focused on variables derived from a theoretical model. Instead, the main methodological thrust was to ensure representative sampling and a high response rate to questions related to demand, use, and satisfaction. The research provided a two-year perspective on the implementation of an educational television program called "The Electric Company," which was aimed at improving the basic reading skills of seven- to ten-year-old children. The sampled universe was that of elementary schools (organizations), but the decision to adopt was treated as the number of individual teachers who decided to use the innovation in their classrooms.

Method

The study involved longitudinal data taken during two different periods by the same research organization. The surveys covered the first and second television seasons of "The Electric Company." Both surveys were national in scope and included public and private schools. Computer-accessible lists of such schools in 1970-1971 provided the basic information from which a sampling frame was constructed. Five dimensions of stratification were imposed on the sampling frame: geographic region, community size, socioeconomic level, school size, and public versus private auspice. A major addition in the study of the second season was a postcard survey of the sampled schools to determine if the school had used "The Electric Company" in both seasons, had used it in 1970-1971 but discontinued it the following year, had used it in 1971-1972 but not in the previous year, or had not used it at all.

In addition, this study includes a methodological study aimed at determining the accuracy of the data reported by school principals in the 1972-1973 survey. The methodological study consisted of interviews of 277 teachers in thirty southeastern schools. There is no rationale given for the regional selection, but the sample was stratified by size, and two schools were randomly chosen from fifteen size categories. The field interviews are not described in the report, but it is stated that the principals were accurate in reporting the total number of teachers in the target grades, the total enrollment, the number of teachers using "The Electric Company," and the number of pupils viewing "The Electric Company."

Findings

The number of users of "The Electric Company" increased from 18,811 in the fall of 1971 to 25,735 in the fall of 1972. There were regional differences, with the Southeast recording an increase well above the national average (a 26 to 30 percent increase compared to a 25 to 40 percent increase). There is some indication that schools shifted from their initial target grades to higher or lower grades. Low socioeconomic status (SES) communities increased their rate of adoption more slowly than middle- and high-income communities did. The most important finding was that there was substantial continued use of "The Electric Company." Seventy percent of the respondents who had ever used the innovation used it for both seasons. In addition, the series found its way to its intended target population, with an estimated 685,000 viewers reported by principals as being "behind grade" in reading skills. However, pupils in low SES and rural areas in the Southeast were less likely to be viewers if they were behind grade than if they were in pace with their grade levels.

The major barrier to the use of "The Electric Company" during its first season was access to television. Forty-nine percent of the nation's schools could not receive television signals in the first season, with the figure dropping to 40 percent in the second season. However, the improvement in capability did not occur in low SES communities, which suggests an explanation in the slower adoption rate. With respect to the decision to adopt or not to adopt, few principals cited pedagogical or ideological reasons for not adopting. In fact, principals had positive attitudes toward the innovation, even in schools that did not adopt it. The report states, however, that principals play a minor role in the adoption decision, since individual teachers actually make the choice.

Principals heard about the innovation from other principals or from the media. There is no indication of how teachers found out about "The Electric Company." The least informed teachers were those in the small cities in the rural Southeast, but as they became informed and the schools became technically capable of receiving the program, the adoption rate increased dramatically. Fifty-four percent of the schools made scheduling changes to increase the number of pupils viewing the program during the second season, and 17 percent of the adopters used upgraded TV equipment.

Conclusions

In summary, the report concludes that:

By midway into the second season, over 50 percent of technically capable schools were using the innovation;

Increase in access capability resulted in the greatest increases in adoption;

The success of the first season increased in the second, with use increasing by 53 percent;

Private and parochial schools were late adopters compared with public schools, but began to catch up in 1972; and

There was little loss of adopters, since only 6 percent of the adopters in 1971 were not users in 1972.

Comment

This report is paradoxically both sophisticated and naive. The sampling methods are rigorous and minutely detailed to ensure representativeness, and the estimation procedures are described in great detail. However, the findings and conclusions are based on data primarily from principals who admittedly were *not* making the decision to innovate. Fifty-three percent of the principals in schools capable of receiving the program approved of the innovation, yet their teachers were not adopters. The analysis at no point explains the attitudes of the actual adopters—the teachers. Teachers in nonadopting schools were not even included in the survey, which is a major flaw in the research.

Another serious flaw is the lack of analysis of the data obtained from existing teacher surveys. An appendix includes teacher responses to fifty-six items ($N = 15,420$ in 1972-1973 only and 112,233 in both seasons) not systematically dealt with in the text of the report. In contrast with the report's portrayal of teacher autonomy in the classroom, the actual teacher responses showed that teachers perceived adoption to be an organizational response in which they participated, not an individual decision to innovate. For example, more than 40 percent felt that the school superintendent, the curriculum coordinator, and the principal participated in the decision to innovate. These data are clearly at variance with the individual-teacher adoption model presented in the text.

Study: Lawrence B. Mohr, "Determinants of Innovation in Organizations," *American Political Science Review* 63 (March 1969):111-126.

This study identifies the determinants of organizational innovation and develops a theoretical and mathematical model of innovative organizational behavior. Innovation is nontechnologically defined as "the successful introduction into an applied situation of means or ends that are new to that situation." Innovation is also thought to carry costs, in the sense of both materials used and time expended. These costs are conceived of as obstacles to innovation, since without financial resources an organization is unable to innovate.

On the basis of the foregoing, the following three-dimensional hypothesis is specified: Innovation is directly related to the motivation to innovate, inversely related to the strengths of the obstacles to innovation, and directly related to the availability of resources for overcoming such obstacles.

The study group for the research included all full-time local health departments located in Illinois, Michigan, New York, Ohio, and Ontario; serving a jurisdiction no greater than 600,000 in population; and having a chief executive who had occupied his current position from 1960-1964. One health officer refused to participate, reducing the total to thirty-three units.

Two working definitions of innovation were employed: one was the total number of nontraditional services adopted by the department; the second was the total number of personnel units (measured in person-years or the equivalent in dollars) that were added to nontraditional programs during 1960-1964. The second definition was termed *progressive programming*.

For the motivational dimensions, two notions were used: ideology and activism. *Ideology* concerned the attitude of the public health officer toward the proper scope of services that should be offered under public (versus private) auspices. *Activism* concerned the officer's perception of the extent to which his role requires interaction with others—especially outside the department—to obtain ideas, support, and resources for departmental programs. Both ideology and activism were measured by Likert-type scales (twenty-six and twenty-three items, respectively) completed in the presence of an interviewer. The activism scale was designed to measure opinions of four role activities: influencing the health power structure, obtaining support beyond local appropriations, emphasizing interagency affairs, and problem seeking. The ideology scale was designed to determine conservatism or liberalism by asking the respondents about their opinions on the proper locus of services in twenty-six areas. For the purposes of analysis, the scales were added to create an activism-ideology variable.

With respect to obstacles, social class (based on the percentage of the population twenty-five years of age and over who completed high school) and percentage of labor force in white collar occupations were taken as indicators of community readiness to accept or resist change. Organizational obstacles were measured by the extent of public health training of lower echelon employees.

The primary operational definition of resources was the level of 1959 expenditures.

Findings

Activism-Ideology. The correlation between activism-ideology and progressive programming was $r = 0.36$. Community size made no difference in the relationship.

Obstacles. The educational level of the community correlated very slightly with innovation when community size was controlled. Similarly, controlling for size, there was a significant relationship between an organizational factor—the training of supervisors—and progressive programming.

Resources and Community Size. The correlation between expenditures and progressive programming was $r = 0.60$; the total for nontraditional services was $r = 0.65$. The partial correlation that appeared when community size was controlled was $r = 0.27$, indicating that although the more robust correlation was partially spurious, there was nevertheless substantial direct influence by expenditures on innovation. Additional analysis, undertaken to place size in sharper perspective, revealed that although the correlation of community size with number of innovative programs was $r = 0.63$, when health department expenditure was controlled the relationship dropped to $r = 0.15$, and when the activism of the health officer and percentage of white collar workers were statistically controlled, it dropped to $r = 0.09$. Thus, for these data, the effects of community size may be almost entirely understood in terms of other variables.

Small versus Large Health Departments. The report states that larger departments adopted substantially more new programs than did smaller departments. Each program was assigned a numerical score based on the median size of the departments adopting it. The highest and lowest thirds of a ranked list were singled out for analysis. The results showed that few observed differences could be accounted for in terms of community size. Disparities in departmental resources, however, seemed to account for the differences. The effective resources were stated to be:

Number of staff

Number of specialized personnel

Stock funds

Accessibility of federal funds

The presence of these resources enables large health departments to adopt many new programs than smaller departments. This difference in the pattern of organizational innovation as a function of size was explained by invoking the concept of "slack innovation." Large departments choose to adopt larger numbers of programs rather than (1) expanding existing ones or (2) adopting fewer on a larger scale because the variety brings the bonus of additional professional prestige. For small agencies, innovations tend to be "problem"-oriented innovations, since the organization may need to expand its services to meet demand. Larger agencies, whose greater resources enable them to meet demands, innovate for status reasons.

Finally, the study compares the fit of a linear additive model and a multiplicative mathematical model to the data. The observations were consistent with the hypothesis that the relationship between motivation and resources is multiplicative, but neither model provided a clearly superior fit. However, the report offers an appealing argument in favor of the multiplicative conceptualization by drawing parallels between innovation and several related forms of behavior that are thought to depend multiplicatively on the motivation of the actor and the net resources available for accomplishment.

Conclusions

The study concludes that the original three-dimensional hypothesis is generally supported by the data, although in some cases the data are weak. The most powerful predictor of innovation was agency size, but the analysis suggests that size is powerful only insofar as it implies the presence of resources.

Comment

This is a thorough and closely reasoned report. However, its argument rests on granting some assumptions that may be open to question.

First is the assumption that the study group is representative of some universe. No argument is made that relates the organizations studied to any wider group, although the report draws several parallels with industrial firms. Second is the assumption that the dependent variable is comparable across cases. Again, this means that "an innovation is an innovation." However, other research (such as that of Mytinger) strongly suggests that this is not the case. Third is the acceptance of the validity of the key variables. The most questionable face validity is found in the use of the proxies for community obstacles to innovation and for organizational resources. The report also fails to distinguish between organizational size and resources. At one point, resources are defined as total expenditures; at another point, size is so defined—yet it is also stated that greater resources accompany larger size. The variable of complexity is not included at all, although in other studies dealing with size it plays a large role in the analysis.

Another difficulty is the lack of a clear relationship between the data and two of the study's conclusions. One conclusion is that large organizations indulge in "slack" or prestige-oriented innovation and therefore adopt new programs rather than expanding existing services. That is one possibility, but there is no attempt to cite evidence that rules out other equally plausible explanations. The second conclusion is that a multiplicative model should be favored. The argument has intuitive appeal, but the actual model tested against the data is not clearly a better fit than is an additive model.

Study: Robert E. Mytinger, *Innovation in Local Health Services,* U.S. Department of Health, Education, and Welfare, Public Health Service, Division of Medical Care Administration, Arlington, Virginia (1968).

This report, a condensation of more detailed research, assesses the relationship of nontechnological innovation in public health departments to three determinants that are frequently encountered in the literature: "the person," "the agency," and "the community."

In the anthropological tradition of Barnett, innovation is conceptualized as a culturally based process of social change. The report provides a theoretical definition of innovation as a "creative art of man . . . deriving from individual experience and initiative, and the cultural setting in which the innovative force finds himself." Empirically, innovation is taken to be major new programs considered by health departments for adoption. The innovating agency is defined as those local and county health departments in California that are administered by a full-time administrator.

Fifty-one variables descriptive of local health officers, their agencies, and their communities were initially constructed from questionnaire and interview data. These produced thirty-three independent variables, including the following, that were retained for analysis against innovativeness scores:

The Man

Age: Health officer's age; Median age of staff.

Incumbency: Health officer's tenure; Predecessor's tenure; Mean staff tenure.

Cosmopolitism: Health officer's professional travel outside jurisdiction during 1964.
Health officer's professional travel outside California during 1964.

Social Status: MPH degree held by health officer.
Board certification held by health officer.
Opinion leadership status of health officer.

The Man (cont.)

Social Status: Breadth of health officer's acquaintance with peers.
(Cont.)   Length of health officer's total medical experience.
Length of health officer's local public health experience.

The Agency

Age: Year health department established.

Size: Number of full-time staff members.
Total population served.
Engagement in residency training.
Engagement in laboratory training.
Engagement in nurse training.
Engagement in field or other training.

Economic Status: Size of total budget administered by health officer.
Budgetary provisions for short-term training for staff.
Budgetary provisions for attendance of professional meetings by staff members.

The Place

Economic Status: Median income of families in population.
Value of owner-occupied housing in jurisdiction.

Urbanism: Physician/population ratio.
Density of population.
Percent of population in urban residence.
Educational level of population (percent that are eighth grade graduates).
Percent of population nonwhite.
Percent of population under five years of age.
Percent of population sixty-five years of age and older.
Growth of population (change between 1950-1960).

The measure of innovativeness selected for this study was a numeric score for each local health department. The score was based on the actual extent of degree (using a series of rating scales) to which the department was engaged in seven innovative public health programs: alcoholism, accident prevention, home nursing, early discovery of chronic illness, medical care service delivery, research and evaluation, and family planning. A second numeric innovativeness score was assigned to each department on the basis of a factor analysis of adoption of a wider array of new programs. Thus the thirty-three "independent variables" were analyzed against two dependent variables.

Method

The sample of agencies included all of California's forty full-time health departments. In-depth data concerning the extent and degree of engagement in the seven main programs were collected through personal interviews with each of the forty health department administrators. For the remaining fourteen programs, shorter interviews supplemented self-rating form that each health officer completed, rating his department's engagement in the programs along a scale from 0 to 10 (0 = no involvement; 10 = comprehensive program). Overestimation of engagement was checked by comparing the extent of engagement observed in the seven programs intensively researched to the extent of the health officer's self-reported engagement in the fourteen others. Further corroboration of self-reported data was also sought from regional program coordinators and officials in the state's Department of Public Health.

Prior to analysis, two health departments were excluded. One was thought to be unique because of its administrative staffing pattern, and the other had recently absorbed an innovative health department and, therefore, its innovativeness score would be misleading.

Findings

The main set of findings related the thirty-three independent variables to the innovativeness scores. Nine characteristics of the innovator were associated significantly ($p \leqslant 0.05$) with higher innovativeness scores:

Health officer's tenure

Predecessor's tenure

Travel outside jurisdiction

Travel outside California

References by others to the innovator being an opinion leader

Years of experience in public health

Number of reciprocal acquaintances with peers

Professional degree (MPH)

Board certification

These findings corroborate those of previous studies on the importance of social status, opinion leadership, and cosmopolitism to innovativeness.

As for other simple correlates of innovativeness, agency size and economic status as defined by the total agency budget were also significantly associated with innovativeness. With respect to the community, the value of housing (related to the tax base) is related to innovativeness, but median family income is not. Three indicators of urbanism are also significantly related to innovation: percentage of the population sixty-five years old and older; percentage of the population under five years old, and percentage of the population living in urban residences.

A second set of findings covered the conditions facilitating and retarding adoption. For the seven programs, external resources were mentioned most frequently as a facilitating condition, followed by advocacy by state consultants or other outside officials and active leadership by the health officer. With respect to barriers to innovation, a different set of categories was employed. The potential barriers were classified as stemming from the health department (staff or organization), the community (opposition, demand, peculiarities), local government (local boards, funds, other), and other organizations. When the kinds of barriers were compared between the eight most and eight least innovative programs, it was found that almost every barrier was salient to the same extent, with resistance by department staff being the greatest barrier.

A third set of findings was based on an effort to use multivariate techniques to tease out the interactive relationships among the independent variables. First, the thirty-three independent variables as a group were regressed against innovativeness scores for the seven focal programs. Six of the thirty-three variables explained 74 percent of the variance. These six were:

Professional trips out of California

Opinion leadership of health officer

Budget size

Residency training

Field and other training programs

Percentage of population living in urban residences

Second, factor analysis using innovativeness scores on all twenty-one programs was performed. It disclosed five factors into which programs seemed to divide:

Administrative (e.g., coordination)

"Limited knowledge" (e.g., early detection of chronic illness)

Traditional (maternal health care)

Medical psychiatric (services for ex-patients)

Contentious (e.g., family planning)

Finally, the thirty-three independent variables were collectively regressed on each of the five program factors. Table F-2 summarizes the results.

Conclusions

On the basis of the data, some implications for the diffusion and adoption of innovations were suggested. Larger and richer health departments were found to be high innovators—a fact suggesting that a broadened population base and an increased level of support are stimulants to innovation. Also, graduate training and cosmopolitism, as well as the length of tenure of the health officer, were linked to greater receptivity to innovation. With respect to advocacy, the study concludes that local health officials of high status who have previously adopted other innovations are the most effective advocates of innovation.

These results lead to the overall recommendation that new pilot projects be placed in large departments that are led by administrators having high reputations. Outside support is seen as sometimes being necessary.

Comment

This is a complicated study whose organization does not lend itself easily to analysis. The two most vulnerable points in the research occur at the initial stage of analysis, where there is no explicit translation of the interview data collected into the variables used in the analysis, and at the final stage, where the models are poorly described. For example, the description of factor construction from raw data is extremely sketchy. A third methodological problem stems from the uncritical assumption of the adoption/diffusion perspective on innovation. This assumption leads to the public health officer being the only decisionmaker studied in the decision to adopt. The study completely ignores the organizational perspective on innovation, and there are no data on service changes, client use and attitudes, or organizational changes in the agency. The overall impression is of a great methodological effort focused on an issue simplistically conceived.

Study: Public Technology, Inc., "Integrated Municipal Information Systems: Program and Projects of the United States of America Urban Information Systems Inter-Agency Committee," prepared for the Office of Policy Development and Research, Department of Housing and Urban Development (January 1975).

Table F-2

Independent Variables that Are Most Closely Related to Innovativeness in Five Program Categories

Type of Innovative Program (dependent variable)	Main Independent Variables*	Percent of Variation in Innovativeness Explained
"Administrative"–type programs		49
Integration/coordination	+Size of staff	
Quality of medical care improvement	+Field/other training	
Data on health status	+Short-term training budget	
Utilization of social sciences	+Percent of population in urban residence	
Joint planning		
Health aspects of total planning		
Hearing and speech		
Home nursing		
"Limited knowledge"–type programs		70
Accident prevention	+Opinion leadership status	
Early discovery of chronic illness	−Age of staff +Density of population −Median family income −Percent nonwhite	
"Basic"–type programs		31
Data on health resources/facilities	+Length of health officer's experience	
Comprehensive maternal/infant services	+Field/other training −Median family income +Median value of housing	
"Medical" or clinical-type programs		61
Services for ex-mental patients	−Health officer's board certification	
Center for community mental health services	+Health officer's out-of-state professional travel	
Suicide prevention	+Residence training program	
Development of rehabilitation services	+Budget for professional meeting attendance	
Psycho/medico-social problems of youth	+Physician/population ratio in jurisdiction	
Direct medical care services		
"Contentious"–type programs		59
Research/evaluation	+Field/other training	
Alcoholism	+Health officer's out-of-state professional travel	

Table F-2 (cont.)

Type of Innovative Program (dependent variable)	Main Independent Variables*	Percent of Variation in Innovativeness Explained
"Contentious"–type programs (cont.)		
Family planning	+Size of budget +Budget for professional meeting attendance −Median value of housing	

*(+) designates a directly *increasing* relationship between the variable and program innovativeness score.
(−) designates an inverse relationship.

This report attempts to address the use of integrated management information systems (a technological innovation) in five cities: Charlotte, North Carolina; Dayton, Ohio; Long Beach, California; Wichita Falls, Kansas; and Reading, Pennsylvania. "Integrated management information systems" (IMIS) are conceived to include the hardware (computers and related data processing and display services) and the software associated with the innovation, as well as the systems-analysis techniques that must be brought to bear to implement the technology. The innovating unit is conceived to be the entire governmental system at the local level rather than any single service agency.

Definitions, Measures, and Method

There is no set of key research questions that is addressed. Instead, the report draws together loosely the experience the consultants have gained in five years' association with urban information programs. The report states that Public Technology, Inc. had regularly received program and project documents since 1970 and supplements this information with a review of selected program and project documents. Mention is made of discussions with "several hundred persons," but no concrete detail is provided on who they were, how they were selected, what was discussed, or how the data were coded or analyzed.

A consortium in each of the five cities was organized so that the municipal government was the prime contractor, with a private consulting firm and a university or research center serving as monitors and conducting selected research and evaluation tasks. The basis on which the five cities were chosen as the implementation sites is unspecified in the report.

Findings

The report does not present findings in any systematic way. In an extensive section on the techniques of change, there is a series of general discussions about technological, financial, psychological, jurisdictional, political, governmental, legal, and educational factors. For example, under "psychological factors," it is asserted that "local officials can be expected to view the adoption of IMIS concepts and proposals with caution because of the newness, complexity, and magnitude of the resources and technology involved." However, there is no attempt to relate this generality to actual data collected from any consortium site. When actual data are used, they are part of a casual reference, not directly related to the general assertion. Even in such areas as "governmental factors" and "political factors," where information from the consortia does provide opportunities for comparison and contrast, no reference is made to concrete findings.

Conclusions

The report concludes that the funding agency failed to anticipate the complexities of the design and implementation of integrated information management systems. However, in spite of falling short of its expected accomplishments, the study concludes that:

The project cities appear to be satisfied that the concepts of IMIS are workable and desirable;

The documentation of an array of municipal processes, data, and information flows has been accomplished on a higher level than had been done previously;

There have been serious difficulties in actually *demonstrating* an operating IMIS; and

The differences in data-base management systems, sophistication levels, and computer capacities constrain the ready transfer of the IMIS concept from one site to another.

Comment

The report fails to describe the characteristics of the innovation in anything but the most general terms (e.g., integrated management information systems), and no outcomes are presented concretely. There is no attempt to develop any line of explanation to account for what happened at any site, although one section surveys on a general level factors thought to be important for unspecified reasons. A diffusion model of the innovation process is outlined at one point in the report, but no effort is made to link the model even to the general observations about important factors.

In summary, this report is a poorly organized amalgamation of information gathered largely from secondary sources. There is scant use of primary data, and nowhere is there a systematic link between either primary or secondary data and the report's conclusions.

Study: Martin M. Rosner, "Economic Determinants of Organizational Innovation," *Administrative Science Quarterly* 12 (March 1968):614-625.

This study concentrates on the relationship between organizational slack, economic orientation, and innovativeness in hospitals. Slack is measured by the proportion of the beds used to the total annual hospital bed-days, since higher proportions provide more income and hence more slack resources. Economic orientation, defined as the degree of preference an organization has for low costs, is measured by the drug cost per in-patient day (the less spent, the more concern with costs) and by the drug inventory turnover rate (the costs of drugs for the latest fiscal year divided by the average value of the inventory). Innovativeness is measured by the frequency with which a hospital tries new technology (drugs) and the promptness of the trials, measured by the time gap between when a drug is released and the hospital's first trial use of it.

The hospital sample consisted of twenty-four non-teaching, short-term voluntary hospitals located in Chicago. The hospital's capacities ranged from 216 to 393 beds. The report does not describe how either the hospital sample of the questionnaire respondents were selected. Neither the number of respondents nor the response rates is given. The research instrument was described only as "a questionnaire on drug use." No interviewing was mentioned.

The promptness of use was traced by means of audits of purchase invoices for six sample drugs. Data on economic orientation and slack presumably were gleaned from similar administrative records. The frequency of trial was obtained from questionnaire data.

Multiple regression analysis was used to determine the relationship between a particular dependent variable and the independent variables. To meet the assumptions of the analytic model, a functional transformation of the variables was made to achieve homogeneity of variance. In addition, the following factors were included in the regression model to control for their effects:

Size: measured by bed capacity

Control of medical staff activity: measured by a composite index derived from administrative requirements about treatment and drug therapy

Visibility of care: measured by evaluative programs, including autopsy rate and clinical audits

Staff innovativeness: measured by physician self-rating

The study hypothesizes that as the occupany rate (slack) increases, the frequency and promptness of new drug trial will increase, and that as the economic orientation increases, the frequency and promptness of new drug trial will decrease. The rationale is simply that innovation is costly and an organization must have the slack resources to absorb the cost to innovate, and that a cost-conscious organization will be less likely to innovate.

Findings

The direction of the regression coefficients followed the predicted pattern, but only the inverse relation of frequency of innovation and economic orientation was significant ($p < 0.03$). In contrast, the occupancy rate was positively related to the promptness of innovation, but not significantly. The authors comment that the large proportion of unexplained variance may be because the scores for all six drugs were pooled in the analysis. The analysis of the residuals showed normal distributions, with no systematic relationship to the regression estimates.

Conclusions

The authors conclude that the findings must be considered in the empirical context. A hospital trial of a new drug may be an atypical example of organizational innovation. The economic risks are not so great as in the purchase of a new capital good; economic factors should exert a more marked influence in other kinds of organizations and with innovations that have a more significant economic impact than drugs.

Comment

The indicators used for the independent variables do not have a high measure of face validity, and no argument is made to increase their plausibility. The concepts of "slack" and "economic orientation" have more complexity than the indicators can accommodate. An additional criticism is the unsupported assumption that the effects of the independent variables in the regression model are independent and additive. In fact, a plausible argument can be made for an association between such variables as "control of medical staff activities" and "visibility of care," defined as clinical audit. In the light of this criticism, the use of the analytic technique is questionable.

The conclusions seem to be designed to justify the study in spite of its findings. The data do not address the typicality of hospitals as organizations, the impact of drug trials relative to other forms of organizational innovation, or the relative place of hospitals in the realm of cost-conscious organizations. There are some hints in the narrative that unreported data may bear on the conclusions, but these are left to the reader's imagination.

References

Abert, James G., and Murray Kamrass, eds., *Social Experiments and Social Program Evaluation* (Cambridge, Massachusetts: Ballinger, 1974).

Ahlbrandt, Roger S., Jr., "Implications of Contracting for a Public Service," *Urban Affairs Quarterly* 9 (March 1974):337-358.

Aiken, Michael, and Robert Alford, "Community Structure and Innovation: The Case of Public Housing," *American Political Science Review* 64 (September 1970a):843-864.

Aiken, Michael, and Robert Alford, "Community Structure and Innovation: The Case of Urban Renewal," *American Sociological Review* 35 (August 1970b):650-665.

Alesch, Daniel J., "A Strategy for Developing in State Government the Capability to Change through Science and Technology " The Rand Corporation, R-785-NSF, Santa Monica (1971).

Allison, Graham T., *Essence of Decision: Explaining the Cuban Missile Crisis* (Boston: Little, Brown and Company, 1971).

Anuskiewicz, Todd, "Federal Technology Transfer," report for the National Science Foundation, Office of Intergovernmental Science and Research Utilization, Washington, D.C. (August 1973).

Archibald, R.W., and R.B. Hoffman, "Introducing Technological Change in a Bureaucratic Structure," The Rand Corporation, P-4025, Santa Monica (February 1969).

Baer, Walter S., et al., "Analysis of Federal Funded Demonstration Projects," The Rand Corporation, R-1926-DOC, Santa Monica (April 1976).

Baldridge, J. Victor, and Robert A. Burnham, "Organizational Innovation: Individual, Structural, and Environmental Impacts," *Administrative Science Quarterly* 20 (June 1975):165-176.

Banfield, Edward, *The Unheavenly City: The Nature and the Future of Our Urban Crisis* (Boston: Little, Brown and Company, 1970).

Banfield, Edward, and James Wilson, *City Politics* (Cambridge, Massachusetts: Harvard University Press, 1965).

Barnett, H.G., *Innovation: The Basis of Cultural Change* (New York: McGraw-Hill Book Co., 1953).

Becker, Selwyn, and Thomas L. Whisler, "The Innovative Organization: A Selective View of Current Theory and Research," *Journal of Business* 40 (October 1967):462-469.

Bennis, Warren G., *Changing Organizations* (New York: McGraw-Hill Book Company, 1966).

253

Berman, Paul, and Milbrey McLaughlin, "Federal Programs Supporting Educational Change," vol. I, The Rand Corporation, R-1589/1-HEW, Santa Monica (September 1974).

Berman, Paul, and Edward W. Pauly, "Federal Programs Supporting Educational Change," vol. II, The Rand Corporation, R-1589/2-HEW, Santa Monica (April 1975).

Bernstein, Ilene N., and Howard E. Freeman, *Academic and Entrepreneurial Research: The Consequences of Diversity in Federal Evaluation Studies* (New York: Russell Sage Foundation, 1975).

Blau, Peter, and W. Richard Scott, *Formal Organizations: A Comparative Approach* (San Francisco: Chandler Publishing Company, 1962).

Bogdan, Robert, "Conducting Evaluation Research—Integrity Intact," paper presented at the annual meeting of the American Sociological Association, San Francisco (1975).

Brickell, H.M., "State Organization for Educational Change," in Matthew B. Miles, ed., *Innovation in Education* (New York: Columbia University Press, 1964).

Burns, Tom, and G.M. Stalker, *The Management of Innovation* (London: Tavistock Publications, 1961).

Burt, Marvin, et al., "Factors Affecting the Impact of Urban Policy Analysis: Ten Case Histories," working paper, The Urban Institute, Washington, D.C. (July 1972).

Cahn, R.W., "Case Histories of Innovations," *Nature* 225 (February 1970):693-695.

Campbell, Donald T., "Factors Relevant to the Validity of Experiments in Social Settings," *Psychological Bulletin* 54 (1957):297-312.

Campbell, Donald T., "Reforms as Experiments," *American Psychologist* 24 (April 1969):409-429.

Campbell, Donald T., and Julian Stanley, *Experimental and Quasi-Experimental Designs for Research* (Chicago: Rand McNally and Company, 1966).

Caporaso, James A., and Leslie L. Roos, Jr., eds., *Quasi-Experimental Approaches* (Evanston, Illinois: Northwestern University Press, 1973).

Carlson, Richard O., "Succession and Performance among School Superintendents," *Administrative Science Quarterly* 6 (September 1961):210-217.

Carlson, Richard O., et al., eds., *Change Process in the Public Schools* (Eugene: University of Oregon, 1965).

Caro, Francis G., ed., *Readings in Evaluation Research* (New York: Russell Sage, 1971).

Carroll, Jean, "A Note on Departmental Autonomy and Innovation in Medical Schools," *Journal of Business* 49 (March 1967):531-534.

Carter, Charles, and Bruce Williams, *Industry and Technical Progress: Factors Concerning the Speed of Application of Science* (London: Oxford University Press, 1957).

Clark, David, and Egon Guba, "An Examination of Potential Change Roles in Education," Seminar on Innovation in Planning School Curriculum (October 1965).

Clark, Terry N., "Institutionalization of Innovations in Higher Education: Four Models," *Administrative Science Quarterly* 13 (June 1968):1-25.

Coe, Rodney M., and Elizabeth A. Barnhill, "Social Dimensions of Failure in Innovation," *Human Organization* 26 (Fall 1967):149-156.

Cohn, Morris M., and M.J. Manning, eds., "Dynamic Technology Transfer and Utilization: The Key to Progressive Public Works Management," prepared for the National Science Foundation with the participation of the American Public Works Association, American Public Works Association, Chicago (1974).

Cole, Richard L., *Citizen Participation and the Urban Policy Process* (Lexington, Massachusetts: D.C. Heath and Company, 1974).

Coleman, James S., et al., *Medical Innovation: A Diffusion Study* (New York: Bobbs-Merrill Company, 1966).

Committee on Intergovernmental Science Relations, "Public Technology: A Tool for Solving National Problems," Report of the Committee to the Federal Council for Science and Technology, Executive Office of the President, Washington, D.C. (May 1972).

Committee on Public Engineering Policy, National Academy of Engineering, "Priorities for Research Applicable to National Needs," Washington, D.C. (1973).

Committee on Science and Astronautics, U.S. House of Representatives, "Science and Technology and the Cities," a compilation of papers presented for the 10th Meeting of the Panel on Science and Technology, Washington, D.C. (1969).

Comptroller General of the United States, "The California Four Cities Program," Washington, D.C. (October 1975).

Comptroller General of the United States, "Problems in Implementing the Highway Safety Improvement Program," Washington, D.C. (May 1972).

Corwin, Ronald G., "Strategies for Organizational Innovation: An Empirical Comparison," *American Sociological Review* 37 (August 1972):441-454.

Corwin, Ronald G., "Innovation in Organizations: The Case of Schools," *Sociology of Education* 48 (Winter 1975):1-37.

Costello, Timothy W., "Change in Municipal Government: A View from the Inside," *Journal of Applied Behavioral Science* 7 (March-April 1971): 131-145.

256

Council of State Governments, "Power to the States," Science and Technology Report, RM-485, Lexington, Kentucky (May 1972).

Crain, Robert L., "Fluoridation: The Diffusion of an Innovation among Cities," *Social Forces* 44 (March 1966):111-126.

Crane, Diana, *Invisible Colleges: Diffusion of Knowledge in Scientific Communities* (Chicago: University of Chicago Press, 1972).

Crawford, Robert, "The Application of Science and Technology in Local Governments in the United States," *Studies in Comparative Local Government* 7 (Winter 1973):1-19.

Cyert, Richard M., and James G. March, *A Behavioral Theory of the Firm* (Englewood Cliffs, New Jersey: Prentice-Hall, 1963).

Czepiel, John A., "The Diffusion of Major Technological Innovation in a Complex Industrial Community: An Analysis of Social Processes in the American Steel Industry," Ph.D. dissertation, Northwestern University (1972).

David, Stephen M., and Paul E. Peterson, eds., *Urban Politics and Public Policy: The City in Crisis* (New York: Praeger Publishers, 1973).

Deal, Terrence E., et al., "Organizational Influences of Educational Innovation," in J. Victor Baldridge and Terrence E. Deal, eds., *Managing Change in Educational Organizations* (Berkeley: McCutchan Publishing Corp., 1975), pp. 109-131.

Digest of Educational Statistics, 1973 (Washington, D.C.: U.S. Office of Education, 1974).

Doctors, Samuel I., *The Role of Federal Agencies in Technology Transfer* (Cambridge, Massachusetts: MIT Press, 1969).

Douds, Charles F., and Albert H. Rubenstein, "Review and Assessment of the Methodology Used to Study the Behavioral Aspects of the Innovation Process," in Patrick Kelly et al., eds., "Technological Innovation: A Critical Review of Current Knowledge " vol. 2, Advanced Technology and Science Studies Group, Georgia Tech, Atlanta (February 1975), pp. 185-269.

Downs, Anthony, *Inside Bureaucracy* (Boston: Little, Brown and Company, 1967).

Emerson, Luther, et al., "Acceptance of Family Planning among a Cohort of Recently Delivered Mothers," *American Journal of Public Health* 58 (September 1968):1738-1748.

Emery, R.E., and E. Trist, "The Causal Texture of Organizational Environments," *Human Relations* 18 (1965):21-31.

Ernst, Martin L., "Public Systems Analysis: A Consultant's View," in Alvin W. Drake et al., eds., *Analysis of Public Systems* (Cambridge, Massachusetts: MIT Press, 1972), pp. 31-44.

Ezra, Arthur A., "Technology Utilization: Incentives and Solar Energy," *Science* 187 (February 1975):707-713.

Fainstein, Norman I., and S.S. Fainstein, "Innovation in Urban Bureaucracies: Clients and Change," *American Behavioral Scientist* 15 (March 1972):511-531.

Farkas, Suzanne, "The Federal Role in Urban Decentralization," *American Behavioral Scientist* 15 (September/October 1971):15-35.

Federal Council for Science and Technology, "Public Technology: A Tool for Solving National Problems," Executive Office of the President, Washington, D.C. (May 1972).

Feild, John, "Science and Technology for the Cities," National League of Cities/U.S. Conference of Mayors, Washington, D.C. (July 1972).

Feldman, M.L., et al., "Applications of Aerospace Technologies to Urban Community Problems," General Electric Company, RM-65-TMP-53, Santa Barbara (September 1965).

Feller, Irwin, et al., "Diffusion of Technology in State Mission-Oriented Agencies," Institute for Research on Human Resources, Pennsylvania State University, University Park (October 1974).

Ferman, Louis A., ed., "Evaluating the War on Poverty," *The Annals* 385 (September 1969): entire issue.

Fliegel, Frederick C., and Joseph E. Kivlin, "Attributes of Innovations as Factors in Diffusion," *American Journal of Sociology* 72 (November 1966):235-248.

Fliegel, F.C., et al., "A Cross-Cultural Comparison of Farmers' Perceptions of Innovations as Related to Adoption Behavior," *Rural Sociology* 33 (December 1968):437-449.

Frohman, Alan, et al., "Factors Affecting Innovation in the Fire Services," Pugh-Roberts Associates, Cambridge, Massachusetts (March 1972).

Galbraith, John Kenneth, *American Capitalism* (Boston: Houghton Mifflin Company, 1956).

Gayer, Gordon K., "A Bibliography of Case Studies of Innovation," IIAP/PPST (Innovation Information and Analysis Project, Program of Policy Studies in Science and Technology) Special Report, The George Washington University, Washington, D.C. (1974).

Gilbert, John P., et al., "Assessing Social Innovations: An Empirical Base for Policy," Harvard University, Cambridge, Massachusetts (December 1974).

Gordon, Diana R., *City Limits* (New York: Charterhouse Books, 1973).

Gordon, Gerald, and Edward V. Morse, "Evaluation Research," *Annual Review of Sociology* (Palo Alto: Annual Reviews, Inc., 1975), pp. 339-361.

Gordon, Michael, *Sick Cities* (Baltimore: Penguin Books, 1965).

Griliches, Zvi, "Hybrid Corn and the Economics of Innovation," *Science* 132 (July 1960):211-228.

Gross, Neal, et al., *Implementing Organizational Innovations: A Sociological Analysis of Planned Educational Change* (New York: Basic Books, 1971).

Hadden, Jeffrey, et al., eds., *Metropolis in Crisis* (Itasca, Illinois: F.E. Peacock Publishers, 2nd ed., 1971).

Hage, Jerald, and Michael Aiken, "Program Change and Organizational Properties," *American Journal of Sociology* 72 (March 1967):503-518.

Hage, Jerald, and Michael Aiken, *Social Change in Complex Organizations* (New York: Random House, 1970).

Hage, Jerald, and Robert Dewar, "Elite Values versus Organizational Structure in Predicting Innovation," *Administrative Science Quarterly* 18 (September 1973):279-290.

Haire, Mason, "Industrial Technology and Urban Affairs," *Technology Review* 71 (February 1969):22-27.

Hallman, Howard W., *Neighborhood Control of Public Programs* (New York: Praeger Publishers, 1970).

Hallman, Howard W., *Neighborhood Government in a Metropolitan Setting* (Beverly Hills: Sage Publications, 1974).

Hamilton, Edward K., "Productivity: The New York City Approach," *Public Administration Review* 32 (November/December 1972):784-795.

Hargrove, Erwin C., "The Missing Link: The Study of Implementation of Social Policy," The Urban Institute, Washington, D.C. (July 1975).

Harrison, Bennett, "The Participation of Ghetto Residents in a Model Cities Program," *Journal of the American Institute of Planners* 39 (January 1973):43-55.

Hatry, Harry P., "Status of PPBS in Local and State Governments in the United States," *Policy Sciences* 2 (June 1971):177-189.

Hatry, Harry P., et al., *Practical Program Evaluation for State and Local Government Officials* (Washington, D.C.: The Urban Institute, 1973).

Havelock, Ronald G., "Planning for Innovation through Dissemination and Utilization of Knowledge," Center for Research on Utilization of Scientific Knowledge, Institute for Social Research, The University of Michigan, Ann Arbor (July 1969).

Havelock, Ronald G., and Kenneth D. Benne, "An Exploratory Study of Knowledge Utilization," in Warren G. Bennis et al., eds., *The Planning of Change* (New York: Holt, Rinehart and Winston, 1969), pp. 124-142.

Hawkes, Robert W., "The Role of the Psychiatric Administrator," *Administrative Science Quarterly* 6 (June 1961):89-106.

Hawley, Willis D., and David Rogers, eds., *Improving the Quality of Urban Management* (Beverly Hills: Sage Publications, 1974).

Hayes, Frederick O'R., and John E. Rasmussen, *Centers for Innovation in the Cities and States* (San Francisco: San Francisco Press, 1972).

Hodgson, David A., et al., "The Uniform Hospital Discharge Data Demonstration, Summary Report," U.S. Department of Health, Education, and Welfare, Public Health Service, Health Resources Administration, Bureau of Health Services Research and Evaluation, National Center for Health Services Research and Development, Washington, D.C. (July 1973).

Horton, Raymond D., "Municipal Labor Relations: The New York City Experience," *Social Science Quarterly* 52 (December 1971):680-696.

House, Ernest R., *The Politics of Educational Innovation* (Berkeley: McCutchan Publishing Corp., 1974).

Hovland, C.I., et al., *Communication and Persuasion* (New Haven: Yale University Press, 1953).

Ikenberry, Stanley O., and Renée C. Friedman, *Beyond Academic Departments* (San Francisco: Jossey-Bass, Inc., 1972).

International City Management Association, "Applying Systems Analysis in Urban Government," Washington, D.C. (March 1972).

Kaluzny, Arnold, et al., "Diffusion of Innovative Health Care Services in the United States: A Study of Hospitals," *Medical Care* 7 (November-December 1970):474-487.

Kelly, Patrick, et al., "Technological Innovation: A Critical Review of Current Knowledge," 4 vols., Georgia Tech, Atlanta (February 1975).

Kimmel, Wayne A., et al., *Municipal Management and Budget Methods: An Evaluation of Policy Related Research* (Washington, D.C.: The Urban Institute, 1974).

Knight, Kenneth E., "A Descriptive Model of the Intra-firm Innovation Process," *Journal of Business* 40 (October 1967):478-496.

Kraemer, Kenneth L., et al., *Integrated Municipal Information Systems: The Use of the Computer in Local Government* (New York: Praeger Publishers, 1974).

Kuhn, Thomas S., *The Structure of Scientific Revolutions* (Chicago: University of Chicago Press, 1962).

Lambright, W. Henry, and A.H. Teich, "Federal Laboratories and Technology Transfer," Syracuse University Research Corporation, Syracuse (March 1974).

Laudon, Kenneth C., *Computers and Bureaucratic Reform* (New York: John Wiley and Sons, 1974).

Levitan, Sar A., ed., *The Federal Social Dollar in Its Own Back Yard* (Washington, D.C.: Bureau of National Affairs, 1973).

Lindblom, Charles E., "The 'Science' of Muddling Through," *Public Administration Review* 19 (Spring 1959):79-88.

Lippitt, R., and R. Havelock, "Needed Research on Research Utilization," in *Research Implications for Educational Diffusion* (East Lansing: Michigan State University, 1968).

Lipsky, Michael, "Street-Level Bureaucracy and the Analysis of Urban Reform," *Urban Affairs Quarterly* 6 (June 1971):391-409.

Lucas, William A., "The Case Survey Method: Aggregating Case Experience," The Rand Corporation, R-1515-RC, Santa Monica (October 1974).

Lucey, Patrick J., "Wisconsin's Productivity Policy," *Public Administration Review* 32 (November/December 1972):795-799.

Mann, John, "The Outcome of Evaluative Research," in Carol Weiss, ed., *Evaluating Action Programs* (Boston: Allyn and Bacon, 1972), pp. 267-282.

Mansfield, Edwin, "Technical Change and the Rate of Imitation," *Econometrica* 29 (October 1961):741-766.

Mansfield, Edwin, "Intrafirm Rates of Diffusion in an Innovation," *Review of Economics and Statistics* 45 (1963):348-359.

Mansfield, Edwin, "Industrial Research and Development Expenditures: Determinants, Prospects, and Relation to Size of Firm and Inventive Output," *Journal of Political Economy* 72 (August 1964):319-340.

March, James G., and Herbert A. Simon, *Organizations* (New York: John Wiley and Sons, 1958).

Marris, Peter, and Martin Rein, *Dilemmas of Social Reform* (New York: Atherton Press, 1967).

Marsh, C. Paul, and A. Lee Coleman, "Farmers' Practice-Adoption Rates in Relation to Adoption Rates of 'Leaders,' " *Rural Sociology* 19 (1954):180-181.

McLaughlin, Milbrey Wallin, and Paul Berman, "Macro and Micro Implementation," The Rand Corporation, P-5431, Santa Monica (May 1975).

Menzel, H., "Innovation, Integration, and Marginality: A Survey of Physicians," *American Sociological Review* 25 (1960).

Miles, Mathew B., ed., *Innovation in Education* (New York: Teachers College Press, 1964).

Miles, Mathew B., "Planned Change and Organizational Health," in Richard O. Carlson et al., eds., *Change Process in the Public Schools* (Eugene: University of Oregon, 1965), pp. 11-34.

Mohr, Lawrence B., "Determinants of Innovation in Organizations," *American Political Science Review* 63 (March 1969):111-126.

Mohr, Lawrence B., "Concept of Organizational Goal," *American Political Science Review* 67 (June 1973):470-481.

Myers, Sumner, and Donald G. Marquis, "Successful Industrial Innovations," Report to the National Science Foundation, NSF 69-17, Washington, D.C. (May 1969).

Mytinger, Robert E., *Innovation in Local Health Services: A Study of the Adoption of New Programs by Local Health Departments with Particular Reference to Newer Medical Care Activities* (Arlington, Virginia: U.S. Department of Health, Education, and Welfare, Public Health Service, Division of Medical Care Administration, 1968).

National Commission on Urban Problems, *Building the American City* (Washington, D.C., 1968).

Nelson, Richard, "Intellectualizing about the Moon-Ghetto Metaphor," *Policy Sciences* 5 (December 1974):375-414.

Nieburg, H.L., "The Tech-fix and the City," in Henry Schmandt and Warner Bloomberg, Jr., eds., *The Quality of Urban Life* (Beverly Hills: Sage Publications, 1969), pp. 211-243.

Niskanen, William A., *Bureaucracy and Representative Government* (Chicago: Aldine Publishing Company, 1971).

Niskanen, William A., "The Peculiar Economics of Bureaucracy," *American Economic Review* 58 (May 1968):293-305.

Pincus, John, "Incentives for Innovation in the Public Schools," *Review of Educational Research* 44 (Winter 1974):113-144.

Polgar, Steven, et al., "Diffusion and Farming Advice: A Test of Some Current Notions," *Social Forces* 42 (October 1963):104-111.

"Power to the States," Science and Technology Report, Council of State Governments, RM-485, Lexington, Kentucky (May 1972).

Pressman, Jeffrey L., and Aaron Wildavsky, *Implementation* (Berkeley: University of California Press, 1973).

Radnor, Michael, et al., "Implementation in Operations Research and R&D in Government and Business Organization," *Operations Research* 18 (November-December 1970):967-991.

Reagan, Michael D., *The New Federalism* (New York: Oxford University Press, 1972).

Rein, Martin, and Francine Rabinovitz, "Implementation: A Theoretical Perspective," unpublished manuscript, Massachusetts Institute of Technology, Department of Urban Studies and Planning, Cambridge, Massachusetts (May 1974).

Report of the National Advisory Commission on Civil Disorders (New York: Bantam Books, 1968).

Richland, Malcolm, "Traveling Seminar and Conference for the Implementation of Educational Innovations," Systems Development Corporation, TM-2691, Santa Monica (October 1965).

Riecken, Henry W., and Robert F. Boruch, eds., *Social Experimentation: A Method for Planning and Evaluating Social Intervention* (New York: Academic Press, 1974).

Robbins, Martin D., et al., "Federal Incentives for Innovation," Denver Research Institute (November 1973).

Rockoff, Maxine L., "An Overview of Some Technological/Health-Care System Implications of Seven Exploratory Broad-Band Communication Experiments," *Institute of Electrical and Electronics Engineers Transactions on Communications* Com.-23 (January 1975):20-30.

Roessner, J. David, "Innovation in Public Organizations," paper presented at the National Conference on Public Administration, Syracuse (May 1974).

Rogers, Everett M., *Diffusion of Innovations* (New York: Free Press, 1962).

Rogers, Everett M., with John Dudley Eveland, "Diffusion of Innovations Perspectives on National R&D Assessment: Communication and Innovation in Organizations," in Patrick Kelly et al., eds., "Technological Innovation: A Critical Review of Current Knowledge. Volume 2: Aspects of Technological Innovation," Advanced Technology and Science Studies Group, Georgia Tech, Atlanta (February 1975), pp. 301-368.

Rogers, Everett M., and F. Floyd Shoemaker, *Communication of Innovations* (New York: Free Press, 2nd ed., 1971).

Rogers, M., and A.M. Carton, "Aerospace Technology: Possible Applications to Our Cities," paper presented at the Fifth Annual Meeting of the American Institute of Aeronautics and Astronautics, Philadelphia (1968).

Roos, Noralou P., "Evaluation, Quasi-Experimentation, and Public Policy," in James A. Caporaso and Leslie L. Roos, Jr., eds., *Quasi-Experimental Approaches* (Evanston, Illinois: Northwestern University Press, 1973), pp. 281-304.

Rosenbloom, Richard S., and John R. Russell, *New Tools for Urban Management* (Boston: Harvard Business School, 1971).

Rosner, Martin M., "Economic Determinants of Organizational Innovation," *Administrative Science Quarterly* 12 (March 1968):614-625.

Rossi, Peter H., and Walter Williams, eds., *Evaluating Social Programs* (New York: Seminar Press, 1972).

Rothman, Jack, *Planning and Organizing for Social Change: Action Principles from Social Science Research* (New York: Columbia University Press, 1974).

Rowe, Lloyd A., and William B. Boise, eds., *Organizational and Managerial Innovation: A Reader* (Pacific Palisades, California: Goodyear Publishing Company, 1973).

Rubinstein, Jonathan, *City Police* (New York: Farrar, Straus and Giroux, 1973).

Sapolsky, Harvey M., "Organizational Structure and Innovation," *Journal of Business* 40 (October 1967):497-510.

Savas, E.S., and S.G. Ginsburg, "The Civil Service: A Meritless System?" *The Public Interest* (Summer 1973):70-85.

Schmookler, Jacob, *Invention and Economic Growth* (Cambridge, Massachusetts: Harvard University Press, 1966).

Schoenberg, Sandra P., "A Typology of Leadership Style in Public Organizations," in Lloyd A. Rowe and William B. Boise, eds., *Organizational and Managerial Innovation: A Reader* (Pacific Palisades, California: Goodyear Publishing Company, 1973), pp. 177-186.

Schulman, Paul R., "Nonincremental Policy Making: Notes Toward an Alternative Paradigm," *American Political Science Review* 69 (December 1975):1354-1370.

Schultz, Randall L., and Dennis P. Slevin, "Implementation and Management Innovation," in Randall L. Schultz and Dennis P. Slevin, eds., *Implementing Operations Research/Management Science* (New York: American Elsevier, 1975), pp. 3-20.

Scott, Thomas M., "The Diffusion of Urban Governmental Forms as a Case of Social Learning," *Journal of Politics* 30 (November 1968):1091-1108.

Shepard, Herbert A., "Innovation-Resisting and Innovation-Producing Organizations," *Journal of Business* 40 (October 1967):470-477.

Special Commission on the Social Sciences, *Knowledge into Action: Improving the Nation's Use of the Social Sciences* (Washington, D.C., 1969).

Sundquist, James L., *Making Federalism Work* (Washington, D.C.: Brookings Institution, 1969).

Szanton, Peter, "Analysis and Urban Government," in Alvin W. Drake et al., eds., *Analysis of Public Systems* (Cambridge, Massachusetts: MIT Press, 1972), pp. 19-30.

Taylor, J., "Introducing Social Innovation," *Journal of Applied Behavioral Science* 6 (1970):69-77.

Thompson, Victor A., "Bureaucracy and Innovation," *Administrative Science Quarterly* 10 (June 1965):1-20.

Tulley, Joan, et al., "Factors in the Decision-Making in Farming Problems," *Human Relations* 17 (November 1964):295-320.

U.S. Department of Justice, *Innovation in Law Enforcement* (Washington, D.C., 1973a).

U.S. Department of Justice, *The Change Process in Criminal Justice* (Washington, D.C., 1973b).

U.S. Department of Justice, *Uniform Crime Reports, 1958* and *1973* (Washington, D.C., 1959 and 1974).

The Urban Institute, *The Struggle to Bring New Technology to Cities* (Washington, D.C., 1971).

Utech, Harvey P., and Ingrid D. Utech, "The Communication of Innovations between Local Government Departments," report submitted to Office of R&D Assessment, National Science Foundation, Washington, D.C. (September 1973).

Utterback, James M., "The Process of Technological Innovation within the Firm," *Academy of Management Journal* 14 (March 1971):75-88.

Utterback, James M., "Innovation in Industry and the Diffusion of Technology," *Science* 183 (February 1974):620-626.

Walker, Jack L., "The Diffusion of Innovations among the American States," *American Political Science Review* 63 (September 1969):880-899.

Ward, David A., and Gene G. Kassenbaum, "On Biting the Hand That Feeds," in Carol H. Weiss, eds., *Evaluating Action Programs* (Boston: Allyn and Bacon, 1972), pp. 300-310.

Warner, Kenneth E., "The Need for Some Innovative Concepts of Innovation: An Examination of Research on the Diffusion of Innovations," *Policy Sciences* 5 (December 1974):433-451.

Warren, Roland L., et al., *The Structure of Urban Reform* (Lexington, Massachusetts: D.C. Heath, 1974).

Washnis, George J., *Community Development Strategies: Case Studies of Major Model Cities* (New York: Praeger Publishers, 1974).

Weiss, Carol H., "Utilization of Evaluation," in Francis G. Caro, ed., *Readings in Evaluation Research* (New York: Russell Sage, 1971), pp. 136-142.

Weiss, Carol H., ed., *Evaluating Action Programs* (Boston: Allyn and Bacon, 1972).

Wellington, Harry H., and Ralph K. Winter, Jr., *The Unions and the Cities* (Washington, D.C.: Brookings Institution, 1971).

Wenk, Edward Jr., "The Social Management of Technology," in John E. Mock, ed., "Science for Society," Proceedings of the National Science Conference, Atlanta (October 1970).

Wenk, Edward Jr., "Technology Assessment in Public Policy: A New Instrument for Social Management of Technology," *Proceedings of the Institute of Electrical and Electronics Engineers* 63 (March 1975):371-379.

Wholey, Joseph S., et al., *Federal Evaluation Policy* (Washington, D.C.: The Urban Institute, 1970).

Williams, Walter, "Implementation Analysis and Assessment," *Policy Analysis* 1 (Summer 1975):531-566.

Wilson, James Q., "Innovation: Notes toward a Theory," in James D. Thompson, ed., *Approaches to Organizational Design* (Pittsburgh: University of Pittsburgh Press, 1966), pp. 193-218.

Wilson, O.W., and R.C. McLaren, *Police Administration* (New York: McGraw-Hill, 1972).

Yeracaris, Constantine, "Social Factors Associated with the Acceptance of Medical Innovations," paper presented at the American Sociological Association meeting, St. Louis (1961).

Yin, Robert K., "R&D Utilization by Local Services: Problems and Proposals for Further Research," The Rand Corporation, R-2020-DOJ, Santa Monica (December 1976).

Yin, Robert K., and Karen A. Heald, "Using the Case Survey Method to Analyze Policy Studies," *Administrative Science Quarterly* 20 (September 1975):371-381.

Yin, Robert K., and Douglas Yates, *Street-Level Governments: Assessing Decentralization and Urban Services* (Lexington, Massachusetts: Lexington Books, 1975).

Yin, Robert K., et al., "Citizen Organizations: Increasing Client Control over Services," The Rand Corporation, R-1196-HEW, Santa Monica (April 1973).

Yin, Robert K., et al., "Neighborhood Communications Centers: Planning Information and Referral Services in the Urban Library," The Rand Corporation, R-1564-MF, Santa Monica (November 1974).

Zaltman, Gerald, et al., *Innovations and Organizations* (New York: John Wiley and Sons, 1973).

Index

Index

Ad hoc working groups, 70
Adaptability, 54-55, 59-60
Administrative procedures and support, 2-3, 12, 72, 76, 93, 108, 129
Adopters and adoption behavior, 8-10, 54, 64, 70
Advocate, 97-99
Aerospace program, 3
Agencies: county, 7; federal, 14, 21, 24, 36, 76, 93; local, 14, 53, 56, 93, 109-113, 118, 121, 123, 127; operations of, 25, 35; service, 43, 49, 51, 67, 109, 126; state, 44, 127
Aggregation and analysis, 25
Agriculture and agricultural practice, 8-9, 110, 122
Ahlbrandt, Roger S., Jr., 96
Aid-to-education programs, 88
Aiken, Michael, 68-70, 89, 126
Air and water pollution, 2
Alesch, Daniel J., 24, 96
Alford, Robert, 68
Allison, Graham T., 128
Ambulance dispatch, 44
American Association of State Highway and Transportation officials, 68
Antipoverty programs, 27
Anuskiewicz, Todd, 109
Archibald, R.W., 13, 72
Architectural and Engineering companies, 24
Arizona, 45
Artisans, 1
Audio and visual contacts, 6
Authors, university and nonuniversity based, 35-39
Autonomy, 13

Background factors and characteristics, 52, 67-69, 72-77, 81-84, 123-125, 130
Baer, Walter S., 8
Baldridge, J. Victor, 68, 126

Banfield, Edward, 2
Bankruptcy, 2
Barnett, H.G., 9, 44, 79
Barnhill, Elizabeth A., 55
Becker, Selwyn, 10, 43
Before-versus-after comparisons, 35
Behavioral roles, 3, 10, 14, 69
Benefits, regularity of, 53, 56-57
Benne, Kenneth D., 8
Bennis, Warren G., 70
Berman, Paul, 12-13, 87-88, 95, 117, 128
Bernstein, Ilene, 28, 33, 36
Bibliographic services, 21
Binary categories, 62-63, 75, 101, 115
Blau, Peter, 72
Blind and deaf children, 45
Blood bank inventory systems, 43
Bogdan, Robert, 39
Boruch, Robert F., 28
Brickell, H.M., 8
Budgets, 2-3, 5, 24, 48, 71, 77, 96, 107-108, 111, 125, 129
Bureaucracy: growth and goals, 13, 24, 95, 125; self-interest stereotypes, 90-92, 95-102, 104-107, 115, 120, 124, 127; structure and organization, 3-4, 89, 121, 129
Burglar alarm systems, 6
Burnham, Robert A., 68
Burns, Tom, 69-70
Burt, Marvin, 25, 88

Cahn, R.W., 17
California, 53, 109
Campbell, Donald T., 28
Caporaso, James A., 28
"Career bound" workers, 79
Carlson, Richard O., 25, 79
Caro, Francis G., 28
Carroll, Jean, 92
Carter, Charles, 79
Carton, A.M., 109
Case-by-case basis, 6

269

About the Authors

Robert K. Yin is a senior research psychologist at The Rand Corporation's office in Washington, D.C. and has worked at The New York City-Rand Institute. He received the B.A. in history from Harvard College and the Ph.D. in psychology from the Massachusetts Institute of Technology, where he is also a part-time faculty member in urban studies. Dr. Yin's main research interests concern urban neighborhoods and the organization of local government services. He served as Executive Director, Task Force on Criminal Justice R&D Standards and Goals (1975-1976), and has published several books, including *The City in the Seventies* (editor) and *Street-Level Governments*. He has also written numerous articles that have appeared in such journals as the *Journal of Experimental Psychology, Administrative Science Quarterly, Policy Sciences,* and *Sociological Methods and Research*.

Karen A. Heald was formerly a research associate and is now a consultant with The Rand Corporation. She received the B.A. in psychology from the University of Maryland in 1970 and is currently a Ph.D. candidate at the Department of Psychology, University of Pennsylvania.

Mary Vogel is a research associate at The Rand Corporation in Washington, D.C. She previously worked with Abt Associates in Cambridge, Massachusetts, and The Urban Institute, Washington, D.C. She received the B.S. from Georgetown University School of Foreign Service in economics and the M.C.P. in urban planning from Harvard University. Ms. Vogel has recently been a coauthor for a study on crime prevention patrols and is currently examining the impact of federal policies on urban form and patterns of residential settlement.

Selected List of Rand Books

Averch, Harvey A., et al. *How Effective is Schooling? A Critical Review of Research*. Englewood Cliffs, N.J.: Educational Technology Publications, 1974.

Bagdikian, Ben H. *The Information Machines: Their Impact on Men and the Media*. New York: Harper and Row, 1971.

Bretz, Rudy. *A Taxonomy of Communication Media*. Englewood Cliffs, N.J.: Educational Technology Publications, 1971.

Carpenter-Huffman, P., R.C. Kletter, and R.K. Yin. *Cable Television: Developing Community Services*. New York: Crane, Russak and Company, 1975.

Cohen, Bernard and Jan M. Chaiken. *Police Background Characteristics and Performance*. Lexington, Mass.: Lexington Books, D.C. Heath and Company, 1972.

Dalkey, Norman (ed.) *Studies in the Quality of Life: Delphi and Decision-making*. Lexington, Mass.: Lexington Books, D.C. Heath and Company, 1973.

DeSalvo, Joseph S. (ed.) *Perspectives on Regional Transportation Planning*. Lexington, Mass.: Lexington Books, D.C. Heath and Company, 1973.

Downs, Anthony. *Inside Bureaucracy*. Boston, Mass.: Little, Brown and Company, 1967.

Fisher, Gene H. *Cost Considerations in Systems Analysis*. New York: American Elsevier Publishing Company, 1971.

Greenwood, Peter W., Sorrel Wildhorn, Eugene C. Poggio, Michael J. Strumwasser, and Peter De Leon. *Prosecution of Adult Felony Defendants*. Lexington, Mass.: Lexington Books, D.C. Heath and Company, 1976.

Jackson, Larry R., and William A. Johnson. *Protest by the Poor: The Welfare Rights Movement in New York City*. Lexington, Mass.: Lexington Books, D.C. Heath and Company, 1974.

Levien, Roger E. (ed.) *The Emerging Technology: Instructional Uses of the Computer in Higher Education*. New York: McGraw-Hill Book Company, 1972.

McKean, Roland N. *Efficiency in Government through Systems Analysis: With Emphasis on Water Resource Development*. New York: John Wiley & Sons, Inc., 1958.

Meyer, John R., Martin Wohl, and John F. Kain. *The Urban Transportation Problem*. Cambridge, Mass.: Harvard University Press, 1965.

Novick, David (ed.) *Program Budgeting: Program Analysis and the Federal Budget*. Cambridge, Mass.: Harvard University Press, 1965.

Pascal, Anthony H. (ed.) *Racial Discrimination in Economic Life.* Lexington, Mass.: Lexington Books, D.C. Heath and Company, 1972.

Pascal, Anthony H. *Thinking about Cities: New Perspectives on Urban Problems.* Belmont, California: Dickenson Publishing Company, 1970.

Pincus, John (ed.) *School Finance in Transition: The Courts and Educational Reform.* Cambridge, Mass.: Ballinger Publishing Company, 1974.

Quade, Edward S. *Analysis for Public Decisions.* New York: American Elsevier Publishing Company, Inc., 1975.

Quade, Edward S., and Wayne I. Boucher. *Systems Analysis and Policy Planning: Applications in Defense.* New York: American Elsevier Publishing Company, 1968.

Sackman, Harold. *Delphi Critique: Expert Opinion, Forecasting, and Group Process.* Lexington, Mass.: Lexington Books, D.C. Heath and Company, 1975.

Sharpe, William F. *The Economics of Computers.* New York: Columbia University Press, 1969.

Williams, John D. *The Compleat Strategyst: Being a Primer on the Theory of Games of Strategy.* New York: McGraw-Hill Book Company, 1954.

Wirt, John G., Arnold J. Lieberman, and Roger E. Levien. *R&D Management.* Lexington, Mass.: Lexington Books, D.C. Heath and Company, 1975.

Yin, Robert K., and Douglas Yates. *Street-Level Governments: Assessing Decentralization and Urban Services.* Lexington, Mass.: Lexington Books, D.C. Heath and Company, 1975.